G000141297

THE PRICELESS GIFT

Steve Lewis is a writer and bookseller whose website, www.rugbybuy thebook.co.uk, specialises in rugby titles. He lives with his wife in Newport.

STEVE LEWIS

THE
PRICELESS
GIFT

THE INTERNATIONAL CAPTAINS OF WALES

MAINSTREAM
PUBLISHING
EDINBURGH AND LONDON

This edition published in 2006

Copyright © Steve Lewis, 2005
All rights reserved
The moral right of the author has been asserted

First published in Great Britain in 2005 by
MAINSTREAM PUBLISHING COMPANY (EDINBURGH) LTD
7 Albany Street
Edinburgh EH1 3UG

ISBN 978 1 84596 113 8 (from January 2007)
ISBN 1 84596 113 7

A catalogue record for this book
is available from the British Library

Typeset in Caslon

Printed and bound in Great Britain by
Cox & Wyman Ltd, Reading

CONTENTS

'Only one man in a thousand is a leader of men –
the other 999 follow women'
– Groucho Marx

PREFACE

Rugby union has become a much-written-about sport. Where cricket once led the way, based on the number of publications dedicated to it, other sports have caught up, the union game not least among them. With a figure approaching 5,000, the books published on rugby football come in many guises: the autobiographies, club histories, international histories, yearbooks, coaching and fitness manuals, and anthologies. With so many titles appearing over the last 25 years, one could be forgiven for thinking the subject matter has been exhausted, but for the researcher and author there are still pastures new to be explored.

The 125th anniversary of the Welsh Rugby Union is an occasion for celebration; a landmark point in the history of the game in Wales, a game which has come to mean so much more to a nation which, despite the early setbacks, embraced it from day one. It is an appropriate time to look at a previously unexamined faction within the game: the men who have led Wales onto the field of play – the captains. Many of them have been the subject of books before as individuals; now, for the first time, they are recognised collectively. From James Bevan, who led Wales on its first venture into the world of international rugby football at Richardson's Field on 19 February 1881, to Duncan Jones, who was captain for the two-match tour to Argentina in the summer of 2006.

When he led Wales out at the Estadio Raúl Conti in Puerto Madryn, Patagonia, on 11 June, Jones became the 123rd player to do so in a capped international. Others are obviously destined to follow in his footsteps, as he has followed in the footsteps of those who have gone before. Along the way the captaincy will be passed among players who have previous experience in the role as well as new names to be added to the roll of honour. Because of this uncertain sequence it was decided not to review the captains on a purely chronological basis but to find another way of telling their stories, one which would enable the concept of captaincy to be explored and, at the same time, accommodate input from many of the surviving 59 men handed the responsibility, men asked to carry the weight of an ever-expectant nation on their shoulders – a tremendous accolade but so often a thankless task.

The format adopted groups the players by position, with a chapter on each of the ten recognised positions on the field of play. By following this pattern, certain anomalies became unavoidable. Some players led Wales from more than one position and there are those from the days when forwards were simply forwards with little, if any, of the specialisation with which today's followers of the game are familiar becoming recognised until the 1930s. Readers may question why Stephen Morris and Idris Jones are included as hookers but there is sufficient evidence to suggest that on the days they led Wales both players performed in what was the first of the forward positions to be recognised. Similarly, some years later, Jeff Squire captained Wales more from the flank than from number 8 but he is included here with the other number 8s for reasons which will be explained.

Having spoken to many ex-captains, I became aware that there were two glaringly apparent schools of thought: one which favoured the position from which it was most advantageous to lead the team, and the other which focused totally on the individual, regardless of whether he appeared in the front row, at full-back or anywhere in between. Both arguments are strongly contested by those with first-hand experience of the demands the responsibility brings with it and such varying opinions led in a direction not anticipated: an investigation into the development of the game in Wales and the impact its many reincarnations have had on the role of captain.

Writing is by and large a solitary occupation but acquiring a better understanding of captaincy and what it means involved the cooperation of others. I am indebted to the following, who gave of their time and no little patience to satisfy the ramblings of an inquisitive individual who hopefully treated them with the respect and reverence they all deserve: Phil Bennett, Bleddyn Bowen, Onllwyn Brace, Eddie Butler, Terry Cobner, Gareth Davies, Gerald Davies, Jonathan Davies, Mervyn

Davies, Terry Davies, John Dawes, Ieuan Evans, John Gwilliam, Mike Hall, Terry Holmes, Rob Howley, Billy James, Ken Jones, Robert Jones, Arthur Lewis, John Lloyd, Jack Matthews, Bryn Meredith, Richard Moriarty, Bob Norster, Michael Owen, David Pickering, Brian Price, Scott Quinnell, Clive Rowlands, Delme Thomas, Malcolm Thomas, Paul Thorburn, David Watkins, Mike Watkins, Bleddyn Williams, Lloyd Williams, J.P.R. Williams and David Young.

At Mainstream, thanks to Bill Campbell, who went with the idea and remained committed, even after seeing Scotland ship 38 first-half points against a vibrant Welsh XV; the editorial staff – Graeme Blaikie, Ailsa Bathgate, Debs Warner and Barry Kew – who aided and abetted the project as only editorial staff can; and Emily Bland, who designed the dust jacket.

Gareth Ahmun, John Billot, Alan Evans, Howard Evans, Huw Evans, John Jenkins, Mark Lewis, Jim McCreedy, Peter Owens, Les Williams and the staff at Cardiff and Newport central libraries all came to the rescue when needed with their various areas of expertise. Thanks are also due to the captains not listed above, those no longer with us and others who, for various reasons, were unable to contribute, for their role in the history of Welsh international rugby and, more importantly, their contribution to the men who have led Wales onto the field of play. They are part of a small, elite group which it has been a joy to view as a collective and record their various deeds.

Finally, as always, my wife Catherine, who tolerated the ups and downs of the nine-month process with her usual calm and patience, nine months which are the nearest a man will ever get to childbirth. For eight of those months, my constant companion in the confines of a converted attic was a four-legged friend who unfortunately decided it was time to visit the great cattery in the sky before the job was finished and was sorely missed in those final weeks. His earlier contribution is immeasurable.

INTRODUCTION

The SS *London* was the flagship of her owner's small fleet of vessels. Constructed at Blackwell Yard in 1864 for Money, Wigram and Co., the ship was designated the profitable run to Australia and in 1865, on only her second voyage, she broke the record for the journey to Melbourne, completing the trip in an impressive 59 days. At the end of the year preparations were finalised for a third tour, and the *London* set sail from Gravesend on 30 December with only a scheduled stop at Plymouth to take on board more cargo and passengers before once again heading for Australia.

The weather was unusually inclement and even worse come the turn of the year. On arrival at Plymouth, early misfortune struck when a lighter taking two pilots out to the vessel capsized in the rough seas less than a mile offshore and one of the men drowned. All around the southern coast of Britain and into the Bristol Channel there were incidents of small ships floundering in the unusually stormy waters, with many reported lost. Notwithstanding this, on 6 January the *London* was finally ready to set sail and despite concerns that she was lying lower in the water than would normally be the case – the manifest shows a cargo which included 1,200 tons of iron and a further 50 tons of coal – she departed Plymouth with 263 passengers and crew on board.

Less than two days into the journey the steamer encountered storms witnesses later described as being of cyclone or hurricane force, and three of the main masts were seriously damaged. Captain J.B. Martin became increasingly concerned as the ship entered the notorious Bay of Biscay and when the engine-room hatch was detached, he made the decision to put about and return to Plymouth. This decision was taken in the early hours of 10 January. Whether the *London* had survived the worst of the weather at this point is unknown, but what is certain is that the decision to return to port took her back into the centre of the storm. She didn't stand a chance.

By midday on 11 January Captain Martin had advised all aboard of the precariousness of their situation and their slim chance of survival, the ship by then taking on water at a rate which could not be contained. The starboard pinnace and two lighters were lost when attempts were made to launch them and eventually only the port pinnace, carrying sixteen passengers and three crew members, successfully pulled away from the stricken vessel, which sank at 2 p.m., taking the fated 244 unfortunates remaining on board with it. After a day weathering the raging storm, the survivors were picked up by an Italian vessel, the *Marianople*. It was only on their return to Plymouth that the true extent of the tragedy was fully understood in the incident report written by the ship's engineer, John Greenhill.

The *London* catered for three classes of passenger and among those who had elected to travel First Class were Mr and Mrs J. Bevan, who joined the ship in Plymouth. They had been on an extended tour of Europe and although originally from Wales were now heading back to their adopted home of Melbourne, Victoria. Bevan was a wealthy coach proprietor who had emigrated to Australia some years earlier, and waiting for him and his wife to return from their vacation was an eight-year-old son, an innocent victim of the tragedy.

James Alfred Bevan was born on 15 April 1858 at Caulfield, a southern suburb of the fast-growing Australian city. When he returned to Wales is uncertain, but he is next found living in Abergavenny, undoubtedly with relatives, and attending Hereford Cathedral School from where he won a scholarship to St John's College, Cambridge. An accomplished sportsman, Bevan won two rugby Blues in 1877 and 1880, the second match played at Richardson's Field, Blackheath, on 14 December, the annual fixture having been relocated from the Kennington Oval. Two months later on 19 February 1881 Wales faced England on the same ground in their first international rugby match, one which saw the visitors comprehensively beaten by a more experienced England, who won by seven goals, one drop goal and six tries to nil.

The events leading up to this are well documented. How, following a meeting at the Tenby Hotel, Swansea, in March 1880, Richard Mullock of the Newport club received a mandate to arrange an international match between Wales and England at the earliest opportunity. How he subsequently took it upon himself to select the Welsh team, and the criticism that he faced following the comprehensive defeat, criticism which insisted the best available players had not been selected. How, three weeks later, on 12 March, at the Castle Hotel, Neath, as a matter of some urgency, representatives of 11 leading clubs formed the Welsh Football Union, the precursor of the Welsh Rugby Union (WRU).

That the first Welsh team was not truly representative of the strength of the club game in Wales at the time is beyond doubt and when a second match was arranged for the following January, this time against Ireland, there were only four survivors from Richardson's Field. Charles Newman, William Phillips, Frank Purdon and George Harding played in Dublin, while Edward Treharne was later given a reprieve when England visited St Helen's, Swansea. The remaining ten players would not represent their country again, most notable among them the Welsh captain on the day – James Alfred Bevan. Exactly why Richard Mullock appointed James Bevan to lead the side is unclear but whatever his reasons Bevan became the first in a long line of men privileged to lead Wales onto the field of play.

With the criticism of the team's failure largely aimed at Mullock, it is fair to say that a precedent was set on day one of the history of Welsh international rugby football, one which would recur regularly in the years that followed, with team selection and the appointment of captains becoming the subject of much debate. What is of particular interest with regard to the events which took place at Richardson's Field is the fact that while James Bevan was the first player to be given the responsibility of captaining Wales in what became his only representative appearance, there would be many more to follow who, like Bevan, enjoyed the experience of international captaincy only once. In 125 years of international rugby and of the 123 players to captain Wales, a remarkably high 41 would not get a second chance, this despite 17 of them leading winning teams. As we shall see, there have been many valid reasons why so many were given little or, more realistically, no opportunity to settle into the role but the figure undoubtedly accounts for the fact that Wales has had more international captains than any other country.

For comparison purposes we need look no further than New Zealand, unquestionably the most successful rugby-playing nation, a statement borne out by the fact that against all opponents played the All Blacks are the only team to have won more Test matches than they've lost. With a shorter international history than Wales and, until recent years, the lack of an equivalent competition to the International Championship, it is obvious that New Zealand have played fewer Test matches, but it is still possible for a fair comparison to be made. For example, Wales have lost 43 per cent of all matches played, while the All Blacks have been beaten on only a miserly 91 occasions – an impressive 22 per cent. Where Wales have called upon the services of 123 captains, the figure in New Zealand stands at 60, among whom only 10 were not asked back a second time. All of which raises the question – does a successful team throw up a good captain or does a good captain nurture a successful team?

First published in 1927, *Rugger*, by W.W. Wakefield and H.P. Marshall, includes a chapter on captaincy which suggests that:

> captaincy should not merely be an honour, but should go to the best man available. There is a tendency to let the distinction of leading the side go round among the best or most distinguished players, but there is more in captaincy than mere playing skill.

Nine years later in the 1936 publication *The Game Goes On*, an anthology edited by Captain H.B.T. Wakelam, rugby union and England cricket selector John Daniell draws a similar conclusion.

> The good captain is a priceless asset to any side, and this is why I can never understand the mentality of some clubs, and even countries, who keep on changing captains – not apparently in the hope of finding the best one, but just that the honour should go round . . . If you have a good captain stick to him as long as possible.

Between 1906 and 1910, Wales were involved in a run of 16 matches, which perfectly illustrates both observations. Beginning with the devastating defeat by South Africa at Swansea, which saw the final international appearance of captain Gwyn Nicholls, the next seven matches introduced seven different captains, the changes made regardless of the fact that six of the seven games were won and that following five of them the successful captain retained his place in the team. There then followed eight consecutive matches under the leadership of Billy Trew, Wales only failing to win once, against England in the first international to be played at Twickenham. From this we can see that those responsible for team selection were guilty of handing the captaincy by rote to the leading players before finally settling on the more conservative option of giving one individual an extended run. To their credit, it has to be acknowledged that both approaches appear to have been successful, Wales winning 13 of their 16 matches.

* * *

In that first international James Bevan represented Cambridge University and was classified as a three-quarter back, but what of those who followed? Which club did they represent and what position did they fill? At the end of the 2005–06 season Wales had played a total of 563 capped internationals under the leadership of 123 captains. Ieuan Evans held the most appearances as captain with 28, followed by Colin Charvis and Rob Howley, who shared second place, both having led Wales 22 times.

Of all the men to captain Wales, Colin Charvis is unique. Only nine players have led Wales from different clubs: Gwyn Nicholls from Newport and Cardiff; John Idwal Rees, Swansea and Edinburgh Wanderers; Claud Davey, Swansea and London Welsh; John Gwilliam, Edinburgh Wanderers and Gloucester; Jonathan Davies, Neath and Llanelli; Jon Humphreys, Cardiff and Bath; Mark Taylor, Swansea and Sale; and, most recently, Gareth Thomas, who became the first Welsh captain from the Celtic Warriors regional side before moving to Toulouse. Added to which is Charvis, who first led Wales while playing for Swansea, then for French second-division club Tarbes, and in the autumn of 2004 as a Newcastle player. But there were also six appearances at the start of the 2003–04 season when the programme editor had no alternative other than to place 'unattached' next to the Welsh captain's name, Charvis having failed to secure a contract with one of the newly formed regions.

The whole ethos of Welsh rugby changed quite dramatically in 2003 when it was decided that in the interests of the international game a move from the traditional club-based structure was needed. Five regional teams were introduced with no little controversy, as it was perceived by many that Cardiff and Llanelli had retained a stand-alone status while six of the other Premier Division clubs had been drafted into the newly named regions. Could Neath and Swansea successfully join forces and attract the public in any numbers to watch a team named after a seabird? Would the partnership forged between

Bridgend and Pontypridd reap the benefits of the abundance of talent at its disposal, and did anybody seriously expect the Newport and Ebbw Vale marriage to survive the honeymoon period? As for Caerphilly, which would have made an obvious partner for Cardiff, nobody seemed interested enough to include the club in the shake-up.

Two years on and followers of the Neath-Swansea Ospreys seemed to have more than comfortably settled into the same nest and even accepted the abbreviated Ospreys as their recognised name, the Bridgend and Pontypridd liaison had fallen by the wayside – Once Were Warriors – and the rugby followers of Gwent were finding it difficult to follow a regional team based at one club which was greeted onto the field by the traditional Black and Amber supporters' cheer of 'New-port! New-port!' The players were Dragons but to whom did they belong? Nothing had changed at Stradey Park – Llanelli were always the Scarlets – while in Cardiff the addendum Blues didn't really upset the majority of the faithful. It is the fervent wish of the WRU that time will see the Blues, Dragons, Ospreys and Scarlets recognised in the game without further explanation, and that day will probably come, but it will not erase the history of rugby union in Wales and the great Welsh club names that are recognised wherever the game is played.

Since the introduction of regional rugby, eight men have captained Wales: Colin Charvis and Mark Taylor, both already experienced in the role, were joined by Stephen Jones, who became the first from the Llanelli Scarlets; Gareth Thomas and Mefin Davies from the Celtic Warriors; Martyn Williams of the Cardiff Blues; Michael Owen of the Newport-Gwent Dragons; and Duncan Jones of the Ospreys. What then of the previous 115 captains; where did they come from? Not as far as Melbourne, Australia, one can be certain of that.

Travel around the rugby clubs of Wales and no matter how big or small, how famous or otherwise, they all have a focal point – the clubhouse. And within the four walls of these hallowed premises is to be found the club's Hall of Fame. Photographs of teams and players from a bygone age fill the walls, while cabinets hold various items of memorabilia – caps signifying representative honours, likewise jerseys with similar references, and much else besides. There are currently 242 member clubs of the WRU, all able to boast an impressive history, but of these only 17 can lay claim to a player chosen to captain the national team while wearing the club's jersey. Add to these eight non-affiliated clubs and come the start of the 2006–07 season a total of twenty-five clubs can boast some immediate association with the Welsh captaincy, together with five of the regions. There will obviously be many others which can claim some level of input into a Welsh captain's development but those that can count the player among their squad at the time of his selection remain relatively few. And with future captains almost certain to be attached to a region in Wales or playing for clubs elsewhere, statistics relating to the contribution of the various Welsh clubs can be viewed as finite. As some players have led Wales while attached to more than one, each club's impact on the Welsh captaincy is measured here by considering the number of matches in which one of its players has been the man in charge (see Appendix II).

Therefore, when Martyn Williams led Wales onto the field at the Waikato Stadium, Hamilton, New Zealand, on 21 June 2003, it was the 145th and probably the last time a player from Cardiff RFC would be at the helm. It comes as no surprise that the capital city club heads the list and neither is it unexpected to see Swansea, Llanelli and Newport in the top four. Between them these clubs have accounted for 400 matchday captains (73 per cent of matches played), which is quite surprising when one considers the periods of dominance seen over the last 30 years by Pontypool, Neath and Pontypridd. Despite this these last three clubs collectively account for only 56 matchday captains, a surprisingly low figure, particularly in light of the increase in the number of international matches now played.

And the remainder? Bridgend can thank Steve Fenwick and J.P.R. Williams for the majority of its eleven matches, while Penarth are solely indebted to Jack Bassett, who led Wales nine times from full-back. Alun Pask, Bleddyn Bowen, Arthur Lewis and his namesake Charles Lewis, who succeeded James Bevan in becoming Wales's second captain, dominate those from Abertillery, South Wales Police, Ebbw Vale and Llandovery respectively, which leaves Aberavon's Billy James, Cross Keys's Steve Morris, and George Travers, who capped Wales once when playing for Pill Harriers, to make up the numbers.

Outside Wales, Bath, Cambridge University, Edinburgh Wanderers, Gloucester, Newcastle, Sale, Tarbes and Toulouse are to be included together with London Welsh, which for many years competed in the unofficial Welsh Championship, but now, as a result of a decline in fortune on the field, coupled with the location factor, while retaining its membership of the WRU, is to be found competing in the English League. However, it can still lay claim to 11 international matchday captains, thanks largely to the outstanding leadership qualities of John Dawes.

John Dawes captain. John Dawes centre. Centre three-quarters –

two of. Centre is the most favoured position for Welsh captains with 25 players having led the team from the middle of the field. Why? In a 1931 publication, *Rugby Football Today*, by E.H.D. Sewell, the author includes a chapter on captaincy interestingly subtitled 'The only successful substitute for brains is silence'. Having outlined various aspects of play that need to be addressed by the captain, Sewell concludes:

> The best of all positions whence a player can observe such incidentals as those I refer to is from centre three-quarter. A centre gets a better bird's-eye view than any player, not excepting the full-back, who is in any case too far away to captain properly. Was there ever a better captain than E. Gwyn Nicholls? I seek information.

We shall see.

They don't field two centres in New Zealand. In one of the game's great contradictions the All Blacks prefer to field one centre who plays outside a first five-eighth (outside-half) and a second five-eighth (inside centre), and in so doing the New Zealand Rugby Football Union unwittingly helps to retain one of the last bastions in sport of Imperial measurements. Athletes no longer run 220, 440 or 880 yards, but 200, 400 and 800 metres, while all jumps and throws are measured using the metric system. Swimming pools and diving boards are metric, Grand Prix drivers race around circuits measured in kilometres, boxers are weighed in kilograms and stand so many metres and centimetres tall. Contrary to all this, British horse racing guards the furlong with great propriety, and the New Zealand Rugby Football Union continues to ensure that when inches and yards have gone the way of bushels and pecks the good old five-eighth fraction will still be in everyday use, despite the fact that few will have any inkling whatsoever as to its meaning.

So the odds on a New Zealand rugby captain being a centre are immediately doubled, but this has little relevance, as a quick look at the history of All Blacks captains will reveal: of the top ten in number of appearances, nine are forwards. A similar situation is found in South Africa where, despite fielding two centres, eight of the top ten captains are forwards. And the remaining three candidates from these two giants of the game? Scrum-halfs, the little men who the forwards can find within an arm's length if they are not happy with the way the game is being controlled.

Looking elsewhere we find that top of the list in Australia is John

Eales, a second-row forward. Ireland has hooker Keith Wood at the top of the table, while in Scotland it is prop forward David Sole. With typical Gallic flair, the French have two players in joint first place, wing forward Jean-Pierre Rives and Philippe Saint-André, a right wing, the same position as the current top of the pile in Wales – Ieuan Evans. It all looks fairly cut and dried in favour of the forwards, but just when you think it's time to rest the case and propose that all future Welsh captains come from the pack, there's a spanner in the works in the shape of one William David Charles Carling. Not only is Will Carling England's leading captain with 59 appearances, he also leads the competition worldwide with only John Eales and New Zealand's Sean Fitzpatrick in serious contention with 55 and 51 outings as captain respectively. Yes, Will Carling, captain, but more importantly Will Carling, centre. Despite the trends seen elsewhere, the leading international captain is a centre, the position most favoured down the years by those responsible for the selection of the Welsh team.

This inevitably leads to the question regarding the least popular position from which Wales has been led. This is not quite as conclusive as one could be forgiven for thinking. There is obviously an acceptable answer but before heading in that direction it must be made clear that in the game's formative years – and, indeed, well beyond, to the 1930s in fact – there was such a lack of specialisation among the forward positions that most historical documents relating to the period offer little more than the fact that a player was a forward. Twelve Welsh captains fall into this category – while it is not unfair to assume that the Revd. Alban Davies was not a tearaway wing forward in the modern-day understanding of the position, and though listings often have Harry Uzzell as a front-row forward, his physique and reputation as an athlete would suggest otherwise – being more specific is nigh on impossible. The truth of the matter is that for many years forwards were treated en bloc, with hooker becoming the first exception due in no small part to the efforts of George Travers. But this aside, it is not possible to include 12 of Wales's captains as anything other than forwards. Which brings back the question of the least favoured position as highlighted by the various selection panels down the years.

Being hidden in the depths of every scrum and invariably rolling around on the fringes of every ruck and maul would not seem conducive to leadership, but many players at club and international level have proved more than competent leaders from positions which offer such limited visibility of the greater picture. But this has counted for naught in the eyes of the Welsh selectors who, despite favouring 11 hookers, have consistently turned a blind eye to the institution that is the prop forward. Be it tight or loose-head, for many of the game's followers, the art and craft of the position remains a mystery and with only three Welsh prop forwards able to claim the honour of leading their country, there is a suggestion that the ignorance, if that is the right word, reaches further than the terraces. Bridgend's John Lloyd, Cardiff's David Young and, most recently, Duncan Jones of the Ospreys are the inner circle's sole representatives and it will be to this position that we go first in our search for the ideal captain.

* * *

Although the following chapters are primarily intended as a tribute to the players who have led Wales during its first 125 years, the main attributes and responsibilities of the captain are also looked at with the views of many ex-captains considered. What is a captain? What should he bring to the team that no other is deemed capable of, and in which position should he play to get the best possible perspective on how the match is unfolding? The answers to these and many other questions will be pursued and at the end some conclusions may be arrived at regarding the qualities needed by the men selected to breathe fire into the players around them. By looking at each position individually, the successes and inevitable failures of the captains involved will be studied in some depth and perhaps there will be some 'information', albeit late, for Sewell – or maybe not. What we are ultimately looking for is the great Welsh captain, a role model for all future leaders to aspire to when they set about the task of inspiring their charges. Let the search begin.

I

OUT OF SIGHT, OUT OF MIND: PROP AND OTHER FORWARDS

Leadership does not come easily to most, which is probably just as well, as inverted pyramids are not ideal whatever the scenario. Whether it's in the political debating chamber or the boardroom, on the battlefield or the sporting field of play, good leadership relies fundamentally on the same principal factors, not least among them the total and utmost respect in which those who find themselves in command must be held by their peers. Without such respect, all around will soon deteriorate into chaos, and the cause, whatever that may be, lost.

For many, age is a barrier, but the respect of one's elders is necessary if a leader is to succeed in bringing out the best in those who fall under his remit. It must be remembered that the most experienced player, the best performer on the field, the best communicator both on and off it, the most tactically aware and the most respected among a squad of 30 or more players are qualities rarely to be found in the make-up of one individual, all of which points to the fact that the truly great international rugby captains are a very rare breed. These are players who, having gained the necessary experience, are able to combine it with the other essential attributes and come close to becoming the finished article, the complete captain. The leadership qualities of Sean Fitzpatrick or Keith Wood are undoubtedly of the highest order and their competitiveness inevitably brought out the best in those around them. They really did lead from the front; hookers who, together with their two props, can lay claim to playing in the least glamorous of factions that make up a rugby union team – the collective that is known as the front row.

With few exceptions, this breed apart are neither the quickest of individuals nor are they likely to be found on the wish lists of the many females the game attracts, but they represent the foundation stone on which a team's success or otherwise depends. If the three players making up the front row are in harmony and have the ascendancy over their immediate opponents, then all is well and a positive result can more often than not be expected. But despite these extraordinary men laying the platform for success, they are not the most favoured by selectors in search of a leader. Fitzpatrick is the obvious exception, and while many hookers have represented the front row as international captains, the same cannot be said of prop forwards.

This is certainly the case in Wales, where only three players have been awarded the captaincy while playing on either the tight- or loose-head: individuals who were identified as having the necessary leadership skills and qualities to enable them to extract the best performance from their team. The fact that they are small in number suggests that their intimate involvement in the forward exchanges has regularly been viewed as a handicap by those considering the due process of captaincy.

A rugby team can simply be divided into three components: a front, middle and back five – that is, the front and second rows; the back row and half-backs; and the three-quarters and full-back. The front five are expected to gain sufficient possession to enable the back row and half-backs to determine the tactics and implement them in such a way that the three-quarters and full-back are given sufficient space and time to put the points on the board. That is the theory, and despite the likelihood that it will be viewed as simplistic by many who control the way rugby union is played in the twenty-first century, it still holds water. In fact, it is beyond argument, as 19 of the top 20 try scorers in international rugby played in the back five. Neither will many forwards or half-backs appear as the list lengthens, so it is fair to suggest that in real terms the game of rugby still proves the old adage that the forwards win matches and the backs decide by how many points.

Before discussing the three prop forwards who have led Wales, there are the twelve men simply referred to as 'forwards' to consider; men who were very much part of a group who hunted and marauded as one and, when it came to the scrum, packed down at random thereby eliminating any need for specialisation. It used to be said that a blanket should cover all the forwards at any point in the match, such was their common cause, and though no longer applicable it does show how the forward effort was invariably viewed as a whole with few players allowed any individual prominence.

However, there were exceptions and some of those who managed to steal the limelight went on to lead their country. A few even became household names to be uttered in the same breath as Gould, Nicholls and Trew, three players who had already ensured that it was for a certain style of play that Welsh rugby would become revered. The exciting back play that would define a nation may still have been in its infancy in the early part of the twentieth century, but then, as now, it was totally reliant on one thing – forwards who could win the ball.

* * *

In the season before the outbreak of the First World War, Wales had assembled a team which began to look capable of great things. The 1912–13 season ended with three consecutive wins over Scotland, France and Ireland, and despite losing the opening match of the following season, an unlucky one-point defeat at Twickenham, Wales again won the remaining three matches. The forwards were the dominant factor, even well in control against England, and it was no surprise that the pack remained unchanged throughout the championship. The season ended in Belfast against an Irish team boasting a similarly explosive pack and the encounter has become recognised as one of the roughest in the history of Welsh rugby. The Welsh pack were already known as the 'Terrible Eight' and the events at Balmoral on 14 March went further in confirming how appropriate a name it was. In atrocious conditions the two packs literally 'fought' each other to a standstill. At every opportunity rival forwards would square up to one another however far distanced they were from play, the referee choosing to turn a blind eye to all off-the-ball incidents.

Irish forward William Tyrell was a man who would later gain recognition in the field of medicine, be decorated for his exploits during the Great War and eventually be knighted, but in Belfast in 1914 he was hell-bent on beating the Welsh forwards into submission. Reputations counted for nothing when the hard men of Welsh rugby were confronted by a green onslaught that refused to take a backward step. Always at the heart of the battle was the Welsh captain, the Revd. Jenkin Alban Davies. For a doctor of medicine and a man of the cloth, what better way to spend a Saturday afternoon?

Wales scored 14 tries in the 1914 championship and rarely has such a dominant pack of forwards been seen in Welsh jerseys. They set up the platform for the backs to exploit and but for a lapse of concentration at Twickenham in the closing moments, when debutant Willie Watts lost control of the ball which led to a converted English try and a 10–9 victory, Revd. Davies would be included in the small group of captains who have led Wales to Grand Slam glory, which would have been an extraordinary achievement. Oxford University, London Welsh, Cardiff, Swansea and Llanelli had all played host to Alban Davies, but at none of these clubs was he appointed captain. In fact, it is unlikely that he captained any side other than Wales, which he led on those four occasions in 1913–14 and once more in an uncapped match against the Barbarians in 1915. What rare qualities did this man have that enabled him to bring together a pack of forwards made up of players from seven different clubs and forge them into a unit capable of sweeping all before it? Some would have it that divine intervention played a hand, but we are left wondering because it was another intervention, that brought about by the German invasion of Belgium, which prevents any real assessment of Davies's leadership abilities.

* * *

On the resumption of international rugby in 1919, Revd. Davies was in his 34th year. Like so many others, he either chose to retire from the game or was considered too old for its demands at the highest level, leaving the selectors with little option but to rebuild the team around a new captain. It was Glyn Stephens of Neath who was invited to become the first player to lead Wales in the post-war era.

Stephens had won nine consecutive caps in 1912–13, but had lost his place in 1914 when the selectors chose to build a new pack under the Revd. Davies which success dictated remain unchanged. However, with the need to introduce 13 players for their first caps, players with Stephens' experience were in short supply and he led the team against the New Zealand Army in the first post-war international played at Swansea on 21 April 1919.

A scrappy affair was decided by penalty goals, the New Zealand Army winning 6–3, and only four of the Welsh team were retained for the opening match in 1920, which saw the introduction of a further nine new caps. Glyn Stephens was one of the casualties. He'd played his last game for Wales, but the selectors again looked for experience when choosing their next captain, and it was another forward who took over.

Harry Uzzell had been a member of the Terrible Eight and, with Stephens, was one of seven players to represent Wales either side of the war. He had recently celebrated his 37th birthday when invited to captain his country, thereby becoming the oldest player to date to do so. Harry Uzzell led Wales to comfortable home victories against England and Ireland, together with a close encounter in Paris, which saw the visitors triumph by the smallest of margins; however, a 9–5 defeat in Scotland spoilt the opportunity of a glorious return to international rugby.

Glyn Stephens and Harry Uzzell were succeeded in turn by Jack Wetter and Tommy Vile, players who had also won representative honours before the war. This leaning towards experience was perfectly understandable, but at the same time it was recognised that at some stage a new name was going to have to be vested with the responsibility of leading the team – it was time for change.

Tom Parker was one of the new faces against the New Zealand Army, and two years and six caps later he led Wales for the first time against France at Cardiff Arms Park. He led the team with a skill and passion that proved difficult to replace once he retired in 1923, when Wales fell into rapid decline. But his record stands alongside that of any of the more well-known great captains and none has led Wales in more matches without experiencing defeat. The fact that three of the victories were against France cannot detract from a record of six wins and a draw, and that his retirement was immediately followed by the worst period in the first hundred years of Welsh international rugby must surely add to Parker's achievement.

Tom Parker was the 33rd player to captain Wales and of the 32 who preceded him, 21 were backs, a ratio which has changed little. The first forward to captain Wales was Henry Simpson of Cardiff, who was only appointed when half-back Charlie Newman got injured. Simpson led Wales against Ireland in the first international to be played at Cardiff Arms Park on 12 April 1884, a match won by the home side. It was 1887 before another forward was handed the reins when Bob Gould stole a march on his more famous brother by becoming the first of the siblings to lead Wales – Arthur would have a two-year wait before his opportunity came.

In Edinburgh Bob Gould led Wales to a defeat of mammoth proportions, one to rival that first match in 1881. Scotland ran in twelve tries, George Lindsay scoring five of them (still a record for the championship), but it was a day of huge disappointment for Gould, with Wales failing to score.

The captaincy remained in the care of the forwards with Tom Clapp and Frank Hill in charge for the next five matches. Clapp claimed two wins in his three outings, including a victory over Ireland in a 'home' match played at Birkenhead Park to avert the additional travelling costs of getting the Irish team to South Wales. However, Hill, who eventually led his country four times, experienced success only once, but that in a match of some significance – Wales's first encounter with a team from the Southern hemisphere.

The New Zealand Native team undertook a tour that makes most others look like long weekends. A total of 107 matches were played over the course of a year, 74 of them in the British Isles. A privately sponsored tour, the original idea was that twenty-six players of Maori origin would make up the squad, however four players were included who could not claim any Maori ancestry, but were deemed native to New Zealand, hence the name. As was the custom in New Zealand rugby, the team fielded eight forwards. To combat this, there was a change in the composition of the Welsh XV selected to face the tourists at Swansea on 22 December 1888. Where Simpson, Gould and Clapp had each led a side which included nine forwards – the preferred format of the day – under Hill, Wales now reverted to an eight-man pack; the days of only six backs being selected were laid to rest for good following a comfortable home victory by one goal and two tries to nil.

After ten seasons of international rugby Wales had yet to find a captain who looked like making the position his own for any length of time, but by 1890 the young Newport centre Arthur Gould was looking the most likely candidate to establish himself as a long-term leader. When his business interests took him overseas for 12 months, the Welsh selectors were forced to look elsewhere and elected to go with William Bowen of Swansea. After one match, he was replaced with Llanelli's William Thomas. Both players were experienced campaigners and both were forwards. Thomas in particular had played at the highest level when he was the only Welsh representative on the ground-breaking British Isles tour to Australia and New Zealand in 1888 – the trademark name 'British Lions' was a long way off. Unfortunately neither player did much to strengthen the case for the forwards when, after losing at home to England under Bowen, Thomas fared little better, experiencing defeat in Edinburgh before claiming some consolation when Wales defeated Ireland in the last match of the season, played on his home ground, Stradey Park.

As Welsh rugby entered the twentieth century and the start of its first 'Golden Era', there was sufficient confidence in the team's abilities to enable the selectors to treat the captaincy as a reward for services rendered and several distinguished players were given the honour of leading Wales once. Arthur Flowers Harding was one such recipient but on closer inspection here was a player who could well have merited much more recognition. His only appearance as captain came in 1908 against England in Bristol, a match Wales won 28–18, but his leadership credentials suggest that he should not have been one of the many denied further opportunity.

Arthur 'Boxer' Harding played his club rugby at London Welsh, had captained the club in four consecutive seasons, 1903–07, and was a member of the British Isles team which toured Australia and New Zealand in 1904. Therefore, he was a man of considerable experience when he was finally chosen to captain Wales on the occasion of his 19th cap. That Boxer Harding was also chosen to captain the Anglo-Welsh team which toured Australia and New Zealand in the summer of 1908 adds no little credibility to his leadership qualities and yet he only captained his country once, and that more as a thank you than by right.

The last 'forward' to captain Wales was Jack Whitfield, who had the misfortune of leading the team against Scotland in Edinburgh on 2 February 1924, a day which saw the worst defeat inflicted on Wales since Bob Gould's shattering experience in 1887, almost 40 years earlier. This was the lowest point in a five-year period that saw Wales struggle against all opponents with the exception of the French, who still had a lot to learn about the international game. Jack Whitfield was a big, naturally athletic player and the fact that he scored over forty tries for Newport and five more in his twelve Welsh appearances suggests that he was a forward of the looser variety, but without sufficient evidence he is the last player to lead Wales from an unspecified position. There has been a suggestion throughout the preceding pages that several of the players discussed were probably the equivalent of the modern-day prop forward, but be that as it may one thing is certain – it would be almost 50 years after Jack Whitfield led the team onto the field before the first designated prop forward captained Wales and a further 28 years would pass before the arrival of the second.

* * *

Bridgend RFC was founded in 1878, two years before the WRU, but it was ninety-four years before the club could boast a Welsh captain. John Lloyd won his first cap in 1966 and had increased his tally to 19 when, after leading Wales in an uncapped match against Canada, he was invited to continue in the role come the start of the 1972 championship. Wales were blessed with a number of international-class props during this period, the emergence of Barry Llewellyn and the ongoing career of the ever present, evergreen Denzil Williams dictating that the versatile Lloyd appear in both the loose- and tight-head positions in the front row. Llewellyn and Williams had played throughout the previous season, which saw Wales win a sixth Grand Slam, but with Williams and captain John Dawes now retired, the selectors had to find a new leader, somebody who would carry the weight of the Welsh public's desire for back-to-back Grand Slams. John Lloyd was duly recalled to replace Williams in the scrum and take over the mantle left by Dawes.

It was a surprise. Although he was not immediately involved, it was Carwyn James who first suggested to me that there was a possibility I could be made captain. This happened at a meeting of the WRU held at the Afon Lido, but I seriously doubted that I was in the running. Carwyn was proved right when the chairman of selectors, Cliff Jones, eventually asked me if I was interested in taking over. I was thrilled. It is a great honour to be invited to play for Wales but to then be asked to captain the team is very special indeed.

In his fifth term as Bridgend captain Lloyd was no novice in the art of leadership. The club had won the Welsh Club Championship in the previous two seasons, playing the open, expansive game which the national team favoured, but it was several years earlier that the future Welsh captain was first associated with the role.

I had always been interested in leadership. I was comfortable with it from a very early age, captaining school teams and district sides, and I was always a great believer in rugby as a 15-man game and made sure I was involved with the whole team. At Pontycymmer Grammar School there was a teacher called John Rees who influenced me a lot. He was a great man for basic skills, running with the ball, passing, tackling and emphasising how as a front-row forward above all else you have to be a solid scrummager, and it was John Rees who made me learn to play either side of the scrum. There have been many props who could never play on both the loose- and the tight-head and I feel I owe a lot to him because he instilled in me the basic scrummaging skills which enabled me to do so.

When I went to Cardiff Training College I met two men who also had an enormous influence on me: Leighton Davies and Roy Bish, men who wanted to play a fluid game, wanted to spread the ball using both forwards and backs. But again the emphasis was on the basics, the forwards focused on winning only quality ball from the set pieces, rucks and mauls.

After leading Wales to a comfortable victory over Canada in an uncapped match, John Lloyd could have been forgiven for thinking he was in a no-win situation when he was elected to continue in the role, such was the expectancy in Wales at the time. He need not have worried. Despite being denied the chance to lead Wales to a seventh Grand Slam when politics in the shape of the IRA forced the cancellation of the match in Ireland, Lloyd can claim a perfect record as captain, Wales winning the season's other three matches with an unchanged team. At Twickenham a dour encounter was followed by the appearance on the touchline at the final whistle of Eamonn Andrews with his big red book.

Following the England match we went straight to a television studio where an episode of *This Is Your Life* was recorded. Barry John was the recipient and the whole team was invited to join with family and friends in the celebration. Then we played some good stuff against Scotland – that wonderful try of Gareth's, following a kick and chase, which ended in the mud in the corner stands out. We won the game well and seven weeks later were in similarly good form against France but the season was marred by events in Ireland.

The cancellation of the match in Dublin was particularly disappointing, but the WRU, like the SRU, decided that it would not be sensible to travel.

There were letters sent to a number of the players and the WRU had to convene, the outcome of which being that the committee decided we shouldn't go. It was disappointing, but at the end of the day they had to make a decision. Whether it was the right or wrong decision doesn't matter – it wasn't to be.

What would have happened at Lansdowne Road we will never know and great as Welsh expectations undoubtedly were, it should not be forgotten that Ireland recorded two creditable away victories in 1972 at Stade Colombes and Twickenham, and can similarly wonder if Lady Luck may have been on their side had the season not been so rudely interrupted.

The years since John Lloyd captained Wales have witnessed many changes in the game of rugby union, changes which have impacted not only on the Laws of the game and the way it is played, but changes which have also impacted on the role of captain. As he had succeeded John Dawes as Welsh captain, so too, eight years later, did John Lloyd succeed Dawes as coach to the national team, a role which is now hugely instrumental in selection and preparation.

Coaches now have a much bigger influence on the game than their predecessors did. You have a situation where messages can be quickly relayed onto the field, information modern technology provides within seconds, all of which can be passed to the players, and there is also the half-time period which allows the coach access to the team. The last five or six years have seen the coach become far more powerful than those who went before and because of this he does perhaps have more influence on the match than the captain. You certainly still need a leader on the field, but I feel the role has been diminished, largely because of technological advances.

The 1972 championship is well remembered in Wales: Gareth Edwards's try in the mud; Derek Quinnell's rush down the tunnel to get onto the Arms Park for the last few minutes against France and a much deserved first cap; the retirement of Barry John; the threat posed by the IRA – but how many remember that for the first time a prop forward captained his country and that he led an unbeaten team? John Lloyd made two further appearances for Wales, neither as captain, and it was 28 years before another cornerstone of the scrum would be asked to take charge.

* * *

Like good wine, prop forwards mature with age. Nowhere is the difference in age between a young player and his opposite number as disconcerting as in the front row, and particularly at prop where the pressure in the scrum for lesser mortals is unimaginable. Does a 19-

year-old wing care if his opposite number is 33 with hundreds of
matches under his belt? Of course he doesn't; neither would any other
player on the field show much concern for the age of his opposite
number. But if you are 19 years of age, preparing for that first scrum,
and the guy staring you in the face, probably salivating at the prospect
of an easy 80 minutes' work, has been round the block a few times and
got the scars to prove it, you bet your life it matters if he's 33 years old
and a seasoned international to boot. This is the coalface, the sharp end
with nowhere to hide, and for those foolish enough to have chosen this
position ahead of the glamour to be found elsewhere on the field, it's
time to stand up and be counted.

When Wales met England at Ballymore, Brisbane, in the quarter-
final of the 1987 Rugby World Cup (RWC), Welsh tight-head prop
David Young was 19 days short of his 20th birthday and Paul Rendall,
England's loose-head prop, was 110 days into his 34th year – in such
situations age matters!

Age certainly does come into it. The position demands a level of
maturity and experience and I'd be lying if I said I didn't have
certain reservations going into that first game. Where I had the
edge perhaps was that I had adopted a professional attitude which
was maybe ahead of its time. I was one of only a handful of players
who regularly trained with weights, whereas Paul and most other
props would not have taken the benefits of such training on board.
Wales had three squads in preparation for the World Cup under
the guidance of fitness coaches J.J. Williams and Lynn Davies. I
was in the C squad, which was based around development players,
but of everyone involved I think only David Pickering, Richie
Collins and myself were doing any regular weight training. From
a young age I had placed a great importance on fitness, always
playing a year ahead of myself through school, and when the
rugby league clubs started to show an interest in me at 22 years of
age, I'm sure my all-round game was taken into consideration
because scrums don't play a big part in league. I remember Bobby
Windsor commenting when I signed for Leeds that Wales didn't
need a sidestepping, round-the-park type of prop and I was better
off going north. It's comical really. When I started out I was told
that I was too young, couldn't scrummage and was too loose, and
when I finished playing I was too old, too tight and not mobile
enough.

For Dai Young, the years following that first taste of international rugby included a British Lions tour, more representative honours with Wales, the move to rugby league, more honours, and on the advent of professional rugby union a much vaunted return to his roots and more of the same.

I hadn't given any thought to playing league but when I returned from the Lions tour in 1989 and Leeds started to show an interest, I made the decision to sign purely and simply for financial reasons. I was concerned about the fact that I needed a career, not one that was dependent on my name and would be over as soon as the next Dai Young came along, something that would look after me when I finished playing. It wasn't easy getting anything suitable because even though I was playing rugby at the highest level with Wales and was a British Lion, the first thing any prospective employer wanted to know was how much time I would need off.

I found it very difficult to find what I was looking for: something which would enable me to carry on playing rugby, which obviously didn't pay the bills. So when the opportunity to join Leeds came along, I grabbed it, not thinking for a moment that there would ever be a way back. Life at Leeds was difficult. Not only did I have to learn a totally different game, but my playing time was limited because the club had four international props on the books. I went on loan to Salford for what was originally meant to be a year, but I settled and spent five good years there, captaining the club for three seasons and, I believe, playing the best rugby of my career.

The player who returned to union in 1996 wasn't the same one who had gone north in 1989. My body was wrecked and I don't think I ever reached my true potential again, largely because of a string of injuries which held me back. Kevin Bowring fast-tracked me into the Welsh team but I wasn't really ready, and when the calf injuries started to take their toll, others got their chance and I struggled to keep my place. At one stage I was out for five months, back for four weeks and then playing for Wales, but I was never 100 per cent fit. It was very frustrating being good enough to play for Wales but not able to fully do myself justice.

Thirteen years on and the start of a new millennium, it was Dai Young who was going into that first scrum salivating and looking as if he had been around the block a few times; and in February 2000 against France at the Millennium Stadium, Cardiff, now 32 years of age, he became the second prop forward to captain Wales. Graham Henry had felt the need to change the captain following the 1999 RWC and it was Dai Young whom he asked to succeed Rob Howley at the start of what, with the inclusion of Italy, had become the Six Nations Championship.

Young was in a position not dissimilar to that in which John Lloyd had found himself. After a run of ten successive victories Wales had disappointed in their last group match of the 1999 RWC, losing to Samoa, and were eliminated at the quarter-final stage by eventual winners Australia. The expectation was still there come the turn of the year and with the increased profile rugby had experienced since Henry's arrival, coupled with Wales hosting the game's biggest tournament, the focus of the nation was firmly on the national sport – but there the similarity ends.

It was almost as if it happened overnight. Welsh rugby was in turmoil, freefall, and Dai Young, from being a senior member of the squad who could be relied upon to go about his job in workmanlike fashion, was now in the firing line. And it was the media who were firing the bullets and rarely missing, having had much practice in recent years. Graham Henry was under fire, fitness guru Steve Black was being criticised for his methods and there were allegations concerning the eligibility of certain players to represent Wales.

When I took over as captain, the honeymoon period was well and truly over. After being put on a huge pedestal, Graham was beginning to come in for some criticism. The results started to turn against us, which he found difficult to cope with, and then Steve Black, who had played such a big part in the success, left suddenly. It was only because of my previous experience of such problems as captain at Salford and similarly with the Welsh rugby league team that I managed to come through it.

On retiring from the game David Young pursued his coaching ambitions and after starting the new career with Cardiff became coach of the regional team, the Cardiff Blues, in 2003. It was not an easy introduction to the unique demands put on coaches, where the fine line between success and failure seems to hang on their decisions. The Blues failed to live up to expectations for a variety of legitimate reasons which unfortunately count for naught when the bottom line is considered. What his new role did was allow Young to view the playing side from a different perspective and not least among the issues he had to consider was the role of captain.

There is no doubt in my mind that prop forward was not the best position on the field from which to captain the team but the game has moved on. Now there are several decision makers, players who are in positions from which they can see their particular area of responsibility, and this has impacted on the captaincy. It is still a huge responsibility for a player, who has to be totally respected by the rest of the team and able to get the best out of them. He has to be as prominent, possibly even more so, in the off-field activities, leading by example in training and general team preparation, keeping a good level of discipline and ensuring that the overall environment is one which will enable the players to flourish. He also has to be able to get to know the players quickly, get to know what makes them tick; find out who among the squad will respond to gentle encouragement and which of the players needs a kick up the backside. Everybody is different and if the captain doesn't understand his players' various traits, he cannot get the best out of them. This can take time, which is why I believe that a captain should get a run of matches to enable him to make his mark. When he made me captain, Graham Henry saw it as an appointment that would last a couple of seasons, but his problem had always been that, while I may have made a suitable captain in the past, he felt that I couldn't always be guaranteed my place in the team.

Dai Young proved that the unfavourable attitudes towards the prop as captain should be reviewed. Where once it was deemed unsuitable for reasons that are self-explanatory, it is no longer the case, and if the right man is shoring up the scrum, it shouldn't be seen negatively. With the British Lions in Australia in 2001 Young led the tourists in four matches, led teams which boasted a wealth of experienced players – Lawrence Dallaglio, Scott Murray, Jason Leonard, Matt Dawson and Scott Quinnell among them. In doing so he made a big statement for the forgotten men of the front row.

* * *

The 1999 Under-21 Six Nations saw Wales claim a Grand Slam. Stephen Jones was captain, Gareth Cooper his half-back partner. Craig Morgan and Matthew Watkins were outside them, and the pack included Andy Newman, Alix Popham, Gavin Thomas, Nathan Bonner-Evans and Deiniol Jones, but it was another Jones who would go on to become Wales's 123rd captain, loose-head prop Duncan Jones.

It may have started in a style which John Lloyd and David Young would have been comfortable with but no more. Circa summer 2006 Duncan Jones, the latest player to be given the honour of captaining Wales, sports a blond-afro hairstyle which ensures that his every deed on the field of play is highlighted. This doesn't present a problem to a player who is a complete footballer: comfortable doing his job in the depths of the scrum; happy supporting in the lineout; capable in the loose with ball in hand; and a player who is often seen making try-saving tackles. He is the finished article for the game that rugby union has become in the twenty-first century.

From Neath to the Ospreys and Wales, Duncan Jones is rarely seen without his fellow prop and namesake Adam, who boasts similar locks but of a darker variety, which accounts for the fact that, in tandem, the pair have been christened the 'Hair Bears'. All of which gives credence to the argument that in the modern game the forwards have as much right to strut their stuff in the fashion stakes as their counterparts behind the scrum.

Duncan Jones first tasted international rugby at the highest level when he took the field as a replacement against Australia in November 2001. It wasn't until the warm up matches for the RWC in 2003 that Jones got his first starts playing against Ireland and Scotland, before appearing against Canada and Italy in the group stages in Australia. His main rival for the loose-head berth was Gethin Jenkins, and when untimely injuries interrupted Jenkins's career, Jones was ready to step in. Theirs is a healthy rivalry, but since the 2005 British Lions tour to New Zealand, from which Jenkins was one of only a handful of players to return with their reputation enhanced, it has been Jones who firstly claimed pole position and then resolutely hung on to it.

With a summer tour to Argentina his first task as national coach, Gareth Jenkins had a problem. Recognised captains Gareth Thomas, Michael Owen, Stephen Jones and Martin Williams were all taking the summer off, enjoying a well earned rest before the build-up to the 2007 RWC began in earnest. Who should he select to lead the squad? With captain Barry Williams injured, Duncan Jones had led the Ospreys through much of the 2005–06 season. He had comfortably coped with the added responsibilities and had impressed many onlookers, Jenkins among them, so it was no surprise when the party to travel was announced and Duncan Jones was named as captain.

A largely inexperienced side with an average age of little more than 24, playing under a new captain, was always going to have its work cut out in what is recognised as one of the toughest places to tour. Seasoned forwards form the basis of the Argentine approach to the game, and with some world-class backs, the Pumas were expected to account for Wales with something to spare. However, in Puerto Madryn, Patagonia, Wales put all such pessimism to rest with a spirited performance which saw them narrowly defeated 27–25 in a game in which they were generally regarded as having been the better side. Unfortunately, the gloom mongers were proved right when Wales had little answer to a fired-up Argentina in Buenos Aries, the home side running out comfortable winners.

Despite two defeats, there were many plusses for Gareth Jenkins to mull over on the journey home. Two exciting young forwards in particular had adapted to the international arena with credit, while behind the scrum there was plenty for the new coach to work with for the future. But not least of the positives to come out of the tour was the way in which the captain had impressed. Duncan Jones had brought his team together, both on and off the field, and there are many who feel that he perhaps did enough in Argentina to be allowed to continue in the role. Time will tell, but with so many leading candidates now putting their hand up for the job this is the type of problem coaches relish. However, one thing seems almost certain: at some future date, Duncan Jones will lead Wales again.

* * *

Through the following pages we shall see a strong argument unfold in favour of the character of the individual being the main criterion, the only factor to consider when appointing a captain. Many respected opinions place total importance on this sole attribute, which suggests that the prop forward should not be overlooked in the manner of the last 125 years, that he should be viewed as an equally serious contender for the captaincy as those players found in the favoured positions, but until such apparently radical thinking is allowed to surface it is down to the third member of the triumvirate to push the case for the front row.

II

HOOKING FOR BUSINESS: HOOKER

In trying to explain the paucity of props who have led Wales, we possibly need look no further than the man in the middle, the one with his arms tightly gripped around his props' shoulders as the front row prepares for a scrum. He is the boss, the organiser, the man in the best position to feel the weight and effort of the forwards around and behind him, the strengths and weaknesses of the opposition scrum – he is the hooker.

There must be something about hanging in the middle of the front row as it waits for the contact of the scrum that focuses the mind, something about grabbing a towel and giving the ball a caressing clean before throwing it into the lineout, something which alerts the player that he is the focus of attention. One almost gets the impression that next to the outside-half the hooker has to be the most confident, even arrogant, player on the field, such are the moments of intense confrontation that he faces, moments in which to come second best is to acknowledge defeat.

In 1934 the Welsh selectors were forced into a complete rethink for the opening match of the championship, a result of several leading players having either retired at the end of the previous season or been ruled out of contention by injury. Among those who had retired was the captain, Watcyn Thomas, which in no small way compounded the problem. When the team to face England was finally announced, it contained thirteen new caps, the most introduced since the first post-war international, and not one player who had appeared in Wales's last match ten months earlier. Included among those making a first appearance was a man not only selected to appear out of his favoured position, but also appointed as captain.

John Raymond Evans was only 22 years of age but had already established himself as one of the leading second-row forwards in Wales. Officials at Newport had wanted him to captain the club, which was going through a particularly lean period, but his business interests had taken priority and now he found himself asked to lead an inexperienced Welsh team and from the position of hooker, one with which he was not overly familiar. That Wales lost to England came as no surprise, but the way in which the match was reported suggests that they were fortunate to avoid a much heavier defeat, having been totally outplayed. Five players, Evans among them, would never play for Wales again after a debacle which left the Welsh public cold.

In miserably wet conditions the pack were taken apart. There was little on the day to give any cause for optimism, Wales losing 9–0 to an England team which went on to win the Triple Crown. The Welsh were castigated by the press: 'any good Welsh club pack would have beaten it easily' and 'rarely – perhaps never – have Welsh forwards been so inferior' summed up the general reaction. In his defence it has to be recorded that during the match Evans sustained a bad injury to his thumb, which prevented him from playing for his club the following week. Nor was he available for selection for the next international, and the selectors never called on him again.

After much persuading, John Evans finally captained Newport between 1935 and 1937 before retiring from the game at the relatively young age of 26. The outbreak of war saw him join the Parachute Regiment, rising to the rank of lieutenant, but in March 1943 he was killed in action in the Middle East, one of two Welsh internationals lost during the conflict; the other, Cardiff scrum-half and Glamorgan and England cricketer Maurice Turnbull.

In his two seasons as captain at Newport, Evans helped to reverse the club's poor form by developing a relatively young pack of forwards into a match-winning eight. Albert Fear, Vivian Law, Tom Rees and Ernie Coleman all gained international honours, but it was a young hooker who caught the eye and he looked particularly familiar to those of an age who could cast their minds back some 30 years. William 'Bunner' Travers followed in the footsteps of his illustrious father, George 'Twyber' Travers, playing for Pill Harriers, Newport and eventually Wales. Both men were hookers and were extremely highly rated by their peers, but it was George who captained his country.

Pill Harriers was the stamping ground for many distinguished rugby footballers and as a club it gained recognition with an invincible season immediately following the end of the First World War. Located in a suburb of Newport that had been founded on the town's thriving docks, the club played regular fixtures against its more fashionable rival on the other side of the River Usk during the 20 seasons between the wars. Many of its finest products inevitably found their way over the river, such has always been the attraction of the bigger pond, among them George Travers, the first specialist hooker to play for Wales.

Twyber Travers won 22 of his 25 caps as a Pill Harriers player, a run of appearances which included his outing as Welsh captain against Scotland at Swansea in 1908 in a match which saw Wales take the second step towards the first recognised Grand Slam. Preceded by Boxer Harding and followed immediately by Teddy Morgan, George Travers was one of the eight players to lead Wales in consecutive matches between 1906 and 1908 and, as such, is another who must be viewed as a flag bearer rather than a leader on merit. Such was the confidence in the Welsh team of the day that the selectors could afford to hand out such laurel leaves, but they could so easily have been caught out in the case of Travers when Scotland failed by the narrowest of margins, a last-minute decision on a possible 'try' being given against them.

Once established as a specialist position, hooker would remain so and it is now possibly one of only two that are unique in this respect, scrum-half being the other. Difficult as it may be, it is far from unusual for prop forwards to be able to play on either side of the scrum, but attempts to convert them to hooker have rarely met with the hoped-for results. Second-row forwards are often found at number 8 and vice versa, while wing forwards can play open-side or blind-side and it is not unusual to see them locking the scrum at 8. Behind, the difference between being full-back or wing seems negligible, with one recent Welsh line-up including a right full-back and left full-back in addition to the recognised number fifteen. Similarly centres can be moved out to the wing or in to outside-half, and although the number ten is the nearest to a specialist position outside scrum-half the demands on it have changed; the individual flair once associated with the mercurial talents who wore the famous jersey now play second fiddle to kicking and tackling ability.

The recent history of Welsh rugby throws up many examples of players who have been selected to play in a position other than that which they occupy week in week out for their clubs. Some are so successful that the change becomes permanent, while for others it has proved to be their undoing, an apparent versatility consigning them to the bench as cover for a couple of positions. Such decisions are now made by one person, following the arrival of the full-time coach, whose selection policies are based on his own interpretation of the style of play he wishes to introduce and the players needed to implement it. In such circumstances it is easy to point the finger when things go wrong, but when more than one individual is involved there becomes a certain safety in numbers – for much of its history Welsh team selection was the responsibility of a panel of five.

It only takes a cursory glance at the record books to see that one of the worst periods in the history of Welsh rugby was the 1920s, when between 1923 and 1928, of the 26 matches played 18 were lost and 17 different captains were chosen in an attempt to reverse the trend, none of whom could claim to have succeeded. It was in 1924–25 that the system for Welsh team selection changed with the introduction of the Big Five, a format which would serve for the next 65 years. Earlier methods had given every committee member his chance to promote the local talent from his region but by narrowing the responsibility it was felt that any local prejudices would be avoided.

In their first season the selectors were called upon five times. The record shows that four matches were lost, five captains chosen and only four of the players who featured in the season's opening match against New Zealand were included in the team that faced Ireland in the fifth, less than four months later. Seven changes were made after the New Zealand defeat and following the reversal at Twickenham there was a general feeling the selectors were going to wield the axe again in their search for a winning combination; however, the team that new captain Stephen Morris led against Scotland showed only two changes, both in the forwards. An involvement with rugby league clubs Salford and St Helens saw Jack Gore replaced by Steve Lawrence, and Ron Herrera took over from Cliff Williams. Gore had apparently been on the books at St Helens for a year after playing under a pseudonym, all of which was revealed when Salford showed an interest in the player. An embarrassing situation was defused, Gore being released from his contract with St Helens and allowed to sign for Salford.

With the Welsh selectors trying to establish themselves and find a winning combination which would avert the already mounting public censure of the new process, it was almost inevitable that another defeat would follow and at Swansea Scotland romped to a 24–14 victory, Morris and his forwards taking the brunt of the criticism. 'It is the lack of intelligence of our forward play which is the great cause of the poverty of Welsh rugby,' wrote Clem Lewis in the *Daily Chronicle*, and he was not alone, with most commentators of a similar opinion. The forwards were poor in the scrum, the mêlée and the rush, and the captain's decision to put one of them into the backs as a defensive manoeuvre left them even more exposed to the rampant Scottish eight. Hooker aside, specialisation among the forwards was still in the early stages of its evolution, and despite the recognition given to George Travers, in the wake of the First World War the selectors chose to ignore any advantages that could be gained by introducing such specialisation into other areas of forward play. In fact, they were culpable in the short-term demise of the hooker as a position requiring a particular expertise. Common sense would prevail in the 1930s, when the forward positions with which today's followers of the game are familiar were finally introduced, but until then scrums and lineouts were disorganised free-for-alls and Welsh rugby was the worse for it. Perhaps it was the 'intelligence' of the selectors that should have been questioned.

Stephen Morris was another of the fall guys of the 1920s. An experienced forward of the looser variety he was chosen to play in the front row of the scrum against Scotland, and although he kept his place in the team, when the selectors reverted him to a role in which he performed best, he was not given a second chance to captain his country. He remains the only representative of Cross Keys RFC to have led Wales.

The interesting phrase in the above comment by Clem Lewis is 'lack of intelligence', which, taken in isolation, can be viewed as quite scathing. The fact that it was a generalisation, referring to the forwards in particular, inevitably meant that the burden of the criticism would be borne by the captain. Whether or not this is perceived as fair is irrelevant, but it highlights the added responsibility he takes with him onto the field. Never has a Welsh captain been allowed any serious input into the team selection or the suggested tactics to be adopted during the match, but in the event of failure it would usually be his head on the block before all others – a sometimes thankless task.

The *Concise Oxford Dictionary* defines intelligence as, among other things, 'the intellect, understanding ... the quickness of understanding: wisdom'. Should we expect individuals blessed with an intellectual level that is acceptable in everyday life to take it unaffected into the sporting arena or should allowances be made for factors that are unique to the occasion and can have a detrimental effect on performance? Stephen Morris was an intelligent man, an education welfare officer, and the seven players who made up his pack included four members of the constabulary, a bank official, a docker and an academic completing a doctorate at Cambridge University at the time and who would go on to gain great recognition in the fields of industry and education. All of which suggests that to take the field of play, a rugby player at any level has to be able to embrace a new mental attitude over and above that which he abides by in everyday life, and a captain even more so. As a forward, any individuality has to be tempered to accommodate the collective and this would seem to be where Morris's pack were found most wanting, added to which are disciplines which must be rigidly adhered to, particularly in the modern game, with the introduction of the sin bin and the ability of the goal kicker to punish offenders with unerring accuracy. Rugby union is a team sport. It has a set of Laws, which must be observed, and when analysts look into the reasons for a team's lack of success, they will inevitably identify a lack of communication and discipline within the players high among its failings.

Many would argue otherwise but fundamentally rugby union is a simple game. Certainly the offside Law will always be open to abuse and its different interpretations are a constant irritation to the game's followers, as is the rule regarding advantage, which also varies considerably in its implementation. Then there are the minor offences: the forward pass and the knock on, the crooked feed and the binding in the scrum, which often appear to be ignored by the officials. But basically it's 15 against 15, with the object of the exercise to score the most points by tries and kicks at goal. A simple game, then, but there is no doubt that you have to be intelligent to play it.

For the visit to Belfast in 1925 the captaincy, having passed from Morris to Arthur Cornish for the expected victory at the expense of the French, was now handed to Llanelli's Idris Jones. Recognised by all but the selectors as the best hooker in Wales, Jones's first three caps had been won playing out of position in the second and third ranks of the scrum; it was on his only appearance as captain that he was selected as hooker. It was Jones who was completing his doctorate at Cambridge University and he now led a pack not dissimilar in its make-up to Stephen Morris's, five police officers and two dockers making up the eight. Behind the scrum there was a wealth of the grey matter with three of the backs also studying at Cambridge, but it was all to no avail. They may well have won *University Challenge*, but they couldn't beat the Irish, who were singularly unimpressed, and recorded a comfortable 19–3 victory.

* * *

The first four hookers to captain Wales had one thing glaringly in common – they only did it once. Travers had been given the honour for services rendered, Morris led a team which received scathing criticism, and Jones fared little better. John Evans made up the quartet. With the wisdom behind the Big Five being questioned, many went the same way as before, the selectors continuing their search for a winning combination and the right man to lead it. The fact that only George Travers led a winning team may go some way to explaining why it was a further 26 years before the front row could boast another Welsh captain.

When Bryn Meredith was called upon to lead Wales, he had already won twenty-four caps and been on two British Lions tours. In South Africa in 1955 Meredith played in all four Test matches, a feat he would repeat in 1962. He was denied a Test appearance in 1959 when the tourists visited Australia and New Zealand, having to play second fiddle to captain Ronnie Dawson, who many commentators at the time thought to be the inferior player. Dai Davies, Meredith's predecessor in the Welsh team, experienced a similar situation when he toured with the Lions in 1950 under the captaincy of Karl Mullen, like Dawson an Irishman and also a hooker. Davies fared better, playing in three of the Tests, but despite having good reason to feel aggrieved Meredith never let his personal ambition cloud his commitment to the cause and was always totally supportive of his captain.

It had taken almost 80 years but on the resumption of international rugby following the Second World War props had become props, second rows were second rows and wing forwards and number 8s had found their identity. Similarly hookers were hookers, the specialisation of the position already reinstated by George Travers's son, William, one of only four players to play international rugby either side of the war. All of which meant that when Bryn Meredith was first capped against Ireland in Dublin in 1954 there was no confusion about where he should play, but there was little which suggested a specialist hooker was on the field in the game's opening exchanges.

I was penalised in the first four scrums and the thought went through my mind that this was the first and last time that I would play for Wales, but I didn't change my stance and after the first few scrums everything went right, I didn't lose a head, even managed to pinch a few. Whether the referee's interpretation changed, I don't know, but I certainly didn't change anything.

Six years later Meredith led Wales for the first time. His four matches as captain were spread over three seasons, interrupted by illness and the Big Five's uncertainty about the most suitable man for the job. First chosen to lead the team against Scotland in 1960, Meredith missed the next game in Dublin.

On the morning of the match I couldn't get my breath and after seeing the doctor at about midday I had to withdraw and Norman Gale was called in for his first cap. There was a strong Aberavon contingent in the squad at the time and I later learnt that the night before the match the 'Wizards', as they were known, had held a séance in one of the bedrooms and outside-half Cliff Ashton determined that somebody was not going to play in the match. It was weeks later that they finally told me about this.

Meredith returned to the helm for the last match of the season against the French in Cardiff following which the captaincy was shared among the backs for seven matches before he was asked to take over for the third and final match of the 1961–62 season, France once again providing the opposition. Earlier in the season the Irish match had been called off due to an outbreak of smallpox in Wales but, unlike the fixture ten years later when the IRA intervened, the match was rearranged and played in the following November.

On my return from the Lions tour to South Africa I had decided to retire from first-class rugby. Early in the season Cliff Jones rang me and said the selectors wanted me to play in the rescheduled Irish game, but I told him I was finished and that it would be a good opportunity to find somebody else before the Five Nations. Nearer the match Dai Jones, another selector, rang and said they wanted me to captain the side, but I told him the same thing. They didn't listen and despite having only played a few matches for Newport United I eventually agreed to play.

The match was his 34th and final appearance for Wales and his record as captain of two victories, a defeat and an unsatisfactory draw in the rearranged match partly reflects a period during which a multi-talented national team often failed to live up to expectations.

As a player you never think you are good enough to play for the village side, the town side, the county side and certainly not good enough to play for your country, and so when the opportunity comes to captain Wales it is an extreme honour and a very responsible position. But you tend to feel very negative about it because the first thing you want to ensure is that the team doesn't lose. After a while, certainly at club level, you begin to realise that there is potential in the team and it's time to let the opposition do the worrying – a more positive attitude starts to prevail – but rarely is an international captain given long enough to be able to change his views on this. As captain you try to lead by example but I always felt responsible for the outcome of a match and if Wales lost, I took it very personally, as if it was my fault. The responsibility of carrying what has always been a great tradition in Wales was huge and if you let it, the captaincy could easily affect your game.

Take the responsibility out of the equation and I think captaincy was quite easy in my day. You took an overview of events on the field and a generalisation of the way the game should be played. If you were in your own half, you kicked to touch and when you were in the opponent's half, it was time to think about moving the ball, but if the backs were in trouble you kept it among the forwards. As a captain you weren't looking at every individual kick or tackle, you didn't concern yourself with all the game's little nuances, but placed more attention to where on the field the game was being played. My attitude to captaincy was pretty basic: everybody knew what they were supposed to do and the team would play to its strengths; international matches are played to be won and it doesn't matter how dour they are, winning for your country is what counts.

What was a constant throughout the 1950s and early 1960s, however, was the level of performance seen from Meredith at both club and international levels. It is no mean achievement to be selected for three consecutive British Lions tours and play eight Test matches in South Africa on tours separated by a seven-year gap, and but for the selection of Dawson the record may well have been more impressive.

By the end of his career Bryn Meredith had achieved all that the game had to offer and after many years of waiting, the front row fraternity could at last lay claim to the recognition it had long deserved – a Welsh captain chosen from among its ranks who attracted little, if any, criticism and was asked back again.

The role of hooker underwent a great change in the 1970s. No longer were hookers measured purely by their footwork; now they were going to need to be equally adept with their hands. For reasons that have become blurred or forgotten with the passing of time, it became the additional duty of the hooker to throw the ball into the lineout. For the first time he would be seen doing something in the open rather than found in the depths of the scrum and, by goodness, didn't they all come to rue the day. Carwyn James said that the best jumper in the lineout was the thrower-in, and wasn't he right? The communication between thrower and jumper has to be spot-on if the ball is to be won and with teams introducing codes in attempts to baffle the opposition it all became a bit technical. Irish second-row forward Moss Keane summed it up best when in the third or fourth lineout of a match at Lansdowne Road, hooker Ken Kennedy went through his coded routine – A1, B2, C3 etc. – only for all present to hear Moss's dulcet tones utter, 'Oh f***, me again'. Another slant on communication and discipline!

The last hooker to captain Wales who was spared the need to practise his basketball skills was Norman Gale. First capped as a Swansea player in 1960, he was a natural successor to Bryn Meredith, making the position his own in 1963. His international career spanned the decade ending in the last match played in 1969 by which time he had long been a regular at Stradey Park, and it was as a Llanelli player that Gale led Wales against New Zealand in 1967 and England in the first Five Nations match of 1968. The outcome of both matches was influenced by unforced errors: John Jeffery's uncharacteristic lapse of concentration on his own goal line let the All Blacks in for a try, and a knock-on by England full-back Bob Hiller following a penalty attempt saw Wales score a try from the resultant scrum. A home defeat and an away draw: others have fared worse in the job and against inferior opponents – New Zealand anywhere and England at Twickenham are as hard as it gets.

* * *

In 1997 Wales played England in the last international staged at Cardiff Arms Park. Regardless of the fact that the location was the same, when the newly named Millennium Stadium opened in time for the 1999 RWC the pitch had been rotated 90 degrees, there was a retractable roof and the capacity had been increased by some 20,000 – in other words, it bore no resemblance to what had been the spiritual home of Welsh rugby for well over 100 years. The new venue represented a giant, and expensive, leap forward for the game in Wales, where the professional era had struggled to find a sensible structure and focus, which it was felt the Millennium Stadium would help identify. It was instantly recognised as one of the world's grandest arenas and all that was now needed to put Welsh rugby back among the game's leading lights was a team worthy of it.

Captaining Wales for the 17th time in that final international before the bulldozers moved in was Cardiff hooker Jonathan Humphreys. First capped against New Zealand during the 1995 RWC, three matches and three months later Humphreys found himself leading Wales out against the Springboks at Johannesburg in what is recognised as the first international match of the professional era. The 1990s were a difficult time for Welsh rugby with notable victories hard to come by and Humphreys's time in charge was not the easiest of rides; come that final match at the old stadium his tenure looked to be over. Although there were more caps, mainly from the substitutes' bench, there was nothing to suggest that he would be involved with the captaincy again following the appointment of Gwyn Jones to lead the Welsh squad on a summer tour of North America.

Never say never. Italy had finally been invited to join the International Championship in 2000 and the Five Nations became Six. It was not going to be easy for the *Azzurri* and despite winning their first championship match, beating Scotland in Rome, there was nothing much to cheer in the first three seasons with a run of fourteen consecutive defeats putting Italy firmly at the bottom of the table. The first round of matches in 2003 took Wales to Rome's Stadio Flaminio. An ideal start and for Welsh supporters a chance to sample the local culture: the vino, the pasta and pizza, throw coins in a fountain and make a wish, go visit the Pope . . . when in Rome etc.

One thing the 2.6 million inhabitants of the seven hills don't do much of is follow rugby. You have to travel north to find the soccer-mad nation's best known rugby clubs, while in Rome sports enthusiasts generally fall into one of two categories – they follow either AS Roma or Lazio. Italy has a daily newspaper totally devoted to sport, but the arrival of the Welsh rugby team merited few column inches in the build-up to the match. Things were very different come Monday's edition.

Italy 30 Wales 22. The visitors were seen to be lacking in commitment, self-belief and, most importantly, leadership, with captain Colin Charvis firmly in the firing line. All agreed that changes had to be made for England's visit to Cardiff and that a new captain was essential in lifting the flagging Welsh spirits. But who should be chosen to breathe some fire into the team, in particular the forwards who, in the English eight, would be up against the best pack in world rugby?

Jon Humphreys had left Cardiff in the twilight of his career but he had not taken the normal route of the senior player and joined a lesser club, quite the opposite. Humphreys had made the short journey along the M4 to Bath, home of one of the biggest clubs in English rugby. Who better to call on, then, than somebody who had been there before, was a natural leader and had the added advantage of playing with and against the English players on a regular basis.

Wales failed to beat England and four weeks later lost to Ireland in the most frustrating way, an exchange of drop goals in the game's dying moments seeing Welsh euphoria turn to tears in a matter of seconds. But in two matches in charge, Jonathan Humphreys had brought some pride and passion back into the Welsh performance, something for the next in line to build on.

* * *

The modern hooker is a rare breed. If Richmal Crompton had taken her anti-hero through to maturity and if he had taken up the union game, William Brown would have been a hooker. A glance at the glorious artwork of Thomas Henry reveals a dishevelled, scruffy individual with a permanent look of innocence on his face, forever asking 'Who, me?' Where else could he possibly have played? But there was one positive to be found in the young man's make-up and that was his undoubted leadership quality, because no matter how outrageous the scheme, and most were to the extreme, others followed. Jon Humphreys would not look out of place at a meeting of the Outlaws and before him, between 1984 and 1990, a trio of 'Williams' were invited to captain Wales, each already a proven leader at club level.

Michael J. Watkins, whom we might here call William the First, was born to hook. 'Spike' Watkins was born to lead. Put the two together and you have a competitive, in-your-face, inspirational captain who brought the best out of a pack of forwards. Watkins led Newport between 1983 and 1987, a period which saw the club make considerable headway from some particularly lean times. In 1983 he led Wales B to an impressive away victory in France at a time when the senior squad was struggling to gel. Surely the higher honour was his by right? Unfortunately, for some years Mike Watkins had been seen as the *enfant terrible* of Welsh rugby, a rebel, a misfit, somebody the selectors didn't know how to handle – didn't want to handle.

> I'd been around for a long time and had a career at Cardiff before joining Newport. I'd also been involved in the Welsh set-up since 1976, sitting on the bench through two Grand Slams and three Triple Crowns, but I could never get on because Bobby Windsor would never come off! I then had an enforced four-year sabbatical as a result of an accumulation of various misdemeanours. Somebody quite eminent at the WRU told me that no matter what, I would never play for Wales, but when I joined Newport, coach 'Charlie' Faulkner showed great faith in me and started pushing my case again.

An embarrassing defeat in Romania in 1983 had followed a close encounter against Japan in an uncapped match in Cardiff and when the 1984 championship began with a home defeat by the Scots, it was time for a rethink. Three changes were made for the visit to Dublin and the public were left in no doubt as to where the selectors felt the problem lay – the front row was dropped en bloc and in addition to winning his first cap Mike Watkins was chosen to lead the team, only the fifth player to achieve this rare distinction.

> Deep down I always knew that one day I would play for Wales but I never dreamt that I would captain the side. I got a phone call telling me I was in the team to face Ireland and that I was captain – then all hell broke loose! That selection not only meant I was replacing Eddie Butler as captain, but also current hooker Billy James had to make way for me. Other people might have, but I didn't find those circumstances difficult because of my earlier involvement with Wales, which had started before any of the squad members arrived on the scene. Remember, I had played B-level rugby since 1976 and gone on the tour to Australia in 1978 and played in four of the matches.

Lansdowne Road was the stuff of fairy tales, with Wales pulling off an unexpected victory with no little style. The Welsh team, despite a narrow home defeat by the French, saw out the season unchanged, ending with another fine away victory at Twickenham. However, for the WRU and the new captain there was little sign of a harmonious relationship developing.

I'd waited for many, many years to play for Wales and after the game in Ireland, the biggest day of my rugby life, I expected everything to be done correctly, but the WRU didn't have a cap to give me. I had to wait a while before I got one and then there was nothing official about the way it was handed over; basically it was just chucked at me. To play for Wales is everything a young person dreams of. It was my dream and I fulfilled it, but the periphery left a lot to be desired, it was appalling. The night before one of the matches I had a meeting in my hotel room with the forwards and ordered coffee and sandwiches on room service, which I ended up paying £36 for when the union sent the bill to my home.

What people didn't appreciate at the time was that I was one of the few players who was self-employed. I was an owner-driver of a wagon and if it wasn't on the road, I wasn't earning, which makes things difficult when you have a young family. People didn't realise the sacrifices some had to make just to play for Wales. While I fulfilled a dream, it didn't pay the bills and sooner or later the simple economics of the situation were bound to come into play.

Despite the off-field problems Mike Watkins could look back on the 1983–84 season with immense satisfaction: a much improving club, a rare away win in France at B level, two wins out of three with Wales – moments to savour.

'Spike' Watkins is a strong advocate for the captain to lead the team from the middle of the front row.

If a hooker is worth his salt he is the boss of the front row, which may account for why so few props have captained Wales. The props have got a lot on their plate, the tight-head having little idea as to what is happening on the loose-head and vice versa, whereas the hooker has a good feel for both sides of the scrum. He is involved with the set pieces, the scrum and the lineout, always at the point of contact. I made the calls at the lineout, which isn't the case today, but I think the hooker should be involved because whether the ball is won or lost depends so much on his getting it right.

In the early '80s hooker was definitely seen as a very good position to lead from, with Peter Wheeler, Colin Deans, Ciaran Fitzgerald, Andy Dalton and Philippe Dintrans all leading their respective countries, which must mean something. That aside, I think that while all captains are different, equally they are also all the same. They share a single-mindedness that ensures when the bombs are dropping, they can keep a cool head and not get fazed. It comes with experience and hot-headed as I was off the field, I like to think that I showed that quality on it. I was very much a captain who led from the front in both training and during the match, and I always adopted the attitude that I would try and do more than the next man and be seen trying to do it. I would never give up, which I think goes back to why I finally played for Wales when, despite everything that was flung at me, I didn't lose sight of that dream.

It all came to an end in November 1984 when the all-conquering Australian Wallabies took Wales apart in Cardiff, inflicting on the home side a comprehensive defeat which included a push-over try, and the Welsh captain felt that it was time to listen to his bank manager and go back to the day job.

Maybe common sense prevailed with regard to my international career, but I continued with Newport until I retired from the game in 1987. That's not quite true actually – I did play one match for Newbridge at the start of the next season, but I got sent off and that was it.

William the Second was real – well, in so much as his name actually was William. Aberavon's Billy James is the only player from the famous club to have captained Wales and he achieved the recognition in his 21st and final appearance.

I first joined Aberavon as an 18 year old and spent a total of 13 seasons with them. Aberavon was a great club with some outstanding players but by the end of the '80s a lot had changed, players had left and the committee was far from what you would call forward-thinking. I was club captain for five seasons but I'd become totally disillusioned with the lack of vision shown by the committee, and at the end I felt very let down by them. They were inward thinking; rugby was changing but Aberavon just didn't want to get involved. I was captain and coach during my last season at the club, but only eight or nine people were turning out for pre-season training and I wanted more from the game than I felt Aberavon could offer. It was a difficult decision, but I knew that I had a couple of seasons left in me and felt they would be better spent at Swansea. All my caps were won while I was at Aberavon, but I did feel very let down at the end because when I left, I was highly criticised for not showing any commitment to the club. I'd been there 13 years, for goodness sake, but they couldn't see that.

First capped against England in 1983, six solid performances counted for nothing when the selectors decided to replace captain Eddie Butler with Mike Watkins, a decision which cost James his place.

I was told that I had done nothing wrong, not played badly, but that I had to step down. I found that amazing, particularly as I had a lot of time for Eddie Butler, who I thought was a good captain. The press were very anti-Wales at that time and I know that Eddie was far from happy with the situation. Following the defeat in Romania things started to get a bit personal and I think the pressure began to tell. There were personal insults, mostly directed at Eddie, which you don't need in an amateur game, and I have to say I haven't read the *Western Mail* since then, that's over 20 years.

What goes around comes around and Billy James was recalled following Mike Watkins's decision to retire from international rugby and he made the position his own, missing only one match during the next three seasons. The selectors relied on his experience as captain at Aberavon when choosing him to lead Wales in the last match of the 1987 Five Nations against Ireland, whom Wales would play in their opening match in the inaugural RWC two months later. It meant that, if nothing else, there was a psychological advantage to be gained by the winners.

It was great to captain Wales. I didn't have any time to stamp my authority on the job, but it was an experience I relished. I think it was the chairman of selectors, Rod Morgan, who rang me with the news I'd been chosen – what a fantastic feeling. It made up for a lot of disappointment I'd had during my time in the squad, waiting four years before getting capped, being dropped, reselected and then dropped again for Kevin Phillips. It was certainly better than John Bevan telling me I was dropped, which was like a stake through the heart – but all these things are character building. I spent match after match sitting on the bench at a time when the only people in Wales who wanted the team to lose were the substitutes, because it might get them a game. If any of them say otherwise, then they're lying! Sitting on the bench was a nightmare.

I certainly have no problem with the hooker being captain and would argue that it is one of the most important positions on the field. He knows what's going on in the scrums, he's got his finger on the pulse of the forwards, while the backs tend to look after themselves – how the hell do you tell Jonathan Davies what to do? International captaincy is nothing like captaining a club where you are involved in team matters, selection and so on; it's very different. You give a team talk before the game, but by then the coach would have already had his say. During the 80 minutes you make decisions such as whether to kick for touch or goal but all that is self-evident really. Motivation is something that is mentioned a lot but do players need motivating once they have pulled on the Welsh jersey? If myself or any player was in need of motivating – whew! No, I don't see that as a factor; respect, yes, but not motivation.

Despite losing to Ireland, fourteen of the team were included in the twenty-six-man squad for the World Cup with Billy James named as one of two hookers, but injury prevented him playing any part in the tournament and he was replaced in the squad by Alan Phillips.

That was a bit sad. I was selected to play against Ireland in the opening match but ended up being carried off during training. Malcolm Dacey fell on my knee and damaged my cruciate ligaments and I was sent back home, arriving in time to watch the match on television. Following that injury I was out for about six months and I lost my way a bit. I'd been involved in the Welsh squad for ten years and decided to settle for club rugby but looking back I think that decision might have been a bit hasty. I should have regained my confidence and stuck it out a bit longer.

Which brings us to William the Third. It was Neath's Kevin Phillips who packed down in the middle of the front row for the opening match of the 1987 World Cup, one which saw Wales gain revenge for the home defeat seven weeks earlier. As the 1980s rolled into the 1990s the top club in Wales was Neath. Champions in three consecutive seasons between 1988 and 1991, and back-to-back cup winners in 1989 and 1990, the men from the Gnoll swept all before them. Club captain during this triumphant period was hooker Phillips who had first been capped in 1987 and was a permanent fixture in the Welsh team for the 1989–91 seasons. It was during this period that Wales undertook a short tour to Namibia on the back of a mauling at the hands of the All Blacks and a wooden-spoon-winning whitewash in the Five Nations. With the unavailability of ten leading players and a new coach in Neath's Ron Waldron, it was no surprise that the tour party included nine players from the champion club, among them Kevin Phillips, who captained the squad. It might not have been with the ease that many had predicted, but both Tests were won, giving Phillips a 100 per cent record, as he was not called upon to lead the team again. This was rather surprising since the next incumbent was another Neath player, full-back Paul Thorburn.

The story of the first 125 years of Welsh international captains could so very easily have ended at the Gnoll club but circumstances dictated otherwise. Mefin Davies was a Neath player when first capped by Wales but a move to Pontypridd saw him included in the newly formed Celtic Warriors region and it was from there that he became the 121st player to lead Wales, his chance coming in a warm-up match against Romania in the build-up to the 2003 RWC.

The disbanding of the Warriors in the summer of 2004 saw Mefin Davies along with the rest of the squad looking for work elsewhere and surprisingly the incumbent Welsh hooker was the notable name who appeared surplus to requirements. There was the offer of a lucrative move to Stade Français, but this would have meant signing a contract which prevented him playing international rugby, so he began the new season once again with Neath, but in the semi-professional Welsh Premiership League. It was from this famous club that he won further caps, playing with distinction in the autumn internationals and the 2005 Grand Slam-winning team.

Common sense finally prevailed and he was at last offered a contract to play at the higher level, but this did not come from one of the Welsh regions, rather Gloucester, who were quick to capitalise on the former Welsh captain's availability when interest in Wales was non-existent.

Were there really six or seven hookers in the Principality of a higher standing than the one favoured by the Welsh coach?

* * *

There can be no doubting the fact that the hooker is one of the more prominent positions on the field when viewing the game from the terraces. Every set piece highlights his presence. Whether hanging in the middle of the front row waiting for the 'hold and engage' instructions from the referee, a pause in the game which involves a period of eyeball-to-eyeball contact to rival that of prizefighters, or waiting to throw the ball into the lineout, he is the focus of attention. Inexplicably no longer involved in the calling of lineout routines, the hooker has become the fall guy when things don't go according to plan in the aerial gymnastics, but, that aside, in his own way he is the captain of all he surveys and has to possess the qualities readily associated with leadership: a captain in the making, then, but an option rarely taken up.

Of the eleven hookers to captain Wales, six carried the responsibility once, two players had a second opportunity and two others were in charge four times with only Jonathan Humphreys enjoying an extended term in office before a well-publicised return. Unlike prop forward, there are many strong arguments to be found among the other leading nations as to why hooker is a position suited to captaincy but, despite significantly more hookers than props captaining Wales, of the front-row fraternity only John Lloyd can claim any significant success – the championship in 1972 – and it is from behind, so to speak, that the men to lead from the front are more likely to come.

III

WALKING TALL: SECOND ROW

If you want to pick a captain the rest of the players are guaranteed to look up to, pick a lock forward. Once rugby union was a game which accommodated all manner of beast, players coming in all sorts of packages: the fat and the thin; the round and the square; those fleet of foot and those less so; and there were the short and the tall. The tall were to be found in the second row, the boiler room; they still are, but haven't they grown? Where once a six-foot-tall player was automatically shoved into the second row, now he would not look out of place in the three-quarters, six foot six inches and upwards having become the norm for lock forwards whose main *raison d'être* is to jump, or more often than not be lifted, up into the stratosphere.

The lineout is the domain of the lock forward and in recent years the lawmakers have seen fit to challenge not only the Laws of rugby, but also those of gravity in their tolerance of the aiding and abetting of the jumper. Where once a lineout expert leapt for the ball unassisted and, having secured it, determined its destiny, now the Laws allow the jumper to receive support from his fellow forwards once he has taken the initial leap, providing he did not begin his jump before the thrower-in had released the ball. All of which makes something of a paradox in that the taller the lock forward has become, so the Laws have been amended to give him greater assistance in the winning of the ball.

The nine locks to have captained Wales include some of rugby's great lineout jumpers. Artists, masters of their trade who brought great pleasure to and reciprocated appreciation from the terraces, where their skill was always applauded. To watch Brian Price, Delme Thomas and Bob Norster winning lineout after lineout was as special as any Phil Bennett sidestep or Neil Jenkins goal kick. It was their job and nobody did it better, but we must not forget that not all lock forwards are selected because of their aerial prowess. Brian Thomas, Geoff Wheel and Craig Quinnell are representative of the alternative second-row forward – the front-of-line jumper, the spoiler and the ball carrier. Not for them the giddy heights of their partners, rather the more down-to-earth steal at the front of the lineout, the ripping and tearing of the ball from unsuspecting opponents and the welcome opportunity to carry the ball onwards, over the gain line and on to yet more physical contact.

* * *

The lineout is quite simply a way of restarting the match after the ball has gone out of play along either touchline. The ball can be kicked into touch, a player can carry it into touch or be tackled into touch while in possession, all of which will lead to a lineout, but under no circumstances may the ball be thrown into touch; on the rare occasions that this happens a penalty kick is awarded. On such apparently minor indiscretions are matches won and lost, and in Cardiff in 1947, when Australian captain Trevor Allen felt safe in committing the offence on the ten-yard line, he had not taken into consideration the goal-kicking ability of Welsh second-row forward Bill Tamplin, who had taken over the captaincy when injury forced the late withdrawal of Haydn Tanner.

Goal kicking is a skill not normally associated with forwards, particularly those who play in the front five. There have been exceptions, among them Scotland's Peter Brown, Wales's Allan Martin and more recently Australian captain John Eales, but exceptions they certainly are and Bill Tamplin is another who will be remembered as much for his goal-kicking ability as his prowess as a tight forward. He ended his playing career having scored almost 900 points for Cardiff, virtually all with the boot, and in his fourteen international appearances Tamplin scored a further twenty-four points from place kicks, including the six that defeated Australia in his only appearance as captain.

In 1947 the Wallabies were not yet the force in world rugby they would later become but were still good enough to beat England, Ireland and Scotland, scoring 11 tries in the process. Bill Tamplin's two penalties saw Wales home in the only match in which the Wallabies failed to get on the score sheet, but there were opportunities aplenty and the local press summed it up by commenting that in Tamplin 'Wales possessed what the tourists lacked – a goal kicker.' Scarce they may well be, but it was only a few years before Wales produced another second-row forward who not only captained his country but could also lay claim to a conversion among his many achievements in the red jersey.

There have been several instances of siblings playing international rugby, uncles and nephews and fathers and sons. The Quinnell family immediately spring to mind and cover all permutations, with father Derek being followed into the national side by sons Scott and Craig, while uncle Barry John played a bit as well. The list of brothers to represent Wales is quite long but not surprisingly, the one chronicling fathers and sons is somewhat shorter.

Wales's first capped international following the First World War was against the New Zealand Army and at the resumption of fixtures in the aftermath of the Second World War it was England who provided the opposition. Apart from the fact that Wales lost both matches there would seem to be little to link them, but among the forwards the name Stephens appears on both team sheets and therein lies a relationship which is unique in the annals of Welsh rugby.

Glyn Stephens led Wales in that first post-war international in 1919 and later represented Wales on the International Board and became president of the WRU in 1956–57, coincidentally the same season in which son Rees brought his international career to an end, leading Wales to victory against Ireland and France. First capped in the match against England in 1947, Rees Stephens's appointment as captain against the same opponents in 1954 saw him follow in his father's footsteps and to date the pair are the only father and son to have both led Wales in capped matches. Where Glyn Stephens captained Wales once, Rees led the team six times during a career which spanned a decade. Being equally capable in either the second row or at number 8, his time was shared between the two positions, and his matches as captain saw him lead Wales four times from the second row and twice from the middle of the back row.

Stephens won eighteen of his caps, including the six as captain, when he was over the age of thirty and it was this apparent seniority that prevented him from playing once more on the game's biggest stage. A British Lion in 1950 he was undoubtedly a leading candidate for the tour to South Africa in 1955, but the selection committee under the guidance of tour manager Jack Siggins controversially introduced an unofficial age limit. At 33 years old, Stephens was pensioned off along with Ken Jones and Bleddyn Williams, three players who would surely have revelled in the playing conditions found on the high veldt.

The options Rees Stephens offered the Welsh selectors would certainly have been welcome but with such a wealth of talent at their disposal during the 1950s his place in the team was far from certain. John Gwilliam, Roy John, Russell Robins and Rhys Williams were always in contention and it is testimony to his qualities that Stephens ended his career with 32 caps. Aggrieved on the occasions that he found himself not included in the team he may well have been, but some years later Stephens undoubtedly acquired a better understanding of the various ramifications of selection when he was invited to become a member of the Big Five and had his say in the destiny of others.

* * *

Television. In the twenty-first century television is the game's major paymaster, determining when matches are played – not only on which day but at what time – and the powerbrokers at the major networks are rarely concerned with complying with what the rugby-watching public want. It's easy to criticise but impossible to replace, and how unfortunate that television wasn't available much earlier, particularly overseas, where the great tours took place, when the game's followers had little more than the radio commentary and subsequent press reports to create the images for them. And what images they would have been.

Televised international rugby was fairly commonplace in the UK during the 1950s, with those fortunate to have the box in the corner of the room able to watch the big matches, from first Twickenham, and then Cardiff and Edinburgh, but it was much later that the screen welcomed pictures from Auckland and Wellington, Cape Town and Johannesburg, all of which is now very much taken for granted, with virtually every minute of every major match there for all to see. Television and televised sport will always have its detractors but don't you sometimes wish that there was more than just *Pathe News*-style footage of all those great games and great players of yesteryear?

Rhys Haydn Williams was a big man, over six feet tall, weighing in at over sixteen stone, and he could boast a big rugby pedigree to match, from Ystalyfera Grammar School to University College Cardiff, the

Royal Air Force, Llanelli, the Barbarians, Wales and the British Lions, with much else in between – the perfect curriculum vitae. And it is because of players such as Rhys Haydn Williams that one craves the extended television footage that never was. Certainly there are televised reports of the majority of his 23 international appearances somewhere in the vaults at Broadcasting House, W12, but these aren't the matches we want to see. Rhys Williams was at his sublime best when he played in the Southern hemisphere, in South Africa in 1955 and four years later in Australia and New Zealand.

'Had he been a New Zealander he could well have won selection as an All Black lock' – praise indeed from the biographical notes found in the 1960 *Rugby Almanack of New Zealand*, whose editors chose Williams as one of their five players of the year. Following four Test appearances in South Africa, Williams was an ever-present in the 1959 Test team, bringing his total number of British Lions caps to ten, by which time he had made twenty-two appearances for Wales. On his return from the antipodes there was one more cap to add to that total, won against England at Twickenham in 1960, and on this final occasion Rhys Williams was chosen to lead the team. It was a bad day at the office for the Welsh XV. A young English outside-half made an impressive debut which left the visiting back row grasping at shadows for much of the afternoon. What was a glorious introduction to international rugby for Richard Sharp was a desperately disappointing final appearance for Rhys Williams.

A few short months after scaling the heights in front of the game's most discerning observers of forward play, Williams decided to bring an end to his international career and retired from the game at the end of the season. There were other factors which impacted on his decision – family life and a change of job took him away from Llanelli – but the disappointment of a nation and the reaction of the media to the Twickenham defeat also contributed, as Terry Davies, Welsh full-back on the day, recalled:

The tour to New Zealand had been hard and when we arrived home, Rhys and I took a couple of months off and didn't start playing again until December. I don't think we had played more than a handful of matches when we were picked for Twickenham and basically we weren't fit. We had a drink together after the game and Rhys told me then that he was quitting; he couldn't put up with the hassle any longer, knowing that there would be hell to pay after we had lost to England.

Such is the expectancy and pressure that Wales places on her rugby heroes.

* * *

The first cap in 1961 had come as a late replacement against Ireland but eight years later Brian Price must have felt that his international days were over when appendicitis and a cartilage operation ruled him out of the 1967–68 season. Four second rows were selected in the five matches played and four different combinations were tried, but come the end of the campaign none could be viewed as a success and it was back to the drawing board.

Wales's most prominent second-row partnership for many years had been Price and Brian Thomas, a pairing which offered the perfect mix of the Newport man's guile and lineout prowess together with the power and aggression offered by his Neath counterpart. It was a partnership that worked and it was one to which the selectors reverted in 1969.

Rees Stephens contacted me and said that if I got myself back to full fitness playing for Newport, there was a very good chance that I would be asked to captain Wales in the 1969 Five Nations and take the team on the summer tour to New Zealand, Australia and Fiji. I viewed this as pie in the sky, but I started playing well for the club, who were having a great season, and in fairness to him, Rees was true to his word.

The year 1969 was when everybody connected with the game in Wales learnt exactly where Welsh rugby really stood in the great global scheme of things. An eleventh Triple Crown was won, the championship starting at Murrayfield with a match which saw first caps for J.P.R. Williams and Mervyn Davies, while the home matches against Ireland and England were played in front of a reduced-capacity Cardiff Arms Park, where the North Stand was under major renovation. But a sixth Grand Slam was denied to Wales by a French team which clawed its way back into the match to salvage a draw at Stade Colombes after Wales had held an 8–0 half-time lead. Price recalls:

I had to sit out the England match after picking up an injury playing for Newport on Easter Monday, six days earlier. We played London Welsh at Rodney Parade, a huge match, and the

WRU had given special dispensation which allowed JPR, John Dawes, John Taylor and Mervyn, together with Stuart Watkins, Keith Jarrett and myself to play, but during the match JPR cut me down with a tackle and my knees were badly hurt, which kept me out of the team to face England. Gareth took over as captain and Brian Thomas was appointed pack leader. It was the only time I saw one of the selectors in the changing-room with the team before the match. I was invited as I had been appointed captain for the forthcoming tour but Cliff Jones took it upon himself to come and wish the boys well, unprecedented in my experience. Brian Thomas was giving his final briefing to the forwards: 'When I shout Trevor in a Gloucestershire accent, I want you to forget about winning the ball; go through the lineout and trample on Trevor Wintle [the England scrum-half], so that when he takes his jersey off at the end of the match it will look as if he's been sunbathing in the Bahamas in a string vest.' Poor old Cliff Jones just put his hands over his face and left.

Brian Price will always be remembered as one of the finest lineout exponents the game has seen, but he will be equally remembered for that punch, the one he threw at Ireland's Noel Murphy with HRH The Prince of Wales sitting at ringside. By 1969 no Welsh player had been sent off in an international, but Price must have come close that day with what was obviously a reaction to some dastardly deed which had taken place out of sight of those in attendance, unlike the response it triggered which was seen by all.

It's a huge story and there have been so many things said about it. We were training at the police ground in Bridgend and looking at how we were going to stop the Irish back row and in particular Noel Murphy, who was their catalyst. He was always talking and I think it was Benoît Dauga who told me that if you could stop Murphy giving orders and bullying his boys along, you were laughing. So we worked out a plan which involved Gareth going around the side of the scrum and when Noel got him we would all pile in and hopefully shut him up for a while. Somehow it leaked out that we had a 'Murphy Plan' and I did an interview with Peter Walker on the Friday afternoon during which he mentioned it, but obviously I had to deny that such a plan existed.

During the match I went up in a lineout and when I came down somebody from behind scragged me around the eyes and I just turned and flung a punch which connected with Noel, who I don't think was the culprit. Tom Kiernan [the Irish captain] came storming down the field shouting at the top of his voice 'It's the Murphy Plan. It's the Murphy Plan.' I just looked at the referee, Mr McMahon, who shook his head, and I thought that was it, I was off, but he said he hadn't seen what had happened, felt that it must have been retaliation and that I should keep my fists to myself. It wasn't a great punch, actually, and virtually every Irishman that I have spoken to since has said that I should have hit him harder, but Noel and I were good friends before and have remained good friends since.

There's a second part to the story. I was hopeless, couldn't sleep before the match, so I was down for breakfast in the Angel Hotel at about 7 a.m. and McMahon was there as well, complaining of a terrible headache. We had breakfast and went out for a bit of fresh air and when we got back to the hotel I took him to see our physiotherapist, Gerry Lewis, who gave him some tablets to sort him out. We'd had a nice chat. Then the next time I spoke to him he was giving me a telling off – thank God for breakfast! That aside it was a rough encounter; Brian Thomas had stitches for a cut in his head and there was blood coming from everyone in the Irish front row, which I think may have been a bit of Brian's work, but it was a marvellous game of rugby.

It was as European Champions therefore that Wales headed to New Zealand and Australia in the summer of 1969, the summer that saw the first man set foot on the moon and Welsh rugby come down-to-earth with a bang. To be able to report that Brian Price's international career ended with a win against Australia is a pleasure, but the real picture is only seen in the light of the two Tests in New Zealand in which the Welsh team was comprehensively outplayed and forced into submission by the then huge scorelines of 19–0 and 33–12. The All Blacks were the cause of the highest and lowest points in Brian Price's playing career, from leading Newport to victory over the tourists in 1963, to the demise of a lauded team in 1969.

The most disappointing point of my career was after that second Test in Auckland when I had to go up into the stand and say a few words to the enormous crowd that had gathered on the pitch. How nice it had been to be in their country etc. after we had just been walloped by what we mustn't forget was a fantastic side.

Brian Price's season as Welsh captain witnessed some innovative changes to the Laws of the game: replacements were allowed for legitimate injuries, initially at international level, subject to a maximum of two; the dispensation Law restricting the kicking of the ball directly into touch from outside the 25-yard line was introduced as an experiment (it became law in 1970); and while not coming under the actual remit of the Laws of the game, the decision by the IRB to ratify squad-training sessions allowed the Welsh coach and his players to carry on their task in earnest. The coach at the time was Clive Rowlands, who offered a marked contrast to his captain.

> The combination of Clive and myself – Clive being a very outgoing personality, while I tended to be a little quieter – was a contrast of styles I believe helped that particular team. There was a hardcore of seasoned internationals in the front five – Denzil Williams, Brian Thomas and myself – but elsewhere there were a lot of newer names to international rugby. I think we had the balance right to help develop the team. As captain you must have the respect of the players, be one of them, not take yourself away and become almost a committee man playing in the side. You certainly have to be a players' player, gain their respect, talk sensibly and treat them as individuals.

Regarding leading the team from the boiler room Price is of the opinion that there are better positions available, the second row being very dependent on a good vice-captain among the backs.

> Gareth was vice-captain but I feel that if the captain is among the front five then a centre should be involved, as the scrum-half tends to be too involved with the forwards. But what could you say about Gareth? The world's greatest player; we could all see his talent, even at that early stage, and I had no problem with him as vice-captain, other than the fact that he kept on bitching at me that the ball was either six inches too far to the right or five inches too far to the left.

Brian Price was not on his own as a representative of the second-row brotherhood when it came to leading Wales against the might of New Zealand rugby; others followed, all meeting with a similar fate, although Delme Thomas is justified in feeling aggrieved at the outcome of his only experience as Welsh captain. Wales had not lost a match for two seasons and the arrival of the All Blacks was greeted with enormous anticipation – even the late withdrawal of captain Arthur Lewis failed to dent the huge optimism that was prevalent in the weeks and days leading up to 2 December 1972. Llanelli's seasoned campaigner Delme Thomas was entrusted with the captaincy of a team which contained no fewer than five players who were ever-present in the British Lions Test side, which had won the series in New Zealand the previous year, and in John Bevan, Derek Quinnell and Thomas himself, three others who had featured in at least one of the matches.

Captain at Llanelli in its centenary season, Delme Thomas had led the club to a famous 9–3 victory over the tourists at the end of October.

Undoubtedly the highlight of my career – that, and being chosen for the Lions tour in 1966 before I had played for Wales. I was really up against it on that first tour – captain Mike Campbell-Lamerton, Brian Price and Willie John the other second rows – and I was particularly proud to play in two of the Tests. I think my greatest personal achievement was running out for the Lions against the All Blacks in Wellington. Being uncapped I had never experienced anything like it before and really felt that I had achieved something.

Leading Llanelli against the All Blacks in 1972 was different. There is something special about your club. I was in my 13th season with the Scarlets, the old man of the team. I'd played against Wilson Whineray's side in 1963 when we were hammered [22–8] but to beat them in 1972 was special. The atmosphere at Stradey that day was wonderful, there were 22,000 in the ground and that feeling of the crowd almost being on the pitch with you was unique.

Carwyn James had masterminded the Llanelli victory and as was the case with John Lloyd, so it was James who told Delme Thomas of his appointment to captain Wales.

What a shame that the WRU closed the door on Carwyn. They slammed it in his face. He had so much to offer and was so respected by the players, by everybody in the game, not only in Wales, everywhere. What a waste. I wish I could say I captained Wales more than once but what an honour to lead my country out at Cardiff Arms Park. I'm quite an emotional person and when they sang the national anthem, the hairs on the back of my neck stood out. It was a special moment, so very special. Every boy's dream.

Having led Llanelli in what is undoubtedly the famous club's finest hour, Delme Thomas was less fortunate in his sole appearance as Welsh captain. At the final whistle three points separated the sides, five penalties and a try to four penalties and a try: 19–16 to the visitors. But the story doesn't end there, for controversy followed the proceedings. The New Zealand try scored by Keith Murdoch was seen by many to have involved a double movement, warranting a penalty *to* Wales, and a late effort by J.P.R. Williams was denied, the referee awarding a penalty *against* Wales for a double movement.

> We had a wonderful side coached by Clive Rowlands and I still look back on that game as one we should have won. What annoyed me was that both incidents were the same. I know that John was brought down short but many referees would have given the try, allowing for momentum, but Mr Johnson didn't, even though the New Zealand try was awarded under what I saw as identical circumstances. There was no consistency in his refereeing.

Maybe it was payback time for events at the same ground 67 years earlier.

* * *

Sherlock Holmes referred to Professor Moriarty as 'the Napoleon of crime', while the Duke of Wellington wrote of the Frenchman that 'his presence on the field made the difference of forty thousand men'. Pick the pieces out of the two quotes and you have the ingredients of a Welsh captain who often fell foul of authority, but one whom players would follow anywhere.

Richard Moriarty was first capped against Australia in 1981 and scored a debut try that helped Wales to an 18–13 victory. Five years later Wales embarked on a summer tour, playing Fiji, Tonga and Western Samoa, three matches to severely test the physical attributes of the players who would have to cope not only with the hard playing surfaces but the even harder men of the South Sea islands. Tour captain David Pickering was an early casualty and for the Tongan and Western Samoan Tests, Richard Moriarty was called upon to lead the team.

No shrinking violet when it came to the confrontational issues of rugby, Moriarty, who had missed the Five Nations following a dismissal in a club game, was just the man to lead a Welsh team, which took a fearful battering from an over-exuberant Tongan team but maintained sufficient composure to win a bruising encounter before Western Samoa were beaten in a much better-tempered affair. Twelve months later, at the end of a season during which injury had prevented him taking part in any international rugby, Richard Moriarty was chosen to lead a squad of twenty-six players to the inaugural Rugby World Cup held in New Zealand and Australia.

I was troubled by injury during the 1986–87 season and after a third shoulder dislocation had to have surgery. I missed the 1987 championship and hadn't played any international rugby since the summer tour in '86. I was struggling to get myself in any shape to go to the World Cup and in hindsight I did put myself under a lot of pressure to make the squad. In all honesty I wasn't 100 per cent fit at that point in time.

Ireland and Tonga in the Pool stages and England in the quarter-final gave Moriarty five wins in charge, but at Brisbane in the semi-final against New Zealand he and his men fell victim to the tournament's eventual winners, conceding an embarrassing forty-nine points in the process. What wasn't known at the time was that this type of result against New Zealand would become the norm in the encounters that followed. That aside, it was a result which should have set the alarm bells ringing that all was not well in the Welsh game; however, it was camouflaged and forgotten by all concerned when Moriarty led Wales to victory over Australia in the third-place play-off.

Much has been made of the state of Welsh rugby in the 1980s, but it is not something I totally agree with. During my involvement with the Welsh team, I felt that there were enough quality players in Wales and I was confident in our ability to be able to compete with the Northern hemisphere countries. In actual fact I was quite confident about playing Australia. I won my first cap against the Wallabies, played against them on a few occasions at club level and spent the summers of 1984 and '85 playing for Western Suburbs in Sydney, captaining the club and obviously getting a good understanding of Australian rugby. I got to know the players, their abilities and limitations, and on that basis I was sure that as

WALKING TALL: SECOND ROW

a team we were more than capable of beating them. My big disappointment was that David Codey was sent off because that detracted from the win, but I still feel we would have beaten 15 men.

Richard Moriarty won a total of 22 caps and although always in the second row when leading the team, he made several appearances in the back row, either at number 8 or on the flank.

I wasn't a pure-bred second-row forward. My experiences in the back row meant that I played a much looser game than the head-down, arse-up approach that is perhaps normally associated with the position. That experience also gave me a good vision and awareness of the game as it was unfolding and on that basis I would suggest that the back row and half-backs are positions more suited to leading the team from. If the best candidate for the captaincy is found elsewhere on the field, then it is essential that he has a line of communication through the middle five because these are the players who ultimately control the game. In today's game, which is a more structured one, it could be argued that the captaincy has a different emphasis. You have to ensure that the structures within the game are maintained and perhaps the position of the captain is of less important. Having said that we are now seeing the benefits of a Welsh team that is less structured than it has been for some years, which I suppose throws the argument out.

Richard Moriarty led Wales on seven occasions, was captain on the 1986 tour to the South Pacific and a year later at the World Cup. What this inevitably meant was that he didn't experience the thrill of leading Wales out at the Arms Park.

Despite having been in and out of the team over a period of years through either injury or suspension, when it came to the World Cup I felt that my standing within the squad was such that I was among a group of players who would make the cut. I was delighted to be selected to represent Wales at the new competition, but when I was told that I was captain it was a feeling which I am unlikely to experience again.

Mine was a chequered career during which there had been several incidents of poor discipline. They had placed a question mark over my personality and inevitably my suitability toward captaincy, but I think I was honest enough to accept those doubts and criticisms. What changed my attitude were the two summers in Australia during which I began to take a totally different view on the game. Whereas previously any opportunity to get in the flare-ups on the field would see me involved, now I started to look at things in a different light, concentrating on the game as a whole, both on and off the field, appreciating the well-being of the team. I place great importance on the interaction between the captain and the team, which may in some way have changed with the depth of the back-up in place today, but the role of captain remains vital.

* * *

There was no shortage of aspiring locks in the mid-1980s and Moriarty's versatility helped the selectors accommodate the likes of Pontypool's John Perkins and Cardiff's Robert Norster, both lineout specialists with Norster in particular destined to become one of Wales's finest at his craft. Robert Norster, like Brian Price and Delme Thomas before him, was a player who would be likened by a certain commentator to 'a leaping salmon', all three players capable of winning excellent lineout ball as a result of their athleticism long before the IRB decided to make the amendments to the Laws which would allow jumpers some assistance.

First capped against Scotland in 1982 when he partnered Moriarty, Norster, on his retirement in 1989, joined Allan Martin as Wales's most capped second row with 34 appearances. Still actively involved in the game as chief executive of the Cardiff Blues, Bob Norster is fully conversant with rugby football in the professional era and with the politics that continue to drive the game in Wales. This, coupled with his experiences as a former player of some stature, make his observations of rugby union in the twenty-first century particularly significant.

Where injury had seen Arthur Lewis hand over the reins to Delme Thomas and David Pickering likewise to Richard Moriarty, it was on the ill-fated Welsh tour to New Zealand in 1988 that skipper Bleddyn Bowen was similarly forced out of the first Test and Robert Norster nominated to replace him as captain. Like Thomas and Moriarty before him, Norster suffered a similar fate against the All Blacks – another defeat of mammoth proportions, Wales beaten 52–3 – and an injury picked up in the match prevented him experiencing further humiliation in the second Test. Following a tour which no country would have relished, the sacking of coach Tony Gray seemed particularly harsh and premature, but his was a fate several others would experience.

At the time and certainly in hindsight most people saw it as a bad decision but that is not in any way a slight on John Ryan, who took over. Ryan was a good coach with a successful record at club level and he probably deserved his chance, but Tony and his assistant Derek Quinnell really engendered a strong emphasis on senior players taking a hand in training sessions through to the performances on the pitch and I think we started to see a group of players that grew together. The nucleus of the team had come through a tough tour of the South Pacific in 1986 with a lot of credit, had continued to make progress in the 1987 World Cup and then won a Triple Crown, which was so nearly a Grand Slam. We had come through it all as a group and while some of us may have been a bit long in the tooth, we bonded together well, both on and off the field, but we were outdone by a really good, professional New Zealand team.

In 1989 Robert Norster bowed out of international rugby on a high, literally, when his lineout domination allowed Robert Jones to control proceedings against England in foul conditions at Cardiff. This was a seventh appearance against the old enemy and Norster proudly boasts that he was never on the losing side, but it had required a lot of dedication and, more importantly, patience, before he broke into the Welsh team.

I first got involved in the Welsh squad in 1977 but it was five years before I won my cap against Scotland, which is amazing when you think in terms of international rugby today. The great '70s era was in its final stage when I first appeared in an uncapped match against Romania and I was probably one of the least-known names in the team. I was playing in Cardiff by then, but I had originally been introduced into the squad when I was an Abertillery player, something I'm quite proud of.

There may have been more caps added to the 34, but a bad shoulder injury sustained playing for a World XV in South Africa during that country's centenary celebrations brought an end to Norster's playing days. Injury aside he must be viewed as one of the lucky players, one of a relatively small number who have carved a career out of the game following retirement.

It was good for me to have the opportunity to continue in the game, having had my career brought to what I considered a premature end, even though I was 32 at the time. I was given the chance to cut my teeth as an administrator working with Alan Davies, a proud Welshman who was a very capable, technical coach but an unknown when he came into Wales, having spent most of his time coaching in England. We had some memorable times together, culminating in the 1994 championship, but the end [which saw the management team resign en bloc following the 1995 Five Nations] was a shambles, a sad chapter, but it happens. Sport is never perfect.

On the advent of professional rugby, Bob Norster returned to the Cardiff club which he had served so well as a player, this time in an administrative capacity, which eventually led to his current position with the Cardiff Blues, and it is from behind this desk that he observes the state of rugby football, how it has changed and the problems which it has to face.

We are all guilty of looking back at the game through rose-tinted glasses. I recently saw 20 minutes' highlights of a match I played in against Scotland and it looked great, but these were the highlights, and to be honest the rest of it was drudgery: messy ball, a lot of hit or miss. The difference in the game as it was and how it is today is like chalk and cheese. Don't get me wrong, the excitement levels were good, but if you look at the skills and the execution, they were often quite poor and all of this has to be taken into consideration before we form a judgement on today's game. Rugby has become much more focused and when considering the role of the captain, you have to remember that many areas of the game have different players in control – the lineout leader, the scrum doctor, behind the scrum tacticians – but you have to be careful not to break the game up too much. I personally favour a captain in either the back row or at half-back where there's a much better overall perspective, unlike in the second row where vision is restricted.

Where once a brief run-out on the eve of the big match constituted team preparation, thanks to state-of-the-art technology, coaches and analysts are now able to dissect a match and each player's performance to the nth degree, and likewise their opponents. But is such attention to detail excessive and for the betterment or detriment of rugby as an entertainment?

There is no doubt that in certain areas the facilities now available to coaches and their back-up team are invaluable. For example, to be able to sit down with a young, developing forward who has to work on his scrummaging, I don't think you can do enough of it. Discussing his leg positions, how he is using his arms and shoulders, is he communicating with the players around him, telling them what he wants. Similarly, it enables the coach to study the biomechanics of a lineout jumper, his technique and skill. Viewing such detailed information on a one-to-one basis with the coach has to be good but sitting the team down hour after hour reviewing matches time and time again, knocking players because they missed a tackle, that is nonsense and has to be controlled. The technology must be used for the benefit of the players; the mind-numbing number-crunching of people into the robotic exercises that you see all too often on the field highlights where it is being used badly.

After the longest reign of a Welsh second-row forward Norster was not up for selection come the autumn of 1989 and another meeting with those familiar black jerseys, but waiting in the wings was a young man from Neath who in due course would not only go on to break Allan Martin's and Norster's record number of caps for second-row forwards but become Wales's most capped player.

Gareth Llewellyn was twenty years old when he debuted for Wales, selected to face New Zealand following a spirited performance for Neath against the tourists ten days earlier. The international went the same way as the previous three meetings between the two countries, but Llewellyn showed enough to suggest that here was a player who could serve Wales well in the years to come. And serve his country Gareth Llewellyn most certainly did. While Neil Jenkins was rattling up the points, Ieuan Evans scoring the tries and a number of other players breaking all manner of appearance records, Llewellyn was winning cap after cap during a period in which he saw off the threat from several seasoned lock forwards, Chris Wyatt, Craig Quinnell and Mike Voyle among them. On his retirement from international rugby in 2005 he was the proud champion of 90 appearances for his country. This after being written off by large sections of the media and public following the Welsh defeat by Samoa in the 1999 RWC when little went to plan, the lineout in particular coming in for criticism.

Two years in the wilderness and then a return to international duty as a replacement at Twickenham in the 2002 championship tell us two things. First, Gareth Llewellyn became the consummate professional rugby player, a man who immediately embraced the sport when it went open and one of the few at the time who took on board that being a professional sportsman meant more than simply getting paid for playing. Second, that there was a paucity of up-and-coming second-row forwards in Wales, with only Robert Sidoli, domiciled Australian Brent Cockbain, and Michael Owen, a more likely number 8, in the frame. When the hugely talented Chris Wyatt, together with Craig Quinnell, fell out of favour and Ian Gough fell victim to a succession of injuries, the selectors' problems were compounded, which ultimately necessitated Llewellyn's return to the squad. There, he competed for a place in the starting line-up with Andy Moore and Steve Williams before both players retired, leaving Llewellyn to yet again contest the issue with the young guns.

Llewellyn first captained Wales in the summer of 1993 when he led a party to Zimbabwe and Namibia in place of Ieuan Evans, who was touring New Zealand with the British Lions. The three Test matches were won, as was Llewellyn's next outing as captain, this time replacing an injured Evans against more experienced opponents France. His last three matches at the helm also came about when further injury problems denied Evans his place in the team and Llewellyn continued in winning vein, leading the side to victory against Italy before firstly South Africa and then the French brought the run to an end.

It is somewhat ironic that during the 2003–04 season Gareth Llewellyn was discarded by the Ospreys and ended it playing in the semi-professional league, not for Neath but Swansea. Come the 2004–05 season, and having failed to secure a regional contract in Wales, he signed for French club Narbonne, yet was still selected in the Welsh squads for the 2004 autumn internationals and the Six Nations in 2005.

Many second rows arrived on the international scene during Gareth Llewellyn's career, including brother Glyn, but his longevity saw him outlast virtually all of them. One such player was Swansea's Andy Moore, whom Graham Henry turned to when another British Lions tour involved several Welsh players in addition to Henry himself, controversially chosen as coach.

In 2001 Wales went on a six-match tour of Japan and under Andy Moore both Tests were won, matches which saw first caps for Gavin Henson, Jamie Robinson and Tom Shanklin. Japan is no longer a rugby nation to be taken lightly, with an ever-increasing influence of outside players in the club game, which is evident in some very un-Japanese-sounding names on the team sheet. The two Welsh victories were a fine tribute to Andy Moore and his squad, which contained the perfect blend of experience and youth. At twenty-seven years of age Moore fell midway between the two measurements, with plenty still to offer. Although he played for Wales through to the end of the 2001–02 season, winning another nine caps in the process, injuries were starting to tell and he was forced into early retirement aged twenty-eight, an untimely departure from the game.

Such premature retirements highlight the problems faced by so many of the big men who, with assistance and their own body height, can be lifted as much as 15 feet in the air lineout after lineout; the pounding their legs receive on returning to the ground will inevitably take its toll. This is not surprising when one considers the amount of training and lineout practice that also enter the equation. It is a general consensus of opinion that for a multitude of reasons this intricate part of the game has become a largely disorganised and dangerous mess, and the time for the game's administrators to step in and review the Laws governing it cannot come soon enough. Then we will see the return of the lineout jumper, the artist; men who can win the ball as a result of their particular skill not because they are elevated to unnatural heights, but one fears that only serious injury will prompt the lawmakers into action.

* * *

When the players themselves raise doubts about the suitability of the position of second row as one from which to captain a team, then perhaps it is time to look at other options and in particular consider that the position they occupy is not paramount when seeking suitable captains. That Martin Johnson, John Eales and Fabian Pelous have proved successful leading teams 'head down, arse up' is more a reflection on them as individuals than their being great strategists, and it is with this in mind that we move from the tight five to the middle five – the back row and half-backs.

IV

FORWARDS AND BACKWARDS:
WING FORWARD

Wingers, side rowers, flankers, wing forwards, open-side and blind-side, left and right. Confused? All these terms relate to the modern-day wing forward, the players who together with the number 8 marshal the back row of the scrum and the tail of the lineout. They have to possess all the skills found in the other specialist positions, be as strong as a front-five forward, as quick (well, almost) as a half-back or three-quarter, and they probably have to be fitter than any of them. They cover more ground, put in more tackles, are first to the breakdown; they are in support when the backs are making their penetrating runs; they destroy and they create – that's the theory anyway. The wing forward must be comfortable ball in hand, be able to give and take a pass at pace and not be inhibited when the time arrives to kick the ball, put boot to leather, find touch, kick ahead, drop a goal, and on occasion have the awareness to identify the correct time to put in a cross-kick and have the ability to do it.

When Wales defeated New Zealand in 1953 it was a result that went very much against the run of play, the All Black forwards dominant but badly let down by some inept play among the backs. Normally sound in defence, full-back Bob Scott and wing Ron Jarden showed great uncertainty early on and when a loose pass between them went to ground, Cardiff wing forward Sid Judd was on hand to score. Then the New Zealand pack took control. How the home team stayed in contention remains a mystery, but as the game entered the final quarter Wales were trailing only 8–5. The forwards had received a terrible hammering and were not helped in their cause when centre Gareth Griffiths was forced from the field with a dislocated shoulder. This necessitated a reshuffle and left wing Gwyn Rowlands was moved infield, replaced on the flank by wing forward Clem Thomas. Wales hung on and when Griffiths returned for the final ten minutes, the team received a boost that saw them firstly tie the scores with a penalty and then, with minutes remaining, steal the match.

Clem Thomas found himself with the ball inside the New Zealand 22 but close to the left touchline, rapidly running out of space and with few options available – he could either end up in touch or kick the ball cross field. He chose the latter and when his kick bounced kindly for Ken Jones, the right wing, to score beneath the posts, Wales had registered a famous victory. The infield cross-kick is rarely used 50 years on but was very much part of the game in the 1950s with Clem Thomas's the most famous of them all – if you are Welsh that is.

First capped in 1949 Clem Thomas made twenty-six appearances for Wales over a ten-year period, the last nine as captain. His career started and finished with away defeats in Paris and he shared both his debut and swansong with centre and namesake Malcolm.

It is important at this stage to differentiate between open-side and blind-side flankers. The theory is that the quicker of the two covers the largest part of the playing field at the set-piece scrum, the open-side, from which position he can be among the opposition backs as soon as the ball is released. This needs pace if the offside Law is not to be broken, while on the blind-side of the scrum things tend to move a little slower.

Clem Thomas was an open-side flanker, big, hard tackling and particularly quick in his prime but by the time he was asked to captain Wales he had lost some of his pace. Despite his leading a winning team against Australia, the selectors felt that he had been exposed by the Wallabies' outside-half, who had beaten him consistently throughout the match. Thomas kept his place for the visit to Twickenham but the selectors chose to introduce the young, flame-haired Haydn Morgan on the open-side and moved the captain to the blind-side of the scrum from where he played out the rest of his international career.

At the end of the 1950s French rugby was at last beginning to look comfortable on the international stage and a first win at Cardiff Arms Park in 1958 was followed by a first outright championship success in 1959. Clem Thomas led Wales in Cardiff and again at Stade Colombes when France secured the title led by their inspirational captain, second-row forward Lucien Mias. In Mias, French rugby had a player and captain who represented everything the game once stood for, but at the same time was the complete antithesis of rugby captaincy in the twenty-first century.

One of the finest hours in French international rugby came in 1958 at Ellis Park, Johannesburg, when, after a drawn first Test, the Tricolours beat the Springboks 9–5 to win the two-Test series. Twelve hours earlier captain Mias had been found in a hotel corridor clutching an empty bottle of rum and there was no doubting where the contents had gone. Come kick-off he rallied his troops and led by example for the 80 minutes with a performance that had the local press calling him 'the greatest forward ever seen in South Africa'. So what is it that inspires men to go beyond the call of duty in the search of success on the playing field? There is no doubt that where Mias went on that hot August day, there were seven other French forwards who were not far behind, a collective effort certainly but undoubtedly one inspired by an individual. And the rum? Lucien Mias was a doctor of medicine and is reported to have said that he knew of no finer cure for sinus problems! A tale of a long-lost game, a long-lost attitude to leadership: captaincy *laissez-aller* – with unconstrained freedom.

Clem Thomas also graced the playing fields of the high veldt. A British Lion in 1955 he had enhanced his reputation with some outstanding performances after appendicitis had prevented him appearing in the first half of the tour. In the third and fourth Tests at Pretoria and Port Elizabeth, Thomas made up for lost time, and despite defeat in the final Test, which resulted in a drawn series, he was one of the many success stories of the tour.

The third Test at Loftus Verfeld was the first played at the famous ground and in 1998 it staged the final game of a six-match tour by Wales, one which had started with a win against Zimbabwe but had gone off the rails from the first match in South Africa, when the Emerging Springboks comfortably defeated a submerging Wales. One shouldn't be too critical of the Welsh performances on this tour since so many of the leading players had made themselves unavailable – 18 missing through injury or personal reasons – but captain Robert Howley was there to lead the troops even if many of them did look a bit wet behind the ears.

As is all too often the case summer tours to the Southern hemisphere are rarely good ideas and South Africa in 1998 was not the place to be if you were a Welsh rugby player, established or developing. It was a tour to be avoided, as many players obviously realised, but these fixtures are confirmed by the IRB some time in advance with nothing resembling a 'get out' clause. It was a sad story. Throughout South Africa, Wales were bullied, harried and generally outplayed despite some creditable performances but the sheer physicality of the contest took its toll and seven replacements were flown out to join the party. Consequently, there were some very unfamiliar names and faces among the squad as it assembled for the Test against the reigning world champions. Among those injured was captain Howley and after answering an SOS call while holidaying in New Zealand, it was Ebbw Vale wing forward Kingsley Jones who led the Welsh team onto the field at Pretoria.

Fortunately Kingsley Jones has a sense of humour, which he undoubtedly inherited from his father Phil, who, despite this, was better known as manager-cum-mentor of Jonah Lomu than for his stand-up routines. Kingsley needed all his tolerance and patience on 27 June 1998 because there was nothing funny whatsoever in the events that overtook Wales, events which would have had a boxing audience calling on the referee to stop the contest. Unfortunately, the largely Afrikaans crowd was baying for blood and there was no white towel to throw in. Neither Kingsley Jones nor anybody else deserved to have one of the proudest moments of a playing career shattered by such a relentless onslaught. Try after try, 15 in all, and but for a piece of careless ball handling in the game's dying moments it would have been 16 and a century of points instead of the 96 for which the Springboks had to settle.

Kingsley Jones wasn't there at the final whistle. Injury had forced him to leave the field, the captaincy passed on to scrum-half Paul John, who was also forced to retire, leaving hooker Garin Jenkins to try and stem the tide. All seven replacements were used by Wales and of the twenty-two players who took part in the game eight didn't play for Wales again, Kingsley Jones among them.

* * *

That Kingsley Jones captained Wales, albeit in its blackest hour, is something of which he is rightly proud. It will always be an honour to lead the men in red onto the field, regardless of the outcome. Traditionally, teams playing away from home enter the arena first and there are many stadia where the wall of sound that greets the visiting captain as he comes into the view of the awaiting spectators is deafening. Be it Twickenham, Stade de France, Eden Park, Newlands or any of the other major grounds worldwide, the decibel level that is reached by 60, 70 or 80,000 people sets the pulse racing and the adrenalin flowing, but it is nothing compared to the sound that greeted the Welsh team when they took the field at the National Stadium, Cardiff Arms Park. There may only have been little more than 50,000 people in the old horseshoe, but they knew how to upset the neighbours and when it was time for the national anthem, well, is it any wonder they didn't bother putting a roof on the place? It was an atmosphere that has never been replicated anywhere. It was unique. If not quite heavenly, it was certainly unearthly and it was what Welsh rugby was all about – *hwyl*. If leading Wales out at away matches was special, imagine what this was like.

It is unfortunate that all Wales's great captains, and regardless of prejudice and opinion they are all great, could not experience this very special moment but to many it was denied. There were those like Kingsley Jones who led Wales once, away from home: Jack Bancroft, Gerald Davies, Idris Jones and, of course, that pioneer James Bevan, and many more besides. Kevin Phillips and Andy Moore both led Wales onto foreign fields twice, Mike Hall three times, then there were Richard Moriarty's seven matches as captain, which were all played away. Added to these are two players of more recent years who both captained Wales five times but never in Cardiff.

Formerly of Llanelli, Gwyn Jones was a Cardiff player when he led Wales on a summer tour to North America in 1997. Captain in the two Tests against the USA, Jones missed the Canadian Test through injury but come the start of the 1997–98 season he was again in charge for three home matches before fate struck a cruel blow.

Home matches Romania, Tonga and New Zealand may well have been, but they were played at Wrexham, Swansea and Wembley Stadium respectively, the bulldozers having moved into Westgate Street and the Arms Park was no more. The rugby people of North Wales certainly arrived in numbers, filling the Racecourse, home of Wrexham FC, but there was less enthusiasm for the visit of Tonga to Swansea where fewer than 7,000 turned out in support, the smallest home attendance of the twentieth century. Strange, then, that this should be followed two weeks later by the biggest 'home' crowd to date when 78,000 supporters painted Wembley Way red for the visit of the All Blacks.

A certain apathy could be identified among Welsh supporters in the late 1990s, with a general feeling that Wales could be expected to beat the less traditional opponents but would struggle to get the important victories against the established nations, and it would not be unfair to say that the five matches Wales played under Gwyn Jones all had very predictable outcomes – following on from those against the USA, there were victories over Romania and Tonga which, in turn, were followed by another win for New Zealand.

On 13 December, two weeks after leading Wales at Wembley, the Welsh captain lay prone on the ground, the victim of an unfortunate accident in a Cardiff–Swansea league match. A serious spinal injury forced Gwyn Jones's retirement from the game and brought to an end a career which had promised so much. At 25 years of age he had already assumed the confidence and stature of not just a good international player but also a good international captain and his loss to the game in Wales was immense, particularly at a time when Welsh rugby was experiencing such difficulties.

Fortunately Gwyn Jones made a good recovery from his horrific injury to become a respected commentator on the game, with his knowledgeable and forthright opinions earning much praise. Whether through the press or television, his thoughts are always constructive and straight to the point, leaving the more speculative aspects of the game's reporting for others to chew over. Be it in Welsh or English the rugby public of Wales listen to what the former captain has to say and he shows an uncanny rapport with supporters, much appreciated at a time when so much else is taken for granted.

Gwyn Jones was a fast loose forward: first to the breakdown, comfortable ball in hand and an outstanding tackler, all skills which are associated with the modern wing forward. It wasn't always so and, as with most of the forward positions, it was the 1920s or later before the advantages of having such a player included among the forwards were fully appreciated, largely due to the efforts of Llanelli's Ivor Jones, the first of his kind to captain Wales and, coincidentally, the great-uncle of Gwyn.

Regardless of the fact that other countries had adopted a winger or side rower in their forward ranks the Welsh selectors chose to stay with the tried-and-tested format of forwards being treated en bloc, but Ivor Jones remained detached from the mauls which dominated so much of the game in the 1920s, preferring to stay on the fringes waiting for the attacking opportunities which inevitably presented themselves. Due to his expertise the selectors finally adopted the concept and another stage in the game's evolution was put into place.

Welsh captain on three occasions – against New South Wales in 1927, at Twickenham in 1929 and Murrayfield in 1930, all three ending in defeat – Ivor Jones's 16th and final appearance for Wales was the match in Edinburgh, but his finest hour was yet to come. With the British Lions in Australia and New Zealand in 1930, he appeared in all five Test matches and made an indelible impression, particularly in New Zealand, where the wing forward has always been treated with great reverence. That his international career was over at twenty-nine years of age was in keeping with the selection policies of the day, but he continued playing for Llanelli until 1938 and captained the club in eight seasons. A member of the Big Five and Welsh representative on the International Board, Ivor Jones's long service to the game was recognised in 1969 when he was elected as the 21st president of the WRU.

* * *

A round trip of over 25,000 miles. A squad of 29 players. Two matches. That those responsible for such decision making had decided it was in the best interests of the global game that quantity (except of games, perhaps) should take preference over quality is an unfortunate fact that rugby union has to live with and it would certainly be wrong to suggest that it was only Wales who went off on such ludicrous missions. The Northern hemisphere countries spend what for the players should be a period of rest at the end of an already overlong season filling the coffers of their Southern hemisphere counterparts who then reciprocate the gesture in the latter part of the year at the end of their equally demanding season.

June 2003 saw England play three matches in New Zealand and Australia, and France play three in Argentina and New Zealand. Ireland also took in three on their tour to Australia, Tonga and Samoa, and Scotland travelled half the distance for two matches in South Africa, while Wales were also to be found in Australia and New Zealand. The television schedulers must have suffered a degree of apoplexy finalising kick-off times that would enable punters around the world to sit down on a Saturday for a feast of rugby that would take in at least three live matches. The Air Miles were totting up and captains Johnson, Galthie, Corrigan and Redpath were preparing their players for one final effort before a well-earned break, but who was doing a similar job for Wales?

Steve Hansen, Wales's second Kiwi coach, had some strange ideas, ideas that many would have called revolutionary, but surely something can only be seen as revolutionary if it encourages development, progress

– anything else and it is soon forgotten. Hansen seemed to find comfort in numbers; there had been the three full-backs and now there were the four captains. Colin Charvis, Stephen Jones, Robin McBryde and Martyn Williams were all named as Welsh captain for a two-match tour – what were they going to do? Have half a match each! In a stroke, a New Zealander had diminished the role of Welsh captain to something akin to a sideshow. Who was going to do the initial press conference when the team arrived in Australia? Who was named as captain in the reports announcing that Wales were in town? The role of captain now reaches way beyond the field of play and to have named four players who would in some egalitarian way satisfy the antipodean news hounds was simply not going to hold water and probably says more about the coach's thinking at the time than his record ever could. Come matchday it was Cardiff wing forward Martyn Williams who led Wales out at the Telstra Dome, Sydney, and the Waikato Stadium, Hamilton, both teams including the other three 'captains'.

Williams was not new to the job, having been handed the responsibility for the trips to Murrayfield and Paris earlier in the year after Charvis appeared to have fallen foul of just about everybody, following the defeat in Rome, and Jon Humphreys, the man originally chosen to take over, had succumbed to injury. Welsh captain is as good as it gets for most players and regardless of success or failure the honour is rarely less than a humbling experience. Martyn Williams led defeated Welsh teams against Scotland, France, Australia and New Zealand, and he was called upon once more in the 2004 championship, this time for the visit to Dublin, where he again led a beaten team, making his record a disappointing five defeats in five matches played, all away from home.

For a player of the calibre of Martyn Williams not to enjoy any success as Welsh captain was a cruel twist of fate. A British Lion in 2001 and 2005 and voted man of the championship in the 2005 Six Nations confirms his standing in the game but, as is so often the case, there were those who would prefer to see a bigger man on the flank and but for an injury which kept Colin Charvis out of contention for a large part of the season, 2005 could have been very different. That the game has gone big to the exclusion of all else is unfortunate, particularly on the flanks of the scrum where speed is still seen to be of the essence. Neither should we forget the required kicking skills which Clem Thomas so ably demonstrated, Martyn Williams able to boast a drop goal among his many achievements.

* * *

Over 1,000 players have been capped by Wales, a figure which puts in perspective the relatively small number of international players who have continued their involvement with the national game once their playing careers came to an end. This is more noticeable in the period since the Second World War and is attributable in the main to one of two reasons – either the players themselves wanted no further involvement in the game or they weren't asked. In the days of an amateur sport it is understandable that for most the continued involvement in something which had taken up much of their time over many years was not always practical. Careers, business interests and family commitments rapidly filled the free time that was suddenly available and that some did make efforts to put something back into the game is to be applauded.

Generally speaking, however, there is little evidence that in the days before the sport became open ex-players were welcome at the administrative table. Where an ex-player wished to continue his involvement in the game, it was the clubs who were the beneficiaries; when Welsh rugby was in a prolonged period of mediocrity during the 1980s and 1990s, any suggestion of turning to the great names of the past fell on deaf ears. 'The game has changed' or 'We have to look forward not back' were the normal ripostes, but the truth was probably that the players were seen as some kind of threat to the hierarchy and all that it stood for.

Since that August day in 1995 when caution was thrown to the wind and rugby union became a professional sport, the situation has changed. Jobs were created, salaried positions that would benefit from having people with not only the business acumen now necessary but also the experience of playing the game at the highest level. In recent years many senior managerial positions within the structure of the WRU have been filled by ex-players. Coach Gareth Jenkins and his predecessor Mike Ruddock both played senior club rugby, as has general manager Steve Lewis, while team manager Alan Phillips represented Wales and the British Lions. Terry Cobner and Paul Thorburn have also played an active part in the national game at an administrative level and, along with current chairman David Pickering, not only represented Wales but were also appointed captain. As he was so adept at doing, so we must now kick Thorburn into touch – his turn will come later – and focus our attention on wing forwards Cobner and Pickering.

Where, in 2003, Wales took a squad of twenty-nine players to play two matches, twenty-five years earlier Terry Cobner led a party of twenty-five players to Australia for a tour which took in nine. The injuries came thick and fast and by the final match the walking wounded almost outnumbered the hale and healthy and for the second Test Wales were left with no option other than to include full-back J.P.R. Williams in a back row which showed three enforced changes from the first. Terry Cobner was among those unavailable for selection and his number of capped matches as captain remained at one, the 18–8 defeat in Brisbane.

I first led Wales in an uncapped match against Argentina in 1976. Mervyn Davies had been forced to retire and I took over, but come the Five Nations I was recovering from illness and Phil Bennett was appointed and continued for the next two seasons, during which time he captained the British Lions in New Zealand. I don't know what would have happened if I hadn't fallen ill, whether the selectors would have asked me to continue or not, but it was certainly odds-on that whoever led Wales in '77 would get the Lions job.

Australia in 1978 was very difficult. We weren't treated fairly, particularly in the first Test when I felt we were being judged harshly by the referee, but he is the sole arbiter over what happens on the pitch and there is nothing you can do other than get on with it. The tour may have been a bridge too far for some of that particular team but with so many new faces the mix of experience was important but I pretty well knew that it was going to be my last appearance.

Of all the players to captain Wales in the first 125 years Terry Cobner is certainly the most experienced: obviously this is a statement not based on his international record of one match in charge, rather his extraordinary exploits at Pontypool Park, where he led the Gwent Valley club for a record ten consecutive seasons. Leading Wales in uncapped matches together with three outings as captain of the British Lions in New Zealand in 1977 make up an impressive CV of captaincy experience, one which should be tapped into.

The important thing about appointing a captain is to get the right man for the job. Obviously he has to be able to command his place in the team, something which the other players have to accept, the fact that he is there on merit. They have to respect him as a player and as a man, and for his knowledge and understanding of the game.

I wouldn't pick a captain because of the position he played but ideally I would pick a back row forward who had the right qualities.

I fail to understand how a back can control the shape of the game, which I feel is done by the forwards who determine whether the backs have the ball or not. If they don't let the ball out, the backs cannot do anything and I know from my playing days as both captain and pack leader, the backs had the ball that we wanted them to have, no more. The captain has to be a forward because if that area is going wrong, he is in a position to fine-tune it, get to the source of the problem. Being more specific, the captain has to understand the nuts and bolts of the game, how the whole team works. If you ask a centre what is going on in the front row of the scrum or the lineout, he won't have a clue; similarly, a front-five forward wouldn't be the best person to ask about three-quarter play. If you ask the same of a back-row forward, he'll know what's going on in front of him and equally he will appreciate what is happening among the backs because he is in the right position to see and control the whole team. This particularly applies to wing forward where you've got a foot in both camps, a support player for the backs but still involved in the contact areas with the forwards.

There is a very fine distinction between the terms 'captain' and 'leader', one of which Terry Cobner is very conscious. Does the appointment of a captain automatically suggest that the player has leadership qualities? Or is he recognised for his understanding of the game, which doesn't necessarily include the ability to take players beyond normal limits, into the unknown, to coax that little extra out of each individual.

I have only seen two men who I recognise as having all the necessary qualities of both captaincy and leadership. Wilson Whineray was the first and cricket's Mike Brearley the second. Whineray was a man who commanded total respect from his players, a respect which even reached out to the opposition, and to watch Brearley control a cricket team in the field was an education.

Cobner is not wrong in his assessment of two of international sport's finest leaders but consideration should be given to the fact that he probably saw Whineray as a tour captain in the days when teams were away from home for four or five months on a tour which included the thick end of thirty or more matches. The situation is better likened to that of a club captain and Brearley would undoubtedly have been given an extended period of tenure, as is the norm in Test cricket, enabling him to adjust to the five-day Test match and all that such a lengthy event entails. Few Welsh captains have been afforded such luxury, forever looking over their shoulders following a defeat and rarely receiving praise in victory. This is a trait that has often determined the fate of many who could have proved successful Welsh captains given more opportunities. But patience is a virtue rarely found among those involved with the game in Wales. When it is shown, more often than not one is left wondering why. Which leads to another observation made by Cobner – does a run of bad results necessarily equate to a bad captain? Unfortunately, good point as this is, the outcome that usually prevails in such circumstances prevents any serious analysis, since the captain is generally consigned to the ranks or worse.

It took Welsh rugby a little over three years to begin to understand what being a professional sport really meant. Three seasons had come and gone, seasons which witnessed record defeats by England, France and South Africa, massive scores more familiar to cricket followers. Added to this was further misery at the hands of Australia and New Zealand. Kevin Bowring was Wales's first coach of the professional era, a position which proved to be a thankless task due in no small part to the apparent lack of understanding of what was needed to succeed at the highest level. Bowring had many innovative ideas regarding the structure of Welsh rugby but could not convince the decision makers and a parting of the ways was inevitable.

With the appointment of Graham Henry much that Bowring had recommended finally got the rubber stamp and a backroom team was gradually put into place. Among the first appointments was that of team manager, a position filled by Terry Cobner on the 1996 tour to Australia and one now seen as necessary for all matches – someone to field the flak, placate the press, protect the players from any unwanted intrusions. The man brought on board to do what in time became a full-time job was David Pickering.

David Pickering made his debut for Wales against England in 1983 and after a run of fifteen consecutive matches, during which he was one of the team's most consistent performers, he was handed the captaincy at the start of the 1986 championship, the visit to Twickenham. Despite scoring the game's only try, Wales were narrowly defeated 21–18, thanks in no small part to the boot of Rob Andrew, who scored all his team's points, but the selectors had seen enough and decided to keep faith with the new captain for the rest of the season, which saw Scotland and Ireland beaten before France completely outplayed the home side on a desperately disappointing afternoon at the Arms Park.

What had started in 1964 when Wales made a first overseas tour to South Africa became the norm by the twenty-first century, players spending the first month after the end of the domestic season away from home. Following on from South Africa in 1964, New Zealand in 1969 and Australia in 1978 were the major undertakings, but there were also visits to Argentina, North America, Japan and Spain, and in 1986 Wales headed for the South Sea islands and three Tests in Fiji, Tonga and Western Samoa.

David Pickering led a Welsh squad of 25 players to what many may view as an idyllic destination – sun, blue skies, white sand, palm trees and exotic cocktails. A perfect holiday destination but, with the hard grounds, even harder players and soaring temperatures, one which can be quite inhospitable to the visiting rugby team, a fact Pickering can lay testament to following a kick in the first Test in Fiji which saw him return home and take an enforced four-month break from the game. 'Somebody jumped on my head from a great height, which caused me a few problems. I was determined to come back, but these things do affect you, I don't think there is any doubt about that.'

He returned to lead Wales in three of the 1987 championship matches but after winning twenty-three caps and leading his country eight times the selectors decided to look elsewhere. It all came to an end at Murrayfield where Wales were badly beaten upfront, but there were extenuating circumstances.

We lost tight-head Stuart Evans, who broke his ankle in training the day before, and Maesteg's Peter Francis was flown up to replace him. Unfortunately, Peter struggled and at one point, after ten or twelve scrums had gone up in the air, Keith Lawrence, the referee, called me over and said he wasn't happy with our tight-head to which Bob Norster chirped up 'You're not happy!' It was quite funny really, but Peter only had the one cap, which was unfortunate. I was dropped and that was it, but I look back on my time as captain with great pride and affection.

I was brought up in a household steeped in rugby and always received fantastic support from my family. Playing for Wales was a particularly emotional experience, something you can always look back on, and being made captain added to that. You make conscious decisions when you are appointed to lead the side, start to make personal goals again. It becomes another starting point; you want to achieve something as Welsh captain, something for which you will be remembered but, of course, that doesn't come easily. I had a 50 per cent record, four wins out of eight, a fair reflection of a time when Welsh rugby was having to cope with seeing leading players go to rugby league. This was particularly disruptive during the '80s and we did well to build a team that went on to be third in the 1987 World Cup and then went on to win a Triple Crown.

I enjoyed the experience of captaincy immensely and in terms of personal development I'm sure it helped me in my future roles. Leading Wales onto the Arms Park was a wonderful experience but like so much else in the game, it has changed, which I put down to two simple reasons. Emotion now plays a much smaller part in preparation; in fact, the modern thinking is that it should be removed from the equation altogether because, while it can certainly be a strength, it can also be a weakness. When you begin to focus on that higher level, a point where things begin to click in automatically, it becomes a mental state, demands a mental sharpness that can only be achieved by taking the emotion away. We've gone from an emotionally led performance to a scientifically led one, a major advancement. Where once we prepared seven or eight things we might do as a team, now there are huge manuals covering every conceivable aspect. The other factor which has impacted on the occasion is the number of matches now played, anything up to ten or eleven in a season, whereas it used to be four or five.

Inevitably the changes have also impacted on the role of the captain. When I was elected, I had a far more personal role on the field, which isn't the case now. The captain is still a key, influential figure, but he has more back-up off the field and other leaders with him on the field. This was introduced during my time as team manager with Graham Henry and since then there has been a huge philosophical change in the way teams are run. We no longer have the old cricket style of captain, who determined everything that happened; now it's a group of individuals who have specific areas of responsibility and that is down to the change in how the team and squad are managed.

That, in turn, has removed any preconceived notions as to where the captain should play, what position is best suited to the job. When I was playing, I would suggest that he had to be a central figure, somewhere between the second row and the centre, but that is no longer relevant. What hasn't changed is the ambassadorial role which has always been of significant importance and remains so today. The captain has to be more media friendly, show the right attitude and demonstrate a responsibility towards the major sponsors who have become involved; be a great leader both on and off the field. The key to captaincy is to be yourself; you can't be anybody else, just be yourself, give it your best shot and enjoy it.

International rugby behind him, David Pickering left Llanelli to join Neath, where he played a major role in that club's league championship of 1987–88, with performances which suggested that the selectors may have acted too hastily. Ten years later he returned to the international scene in his capacity as team manager and in 2003 he was elected chairman of the WRU, a position which has seen him involved with internal issues that make the Fijian tackling seem lightweight in comparison. The chairman has had to ride out many seemingly no-win situations in the singular belief that the decisions made were for the long-term benefit of the game in Wales. But Welsh rugby being the tribal-based democracy that it is, these have been decisions that usually upset many and appeased few.

The last two years have seen a turnaround of seismic proportions at the WRU. Professional managers are in place at all levels; the disjointed system which existed in the very important area of schools rugby has been sorted out, bringing every promising player into the system; the structure of the game has been overhauled, from the mishmash that it was a few years ago to a system which means we can now compete. There will always be a few players who move elsewhere, but more are looking to stay in Wales, where we have now got state-of-the-art training facilities and the debt problem has been sorted out; we don't exist under a cloud any longer. What was a £2.7 million loss a couple of years ago has been turned into a significant profit. We have to keep working at it but I am very optimistic about the future.

Terry Cobner and David Pickering lay testament to the fact that the door is now open for players to consider long-term careers in the game, careers which can continue after their playing days have come to an end. The fields of coaching and administration offer opportunities that didn't exist before 1995 and players are queuing up to take advantage of them.

Of the seven wing forwards to have captained Wales apart from Martyn Williams, who continues to play the game, the other six all maintained an involvement with the game either in an administrative capacity, through coaching or with the media. What this can tell us about the position is debatable but it does suggests that to a man, they all developed an acute understanding of the game which playing such a complex position probably helped nurture – by being a forward who is a back and a back who is a forward.

V

FIGURES OF EIGHT: NUMBER 8

At the start of the 2004–05 season the role of Welsh captain was under review, or at least if not the role of captain, then the way in which he would be chosen. No longer would one player be immediately identified as the man for the job, handed the responsibility and allowed to get on with it. Now suitable candidates were invited to attend an interview at which they could try to convince coach Mike Ruddock why they were the best man to captain Wales.

The incumbent captain in August 2004 was number 8 Colin Charvis but whether by accident or design he had once again succeeded in alienating many of the game's supporters and the nation was divided over whether he should continue in the role following the summer tour. Charvis had created a furore in Argentina when he refused to speak to the media unless he received financial remuneration for doing so. Former players did not hold back in their condemnation of the captain, but the flames were very quickly put out when Charvis retracted his request and conformed to the expected terms of communication. The damage was done, however, and before announcing the captain for the autumn internationals the coach took the previously unheard of step of inviting six players, Charvis among them, for interviews.

There was a division of opinion over who would be best suited to lead the team. Seasoned campaigner Gareth Thomas was a popular choice but many were still of the opinion that Charvis should continue. Stephen Jones and Martyn Williams had previous experience in the job and Michael Owen and Jonathan Thomas were both being talked of as future captains and by including them in the process Ruddock could only do their confidence some good. In the final analysis Gareth Thomas was appointed to lead the side and a disappointed Charvis confirmed as vice-captain.

A seasoned international, Colin Charvis is the most travelled of all Welsh captains in both his choice of club and the positions he has played. We have already seen that he has captained Wales while at Swansea, Tarbes and even when unattached, and was registered with Zurich Premiership outfit Newcastle Falcons when leading Wales in Argentina and South Africa in 2004, and a first team regular when he was captain against Japan in the autumn. He has similarly played in each of the three very different positions in the back row of the scrum but it is as a number 8 that he is included here. First capped as a replacement against Australia in December 1996, Colin Charvis has won 75 caps, making him the fourth most capped Welsh player despite being involved in some hugely self-destructive incidents, the last of which led to the appointment of Gareth Thomas.

In the build-up to the 2002 Six Nations Championship, Charvis went to Jamaica to visit family, thereby missing the Welsh team's preparations and losing his place in Graham Henry's final squad. The player insisted he had confirmed there would be no training camp during his planned holiday and receiving the OK from Swansea went regardless of Henry's apparent late change of schedule. A heavy defeat in Dublin saw Welsh rugby and Graham Henry part company with the elevation of Steve Hansen to coach, a change which saw Charvis on the bench for the visit to Twickenham and a resumption of his international career when he took the field as a replacement. Rather surprisingly, bearing in mind all that had gone before, Charvis was handed the captaincy for the final match of the championship against Scotland and then led the squad for the two-Test series in South Africa at the end of the season. Despite losing all three matches there was a renewed sense of commitment from the Welsh players, which Charvis took a lot of credit for, particularly the performances in South Africa.

The autumn internationals went much as expected with victories over Romania, Fiji and Canada before the All Blacks were flattered by a final score of 43–17, a long period of injury-time accounting for 21 of the points. There then followed the second of three contentious issues which have marred Charvis's international career: the capitulation of the Welsh team in the Six Nations opening match in Rome. Unfortunately, after being replaced, Charvis was captured by the television cameras sitting on the substitutes' bench with a smile on his face, which under the circumstances seemed inappropriate. The axe fell rather unceremoniously and the nation was divided over the captain and his future. What all this controversy began to hide, and what a large section of the Welsh public became blinkered to, was the fact that Colin Charvis, underneath his myriad of idiosyncrasies, is a fine rugby player.

He was rightly handed back the captaincy for the 2003 RWC and led Wales from the front on their great adventure in Australia. Although there were no shocks on the road to an expected quarter-final against England and an anticipated exit from the competition, Wales were the surprise package of the tournament and fast became the neutral's favourite. And the manner of the defeats against New Zealand in the Group stage and then England suggested Welsh rugby had experienced a kind of metamorphosis Down Under.

Charvis led by example. Tries against New Zealand and England, plus one against Canada, helped win back the doubters and helped put him back in favour with those who, nine months earlier, had foolishly likened him to Osama bin Laden or Saddam Hussein. But little did anyone know in those heady days in Sydney and Brisbane that in eight months' time the proverbial would hit the fan once again.

Is Colin Charvis stupid? Highly unlikely. Is he greedy, looking to fully capitalise on what is undoubtedly a short career? Possibly. For whatever reason the Welsh captain saw fit to close ranks and refuse to talk to the media unless there was something in it for him, something financial which would compensate for the extra demands he felt were placed on him as Welsh captain. The timing of this controversial episode? A couple of days before the first Test against Argentina in Tucamen, June 2004.

The position of Welsh captain is sacrosanct and the high public profile that it inevitably attracts should never be either taken for granted or abused. Colin Charvis must have known that there would be adverse reaction to his holiday, his apparent relaxed attitude in the face of defeat and his financial demands, but this did not prevent him carrying on regardless, and having the captaincy taken away from him would have hurt, particularly as he was probably still the best option available to Ruddock. The merits of a captain at either full-back or on the wing are still to be discussed, but the advantages of leading from the back row are considerable, on top of which the players obviously respected Charvis. If anything, Colin Charvis can perhaps best be described as a victim of the professional era and all that the silver lucre has brought to the game, but his destiny was always in his own hands and ultimately it was the player himself who decided his own fate.

* * *

Professional rugby union may have only arrived in 1995 but there had long since been an alternative for players who were prepared to turn their back on an amateur sport. In the north of England rugby league had been dominant for 100 years, an abbreviated version of rugby union which those Welsh players considered good enough were invited to try their hand at and, for the not inconsiderable sums of money on offer, many did.

Scott Quinnell came from good rugby stock. Father Derek had been a leading back-row forward in the Golden Era of the 1970s, winning twenty-three caps and featuring on three tours with the British Lions, and upon retiring from the game he appears to have gone on a personal crusade by rearing sons who seem to get bigger and bigger. Firstly Scott followed by Craig, both now senior internationals, with the third in line, Gavin, having represented Wales at Under-21 level.

Scott Quinnell was first capped in 1993 in what was an inauspicious start to an international career that would reach the heights, Canada gaining their only victory in the fixture to date. After a further eight caps in 1994, which saw a memorable try against France in Cardiff, Wigan RLFC came waving the cheque book and Welsh rugby lost another blossoming talent. But things were changing and 12 months later events in Paris confirmed an open sport and the player drain to rugby league finally came to an end. Not only did it stop, but there was now an opportunity for those who had 'gone north' to return south, and Scott Quinnell soon took advantage of the relaxed criteria. It was Richmond, however, who initially gained the benefit of his services.

In the autumn of 1996 Wales's prodigal sons started to come back into the international reckoning with firstly Scott Gibbs then Jonathan Davies, David Young and Alan Bateman recalled for international duty, followed by Scott Quinnell, who was welcomed back into the team against the USA Eagles on 11 January 1997. One of six former rugby league players who toured South Africa with the Lions in 1997 his tour was cut short by injury and it would be another four years before he did himself justice in the famous jersey.

Rugby league taught me a lot. I joined a great club at Wigan and was fortunate to play alongside Shaun Edwards, Dennis Betts,

Martin Offiah, Phil Clarke and many other big names, but it was a different way of life. I quickly learnt the demands that training every day places on your body, how to cope with regularly putting your body through the stresses and conditioning it needs in preparation for matchday. I could barely walk in the first three weeks simply because I wasn't used to running backwards, which you tend to do a lot in league.

A little over seven years after winning his first cap, Scott Quinnell was chosen to lead Wales against South Africa in the absence of David Young but another twelve months passed before he was given a second chance, this time hanging on to the job for six matches, including the record defeat in Dublin which saw the end of Graham Henry and then another fifty-point defeat at Twickenham. These were not good days for Welsh rugby, but Quinnell is very focused when considering the role of captain whatever the circumstances.

My feelings toward captaincy are quite simple. If you are the right man for the job, it doesn't matter what position you play. The most important thing is having the players with you, understanding what type of man you are, what you expect from them and then allowing them to get on with their own job. The training field is where you have the opportunity to prepare the structure of the game you want to play, the points you particularly want to get across, and come matchday you have a few words in the changing-room. By this stage there should be a mutual trust and as you go onto the field you hand the game over to the players, and ultimately if those 14 around you are good enough to win Grand Slams and Triple Crowns the team will succeed.

Certainly you decide whether to kick for goal or go for position and when the inevitable indiscretions occur and the referee calls you over, you just hope it isn't you who has caught his eye, but captaincy is all about being part of the team, leading by example and letting everyone else get on with what they do best. Technology has played a big part in redefining the role of the captain. The depth of analysis now available to coaches allows every detail to be examined in depth, how many tackles are missed, how many carries made, how many times you did your bootlace up. Each player is so focused on his own performance, which inevitably takes some of the responsibility away from the captain; players have become so accountable. To counter this, responsibilities off the field are greater. Dealing with the media and all that entails is very demanding and there is also the fact that rugby is a business that has to be sold and the captain becomes involved in the marketing of the product, selling the game and the particular brands involved, all of which has to be got over to the public if the business is to thrive.

In 2002 Scott Quinnell decided to put family first and bring his international career to an end. Long since back with his beloved Scarlets he was content to commit all his hammered body had left to his home club in its search for European glory but in March 2005 further injury forced his decision to retire a few months earlier than planned. A career which had taken in representative rugby at all levels, from schools, youth and the various age groups through to the national team, was brought to an end after 15 years of intense rugby which had finally taken its toll.

Where rugby will be in ten or even five years' time is a matter for conjecture, and where the player of the future will fit into the social strata is impossible to tell. Yet to reach the global reverence in which leading footballers are held or attain the attached wealth and trappings that such superstars take for granted, the high-profile rugby player has a sense of urgency in a career which is ever shortening as the physical aspects of the game increase and the competition for places intensifies. What the prospects are for the vast majority of players once they have hung up their boots is debatable but for the time being there are many young men travelling the world on passports that describe their occupation as 'professional rugby player'. Contrast this to how a leading player from the Welsh teams of the 1920s chose to describe himself.

Rugby-Playing Man is a most suitable title for a player's reminiscences and it was used by Watcyn Thomas when he went to print in 1977, over 40 years after retiring from the game, a title which fully expounds the ethos of the amateur days of rugby union. In his foreword to the book Vivian Jenkins describes Thomas as 'the Mervyn Davies of the late twenties and early thirties' whose 'name was known wherever the game was played'. A big man for his time, standing over six feet tall and weighing sixteen stone, Watcyn Thomas was the epitome of the number 8 – good in the lineout, mobile, and a sound defender who had a vision of the game not readily associated with forwards of his era. That he became the first number 8 to lead Wales is only surprising in that it took the selectors so long to realise that the back of the scrum was an ideal position from which to captain a team, as it represents the perfect link between forwards and backs, a fact that would be taken on board worldwide in the post-war years, particularly in the Southern hemisphere, where it would almost become mandatory.

Watcyn Thomas was first capped in 1927 when he played against England in a Welsh side that came so close to laying to rest what had become the Twickenham bogey, all previous attempts to win at the famous ground having been doomed to failure. His debut may have ended in defeat and it would be a further six years before Wales finally succeeded at HQ, but when the day finally arrived it was a Welsh team captained by Watcyn Thomas that silenced the largely partisan crowd of 64,000, at the time a record for the championship. Thomas led his forwards with great enthusiasm and in their domination of the English eight they laid the foundation for the Welsh win. A story circulated which told of inspirational dressing-room talks – 'If you see a dark object on the ground kick it . . . if it squeals, apologise' – vehemently denied by Thomas, but the captain certainly fired up his forwards if not by words then by his extraordinary deeds.

Under Thomas Wales lost the season's remaining matches against Scotland and Ireland and his international career ended in unsatisfactory fashion when he fell foul of the selectors after taking it upon himself to change two players' positions once the team took the field against Ireland, going directly against their preference, and, of course, Wales losing didn't help.

* * *

Following the heady days at the start of the twentieth century, days that saw Wales capture the Triple Crown on no fewer than six occasions and the Grand Slam three times, the inter-war years were particularly barren. In 1946 it was inevitable that few international careers would be resurrected after six years of conflict and in fact only four Welsh players were capped before and after the Second World War – C. Howard Davies, Les Manfield, Bunner Travers and Haydn Tanner – and on the resumption of the International Championship in 1947 it was the Cardiff scrum-half who guided Welsh fortunes for three seasons. But come the start of the 1950s there was a new name charged with the responsibility of leading Wales back to the forefront of European rugby.

From a first appearance against Australia in 1947, John Gwilliam won six caps while a student at Trinity College, Cambridge, playing in the second row in five of the matches with a rare outing in the middle of the back row against England in 1949. This was about to change, however, a teaching post in Scotland seeing the player in the colours of Edinburgh Wanderers, where he became the regular number 8. For the opening match of the 1950 championship the Welsh selectors chose Bleddyn Williams as the man to succeed Tanner as captain, but injury forced a rethink and Gwilliam was asked to lead the side at Twickenham. But with only one previous victory at the ground and a team that included six new caps, there was little optimism among the travelling support.

My introduction to the captaincy was purely by chance. Bleddyn had been chosen to lead the side but had to pull out and Rees Stephens, the vice-captain, also had to withdraw. I had no idea. I came down from Scotland for the practice on the Friday afternoon at Herne Hill and Vincent Griffiths took me to one side and told me the selectors had decided to appoint me captain adding, 'Play your own game. Don't knock the ball back in the lineout and don't hold it in the back row and don't do these wild passes – just play your own game.' All things that were a part of my game!

When Wales won 11–5, few could have predicted what the next three seasons held in store for the men in red, a period which would see Welsh rugby both scale the heights and plummet to the depths. Calling on a total of 17 players during the season, Wales next defeated Scotland followed by Ireland and finally France at the Arms Park to record a long overdue Grand Slam which had been 39 years in coming. It was also a first Triple Crown since 1911, but the victory in Belfast was overshadowed by the tragic Llandow air disaster which claimed the lives of 80 Welsh supporters returning home from the match.

The respects of the players, spectators and Welsh nation were observed with the sounding of the 'Last Post', followed by a minute's silence before the final match of the season against the French in Cardiff, remembers Gwilliam, played on 'a beautiful, sunny afternoon but we failed to score for a long time, Jack Matthews breaking the deadlock with a try under the posts which saw us 5–0 up at the interval. Then poor Jean Prat had to leave the field with a bad leg injury and we scored three more tries.'

Gwilliam was asked to continue in 1951 and after a comfortable victory against England all roads led to Murrayfield, where more of the same was expected. It wasn't to be, Wales going down 19–0, their heaviest defeat since the 1920s, and following a disappointing home draw with Ireland the captain was dropped.

What happened at Murrayfield was just one of those things. After the 1950 Grand Slam fourteen of the players went on the British Lions tour to Australia and New Zealand and were away for over six months. I had not long got married and we were expecting a baby, so I said I wouldn't go, but when the players came back they were a bit tired, there is no doubt about it. Ben Edwards was brought into the side against Ireland and kicked the goal that earned a draw, but I was dropped after that.

The season ended with defeat in Paris and, as so often happens, Wales had fallen from being the undisputed kings of Europe to also rans in the space of 15 months.

John Gwilliam was recalled to lead the team against the Springboks, but it wasn't easy to reclaim his place, particularly as he was playing his club rugby in Scotland, out of sight of the Big Five.

I had a job to get back into the team. There were lots of trial matches in those days and I was asked to take part in one, which meant undertaking the long journey from Edinburgh, tiring at the best of times but particularly so for a trial. The match was played at Abertillery and I was included in the 'Possibles' together with a lot of other good forwards and our pack knocked spots off the 'Probables' in the first half. At half-time one of the selectors gave me a red jersey and told me to transfer to the Probables – I was back in favour.

Against the tourists Gwilliam failed to extract a winning performance from the Welsh team but was seen to have done sufficiently well to be asked to continue when the championship got under way in the new year. Once again it was to Twickenham and a case of déjà vu when a win was followed by revenge against Scotland and more success against Ireland and France. It was 1950 all over again and a second Grand Slam in three seasons with no obvious explanation for the fall from grace seen in 1951. Suddenly John Gwilliam was up there with the successful Welsh captains who had gone before. Only Billy Trew in 1909 had previously led Wales in each of the four matches during a Grand Slam season and now John Gwilliam had done it twice. Despite three other captains leading Grand Slam sides in the 1970s and a joint effort in 2005 Gwilliam remains the only captain to have enjoyed the experience on two occasions.

The start of the 1952–53 season saw him playing at Gloucester.

After three years in Scotland we decided it was too far to travel with the family and I got a job in Bromsgrove. Newport asked me to play for them but the travelling was still a problem and I decided that Gloucester would be a better option. I was quite happy to finish my career there, as my father was originally from the Forest of Dean.

After a home defeat by England Gwilliam was replaced as captain and although there would be more caps his days as Welsh captain were over. It was an irony not wasted on the player that the man chosen to lead Wales was Bleddyn Williams whom he had replaced three years earlier at the outset of his thirteen matches in charge.

'An awful lot of luck and some brilliant players' are the prime requisites for a captain in the opinion of John Gwilliam.

I would never have been made captain but for injuries to Bleddyn and Rees Stephens, so my selection was very much down to luck, added to which the team had any number of great players. The selectors had no input beyond choosing the team and captain and once that was done we were just left to get on with it. One of the big advantages I had was that many of the players had come through schools' rugby together and knew each other well. One of my traits was that I could never stop talking during a match, but I think players like to be encouraged, referred to on the field by name. Even the likes of Cliff Morgan and Bleddyn responded to a few words of encouragement. You can't just speak when things are going wrong. I'm sure I talked a lot of rubbish but some of it must have got through.

Twenty-four years on from that surprise defeat at Murrayfield the same ground hosted the championship's estimated record crowd of 104,000 when, in 1975, Wales were again beaten by a fired-up Scotland. No 19-point mauling this time, rather a much more respectable 12–10 with the visitors gaining some consolation in claiming the game's only try. However, although it meant no more or less than many another lost cause at the time, barely 12 months later the benefit of hindsight would reveal how desperate a result it really was.

* * *

Mervyn Davies was an unknown to the majority of Welsh supporters when he was selected for his first cap against Scotland in 1969. Playing his rugby at Old Deer Park with the successful London Welsh team, he was distanced from the week-in week-out neighbourly contests that represented Welsh club rugby but his reputation had spread and he joined other exiles John Taylor and J.P.R. Williams, also making his debut, in what became a Triple Crown-winning team. The trademark headband was in place, the moustache would follow, but more importantly the abundance of talent was there for all to see and Welsh rugby had found a superstar.

For 38 consecutive matches the name T.M. Davies appeared at number 8 in the matchday programme, dominated the back row of the team photograph and on the occasion of his 30th cap Mervyn Davies led Wales in the opening match of the Five Nations against France at the Parc des Princes, an intimidating pile of concrete in the south-west of Paris. Wales may well have won at the venue twice in the early days of the fixture back in 1911 and 1913, but in the new all-seater stadium that played host to French international rugby in Paris between 1972 and 1997 they were successful only once in 13 visits, in 1975, the day Davies, now a Swansea player, led the team for the first time.

> My involvement with the captaincy happened late in my career and perhaps I should have been more forthcoming in letting people know I was anxious and needed to captain the side. At that time I felt I was playing some of my best rugby, wanted an extra challenge and, Lions rugby apart, that challenge was to captain my country. It has to be the greatest honour a Welshman can achieve and I felt that it was a little late in coming. I'd no real experience in the role other than leading Surrey a couple of times but I knew I had reached a time where I needed more involvement, more responsibility. As a player you reach a level of confidence where you know you are playing well and that the added responsibility of captaincy isn't going to be a problem, won't make the slightest bit of difference to you, and I knew I had reached that point. I wanted more input, a bigger say in what was going on, how things should be done and what needed to be done.

The appointment of Mervyn Davies came about primarily as a result of a change of national coach. After six years in the role Clive Rowlands had been replaced by John Dawes and inevitably with the new coach came new ideas and a change of leader was among them.

Clive's preference had been Gareth Edwards but when John took over he saw things differently. My rugby career had been synonymous with John's for a number of years, mainly at London Welsh, but also with Wales and the British Lions; we knew each other inside out and knew what we wanted from each other, which I believe had a great bearing on why I was appointed. Looking back, apart from my time with Swansea, I've always been under the influence of Mr Dawes, both on and off the field – but that's another story!

I feel that certain positions lend themselves to captaincy more than others, number 8 among them. You are relatively close to the action unlike wing three-quarter or full-back and while I'm not saying it's impossible to lead from those positions, because many people have done it very successfully, nevertheless if the captain is at the hub of things, in the centre, at half-back or in the back row, you very much get the feel of what is happening both upfront and behind. Then other factors come in for consideration. Gareth was the greatest rugby player the world has ever seen but I think captaincy weighed heavily on his shoulders; he felt he had to do more, which on occasions took something away from his game and I'm sure he would agree. Having said that I will freely admit that when I was captain of Wales at no time did I try to influence Gareth; he was his own man and could do as he liked.

John Dawes's first venture as national coach had ended in defeat. An uncapped match against the All Blacks in November 1974 followed a disappointing season and it was time for change. The Big Five introduced six new caps for the visit to Paris, completely reshaping the midfield with a new outside-half and centre pairing, two props to complete a famous club front row and a new back-row forward. That John Bevan, Steve Fenwick, Ray Gravell, Tony Faulkner, Graham Price and Trevor Evans all subsequently represented the British Lions suggests there was little cause for concern with their selection, but at the time few were of the opinion that Mervyn Davies would have a winning start to his term as Welsh captain.

There were six new caps but those guys had been around the block a few times, they were part and parcel of what was happening. It's so long ago I can't really remember how confident we were but the Parc des Princes was a difficult place to play and the general expectation can't have been high.

The everlasting image of a significant victory is of Graham Price chasing a loose ball over half the length of the field in the game's dying moments for a debut try but the leadership qualities of Davies drew praise from all quarters, remarkable for a player yet to captain a club side. Convincing victories over England and Ireland followed, enough to see Wales end the season as champions, but they sandwiched the defeat at Murrayfield which denied any hopes of a Grand Slam or Triple Crown, and for the captain there was a salutary lesson to be learned from the Edinburgh experience.

St David's Day and 104,000 people. The day it was safer to be on the field than in the crowd. Phil Bennett hadn't really established himself in the number ten jersey and Dawes was of the opinion that John Bevan gave more options behind the scrum. There was also a school of thought at the time that Phil didn't like sitting on the replacements' bench, that he was a player who needed the build-up, that sitting on the bench didn't suit his temperament. David Richards was also in the frame and in fact there was a time when Phil was actually third choice outside-half. At Murrayfield I lost Steve Fenwick and John Bevan through injury and with Richards not in the squad it was Phil who came off the bench to replace Bevan. When I look back on my captaincy and the mistakes I made, this substitution brings about one of the occasions which immediately comes to mind. There was a penalty in front of the posts 30 yards out, easy for Phil and I told him to take the kick. He wasn't happy having only just come on and said he didn't want to take it but being in dictatorial mood I told him to and he missed. I had Allan Martin in the side and should have given it to him, but more importantly I should have listened. Thereafter I changed my whole perception of what goal kickers do because they are vitally important, they keep the scoreboard ticking over, and following that incident I told Phil, Steve and Allan to sort it out between themselves and it worked like a dream. Never again was I dictatorial to a goal kicker.

How near Wales came to playing perfect rugby in 1975–76 is impossible to assess. Many factors enter the equation, not least among them the strength of the opposition, and at the end of the day such hypothetical analysis is best left alone, but this Welsh team under coach John Dawes and captain Mervyn Davies were setting themselves high standards. When Australia were beaten 28–3 and England 21–9 with both coach and captain critical of the performances, it was clear that the expectation from within the camp was high. Close analysis of the matches played show three distinct periods of play.

The first quarter I viewed as the confrontational period, when you sized the opposition up, looked for weaknesses. I'd tell the backs I wanted to spend this period in the opposition half as much as was possible; they could run at their own peril but kicking was a better option. That was all I wanted from them. Yes, we were going to make early mistakes, give penalties away, but better to do it in their half and not concede any easy points. Then there was a period of consolidation by which time you had a feeling how the match would unfold. I was lucky in that the teams I was involved with were nine times out of ten at least as good as the opposition, often better, and by the second half we were usually in a position to control, almost dominant.

What I would say about the Welsh team of the '70s is that I don't think it was the greatest team in the world in the true sense. There were many tremendously gifted individuals within the squad but I don't think we tended to play that well as a team. The perfect example of team play was the first half of Wales against Scotland in 2005. Everybody worked for each other, no balls were dropped, the support play was there and looking at that team as a whole everybody, forwards and backs, intermingled and interpassed very well. We did it in the '70s, but I do think that we lacked that ultimate team set-up because we tended to be catering for individuals – Gareth Edwards, Barry John, Phil Bennett, Gerald Davies, J.P.R. Williams, etc. etc. etc.

Neither Australia nor England had crossed the line, which confirmed the Welsh team was complete in both attack and defence and after Scotland were comfortably despatched 28–6, followed by Ireland 34–9, it was only the Scots who had registered a try. France then outscored Wales by two tries to one in Cardiff, but a final score of 19–13 earned Wales a seventh Grand Slam and Mervyn Davies had led Wales to eight victories in his nine matches as captain.

The French match saw the culmination of everything we believed in ourselves: the never-say-die attitude, the ability to fight to the end. Basically we didn't panic. France played well on the day and were probably the better side, but they took a few wrong options. It was a typical French encounter in which it was my turn for some treatment. Normally they focused on Gareth but at one point the ball was 30 yards away and I had the entire French pack running over me and I probably should have gone off but wild horses couldn't have dragged me, it was that sort of game.

Only now could the relevance of that earlier defeat in Scotland be fully understood; it had prevented back-to-back Grand Slams and a 100 per cent record for the Welsh captain.

These were heady days for Welsh rugby, the nation's emotions were running high and expectancy was huge. As captain it was for Mervyn Davies to maintain a level of equilibrium among the players, be a schoolmaster and one of the boys, as appropriate, and to do this he had to understand what made them tick as individuals.

In the second row we had Geoff Wheel and Allan Martin. Geoff was the most excitable and energetic player who was not in total control of his emotions before a game; the pressure would be getting to him while Allan Martin would be half asleep, totally laid-back. On the morning of the match I would get them into my room and try and take the energy and fervour from Geoff and instil it into Allan and vice versa, take Allan's calm, collected attitude and put it into Geoff, so that they were somehow on a par. I also felt it was important as captain to talk one to one with players outside of the squad system and the coaching sessions. Take them aside and have a word if I felt there was a problem. This was better than the team talk in the changing-room, which I tended to view as something of a ritual, more for the forwards than the backs, but I don't think it touched many players. It was about focus, getting them all on the same wavelength, re-emphasising why we were there, how lucky we were to be representing so many. I used to think about it a lot before matches but came to the conclusion that it was a total waste of time, especially at the National Stadium.

The visiting team would go out first and there was this colossal roar, then we ran out and it was trebled. Absolutely mind-blowing, frightening. I cannot think of anything in my life more moving, more stimulating, more enjoyable and yet more frightening than running onto that field in front of 60,000 people. You'd go through the rigmarole of shaking hands and so on, and when it came to the anthem, there would be players with tears in their eyes, such was its effect. Noise becomes a physical thing on a rugby field, especially when 60,000 are singing the same song, and it moves you. That anthem is so draining, my knees would turn to jelly, the hairs on the back of my neck stand on end and then they would kick off and we would be three points down and I'd wonder why I bothered with all the build-up for it to be shattered by this anthem. If the crowd had kept quiet and they hadn't played the anthem, Wales would have started better. Strange feelings.

Following the 1976 Grand Slam the Welsh public wondered what would be next for their heroes. Mervyn Davies had gone on record as saying that he felt three consecutive Grand Slam years were not beyond the realms of possibility, but it was not to be. At the age of 29, at the height of his athletic prowess and with much to look forward to in the game, Mervyn Davies's playing career came to a sudden and dramatic end. Three weeks after leading Wales to Grand Slam glory Davies was at the helm for Swansea in the semi-final of the WRU Challenge Cup against Pontypool. Played on neutral territory at Cardiff on Sunday, 28 March spectators saw him collapse and be carried from the field in the 27th minute, having suffered what was later diagnosed as a cerebral haemorrhage totally unrelated to any incident in the match. After a long illness Mervyn Davies made a full recovery but his playing days were obviously over and what might have been can only be a matter for conjecture, but suffice it to say that enough had already been achieved to place him among Wales's finest captains.

* * *

Players retire, get injured, lose form and in the 1970s it was far from unusual for players to join the ranks of rugby league and get paid for their weekend toil. The Welsh selectors were well used to all of these eventualities but the tragedy that befell Mervyn Davies was something for which they would not have been prepared. Their captain had years on his side. He was at the peak of his form, his presence in the team was never in doubt and the players around him were gelling together as a body. There was the promise of more great deeds. The captaincy and the number 8 position looked the least of their worries as the Grand Slam of 1976 was celebrated, but circumstances dictated otherwise and for the 1977 campaign there was a new captain in Phil Bennett, and Newport's Jeff Squire was called up for a first cap with the difficult task of replacing Davies.

In his 29 appearances for Wales Jeff Squire moved between number 8 and blind-side wing forward with consummate ease. Wales had several options in the back row and after two caps at number 8 Squire was replaced by Derek Quinnell, but returned for the 1978 season playing on the blind-side of the scrum in all four matches and it was at number six that Squire would continue for a further thirteen matches during which he was appointed captain for the 1979–80 season. With the selectors struggling to find the right balance in the back row Squire's versatility saw him back at number 8 for six matches, two as captain, before ending his career with a final four appearances at number six.

These complicated moves inevitably lead one to ask why Jeff Squire is included here as a number 8 rather than a wing forward. After all, of his twenty-nine caps most were won on the flank; similarly, of his six matches as captain four were at wing forward and the pattern continued in the six Test matches he featured in on three British Lions tours. So why? How can we justify placing an obvious imbalance in favour of the lesser party so to speak?

Readers will have picked up on the fact that each chapter has not dealt with the players it covers in a chronological order, preferring to find a link between them, so the fact that Jeff Squire replaced Mervyn Davies and that later, in his first game as captain, he played alongside a new Welsh number 8 who would himself go on to captain Wales was too much coincidence to ignore. Tenuous or incongruous as some of the links may have been, here were two which could not pass without comment, but for them to work Jeff Squire had to be included as a number 8.

Having celebrated his first match in charge with a home victory over the French, Squire, now a Pontypool player, led an unchanged team to face England in a match which had been hyped up by the media to such a level that it was almost inevitable there would be controversy and recriminations over its outcome. Twickenham on 16 February 1980 was arguably Jeff Squire's finest hour as Welsh captain. Forget the fact that Paul Ringer was sent off in the 15th minute, that goal kicks were missed and that Wales lost the match 9–8. Forget all such incidentals but what must not be forgotten is that after going three points down following Ringer's dismissal, Wales took the game to England, scored two unconverted tries and led the team that would go on to win the Grand Slam 8–6 as the game entered its closing stages. The fact that for 60 frantic minutes 14 Welshmen dominated a much-lauded England on their own patch is in no small part due to the leadership of

Jeff Squire. He led by example, scored Wales's first try and extracted every ounce from the thirteen men around him, and if he left himself open to any form of criticism it was in his decision to share seven kicks at goal between four players rather than persevere with one or two.

Between 1973 and 1986 the Pontypool club was represented in the Welsh pack in 62 consecutive matches. As many as four players were included on several occasions with the Pontypool front row gaining worldwide recognition as one of the finest ever seen, but by the end of the 1978–79 season of the trio only Graham Price remained, together with Squire in the back row. The next Pontypool forward to win international recognition was number 8 Eddie Butler, the player who made his debut when Jeff Squire first captained Wales.

Following the first cap alongside Squire in 1980 a further 15 were won and a late call-up as a replacement in the latter stages of the 1983 British Lions tour to New Zealand saw him make one appearance for the tourists, thereby completing a rugby education which had started at Cambridge University, where he won three Blues.

If you were an aspiring forward in Welsh club rugby during the late 1970s and early 1980s, there was no better place to learn your craft than at Pontypool Park. Breaking into the team would be another matter, such was the wealth of talent at coach Ray Prosser's disposal. Price, Windsor, Faulkner, Cobner and Squire were permanent fixtures, but it was to Pontypool that Butler headed and in time made his mark. He was appointed club captain for the 1982–83 season and invited to lead Wales in an uncapped match against the New Zealand Maoris, still packing down alongside Squire for both club and country. Butler continued as captain for the 1983 Five Nations which, despite seeing a significant Welsh improvement on the previous season, still left questions unanswered, questions which would remain unanswered following an unbeaten five-match tour of Spain, not least among them – was the pack powerful enough?

Autumn matches against Japan and Romania gave the selectors two further opportunities to find the right balance upfront before the '84 championship got under way. Wales failed to capitalise on a comfortable lead against Japan and allowed the visitors to score two late tries which made the final 29–24 score far too close for comfort.

Despite the hollow victory the selectors showed faith in the majority of the team and included six players with an average age of twenty-two for the Romanian match in Bucharest. For the first time caps were awarded against a country not affiliated to the IRB, but the irrational selection policies at forward, where no middle-line jumper was chosen, proved costly. Eddie Butler led the team to an embarrassing defeat which saw the hosts score four tries in a 24–6 victory, Wales having to settle for two penalty goals.

> Arriving in Ceausescu's Romania had an effect on us all. Not knowing what to expect, it was a huge culture shock and we were completely taken aback by what we saw. When it came to the match we just couldn't get our hands on the ball. They had the biggest pack I ever played against, four jumpers standing at six foot eight, and they just worked the touchlines. We knew this was likely and our plan was to opt for short lineouts wherever possible and throw the ball to Mark Brown, a rangy, lightning-quick wing forward, but he injured his neck in the first minute, so our great lineout secret weapon was gone. It was a haunting experience and whenever I meet any of the lads we always talk about Romania.

To have conceded a total of eight tries against what had to be recognised as lesser opponents certainly gave the selectors much to consider and if you listened closely you could hear the knives being sharpened. What had once been the greatest fortress in the Five Nations, the National Stadium, Cardiff Arms Park, was no longer held in awe by visiting teams, no longer worth six points and no longer the theatre of dreams it had become in the 1970s. When Scotland took the spoils it was the front row which took the brunt of the selectors' wrath, all three players replaced in the only positional changes made for the trip to Ireland. But there was one other difference in the team – Eddie Butler was no longer Welsh captain.

Despite retiring from the game over 20 years ago Eddie Butler's credentials as captain of Wales are still often questioned largely as a result of his television work in which he is never less than controversial in his opinions and seen by many to have become Anglicized, spending much of his time watching the English game at club and international level as rugby correspondent for *The Observer*. It seems a strange way to attack a commentator who doesn't always say what the public want to hear, but people have to accept that there were many Welsh captains who never led a winning team and Butler's two wins and a draw with three matches lost is nowhere near the worst record. He was no novice when it came to captaincy, leading Pontypool to great success during 1982–85, a period which saw the club runners-up in the Welsh Club Championship before winning it in consecutive seasons. This was a period which saw 101 of the 114 championship matches played won – a record which suggests that somebody was steering the ship.

By the time I took over at Pontypool I had been with the club six years. I was part of the furniture in a side which didn't want to change or do anything different other than introduce a couple of hand-picked players, such as David Bishop, but by and large we were very settled and at ease with each other which was in stark contrast to the Welsh team I was involved with. International rugby is a very competitive business and captaincy at that level is extremely difficult. You have to try and put enough pressure on people to avoid any complacency but you also have to try and build some sense of confidence and continuity. It is a very difficult job.

The fact that during the early 1980s in particular Wales was riven by inter-club jealousies didn't help. Pontypool were regularly slammed by the *Western Mail* and we received a warm welcome everywhere we went. We played a certain style of rugby and weren't the most popular team outside our boundaries, which suited us fine; we were very comfortable with that. Being captain of that travelling, very tight group of players was far different from trying to combine all the clubs within the parish who basically hated Pontypool, but the perception among the players is far different than when you are looking at it from the outside, the spectators' point of view. The players all got on well together but the media insisted on building up various issues and it was very tough to control. John Bevan was Welsh coach, a man who was ahead of his time and who I feel didn't get the credit he deserved, but he was a truculent character and not an easy person for the media to deal with which meant he got a bad press because he would basically tell the papers where to get off. This had a great bearing on why I went into journalism. I really didn't approve of the way the Welsh media reported on Welsh sport, which was written from a viewpoint of pure ignorance, but I have to say that it has improved of late, a bit more sympathetic to the spirit of the players. You certainly don't want to become part of the establishment furniture like J.B.G. Thomas, but you do have to be more sympathetic to what's going on than they were in the early '80s. They crucified us at Pontypool – not that I'm bitter and twisted, you understand!

For 16 consecutive seasons Pontypool were led from the back row of the scrum, Butler following in the footsteps of Terry Cobner and Jeff

Squire, and it is no surprise that he favours the position of number 8 as captain.

It's a good position. The front five have certain things to do, are heads down for much of the time, and the three-quarters should be left to do what backs do, indulge themselves in intrinsically selfish things, while in the middle five you find all the play-makers, but I think the half-backs are generally too busy, which leaves the back row.

Captaincy is a very tricky, fluid role. You can't expect a Phil Bennett to do the same as a Martin Johnson; it has to be a reflection of the individual's character. He has to be able to do something for the team; one person who makes the collective feel good. He doesn't have to be loud, but he has to have a presence. It certainly isn't rocket science, a case of making decisions out there that are going to split atoms, but it is important. England would not have won the World Cup if it hadn't been for Johnson and his figurehead role as captain. Clearly, the better the team, the less you are going to need somebody hauling you forward, but we all have bad times and you need somebody to bring you through. It's also a learning process; you don't approach it in game six in the same way that you did in game one.

The role has probably changed a lot in recent years. The players spend so much time together, the captain has to be more sensitive to feelings within the camp because they are on top of each other so much. Players are breathing rugby 24 hours a day and there is the additional problem of the boredom factor to contend with, which creates a massive off-the-field job in simply keeping the troops happy. The captain is so important here because between the bouts of high intensity the players are bored rigid. It's part of the trigger mechanism to keep them bored, so that when you unleash them they are champing at the bit – all very different to working during the week and simply looking forward to playing a game on Saturday.

* * *

The only link between Eddie Butler at Pontypool in 1983 and Alun Pask at Abertillery in 1966 was and still is a road – the A472 which leads to the A467. Abertillery is no more. Certainly there is still a town steeped in Welsh history which thrived during the days of coal, a town which can still boast one of the prettiest rugby grounds in Wales, but sadly the famous old club no longer plays on it. A victim of the professional era Abertillery RFC withdrew from the league in 2004, no longer able to fund a squad of players, and has since been replaced by an amalgamation of clubs who play as Abertillery Blaina Gwent. But it was all so different in 1966 when Abertillery RFC boasted three players in the thirty-strong British Lions team which toured Australia and New Zealand – scrum-half Alan Lewis, open-side wing forward Haydn Morgan and number 8 Alun Pask.

Undoubtedly a player ahead of his time, Pask was a supreme ball handler. There was no finer sight than him running in open play with it firmly gripped in one hand, throwing dummies in every direction, while his deceptive pace made huge inroads into opposition territory. His defensive qualities were equally outstanding, with the outcome of many matches decided by his magnificent tackling. Pask won twenty-six Welsh caps, made nine Test appearances on two tours with the Lions and was another player equally at home on the blind-side of the scrum, although his six games as captain saw him at number 8.

By 1966 Wales had yet to provide a British Lions captain. True, Arthur Harding had led the 1908 Anglo-Welsh team to Australia and New Zealand, a tour which is now included in Lions history, but Wales still awaited the leader of a team drawn from the four home countries, and the feeling was that Alun Pask would be that man. When England were beaten at Twickenham in Pask's first match as captain, followed by Scotland in Cardiff, the trip to Dublin was expected to be a formality which would bring an 11th Triple Crown and set up a Grand Slam clash with France. It would also install Pask as firm favourite to skipper the tourists when the party was announced immediately following the championship. Ireland failed to beat France in 1966, they missed out at Twickenham and failed again in front of a despondent Lansdowne Road when Scotland visited, but they beat Wales and any thoughts of a Welshman leading the British Lions were quickly forgotten despite Wales recovering some poise with a last-gasp try to beat the French.

Every now and then the selection of the Welsh team will divide the nation. This usually happens when two players are in contention at outside-half, which was the case in December 1966 when Australia arrived in Cardiff, the selectors awarding a first cap to Llanelli's Barry John in preference to the more experienced David Watkins. The arguments raged and it would not be an exaggeration to suggest that for one day only much of the Welsh support, specifically that from

Newport and the Monmouthshire valleys, was divided in its loyalties. It was down to Alun Pask to lead the side in such unusual circumstances and when the tourists registered a 14–11 victory the captain's cavalier approach to the game came under fire. When the better option would have been to close the game down, Pask was happy to enter into an open spectacle which cost Wales dearly.

Despite the manner of the defeat Pask was selected as captain for the visit to Murrayfield, but leading a team which included six new caps proved a thankless task and following the almost inevitable defeat Pask was relieved of the captaincy and made only one further appearance in the side. The general consensus of opinion regarding this ball-handling number 8 is that he was ahead of his time, a theory possibly confirmed by one of the Wales's most recent captains, one who plays the game much as Pask did, with great thought and great skills, none better than his ability ball in hand.

On 6 June 2002 Welsh rugby reached a milestone. At the Orange Free State Stadium in Bloemfontein, the team which lined up against South Africa in the first of two Tests included a new cap at blind-side wing forward. Michael Owen was a product of Pontypridd, a player who had represented Wales at all levels before this first appearance in the national team, and when he took the field against the Springboks he became the 1,000th Welsh cap.

More caps followed and, with opinion divided over which position best suited him, Owen also appeared in the second row before finally getting an opportunity in his favoured position of number 8, which he set about making his own.

I played all my early rugby at number 8, through school, at youth level with Beddau and Pontypridd, and in various representative teams, the Welsh Schools, Wales Under-21 and Wales A. To finally play for the senior team and become the 1,000th cap was a dream. After four or five matches I was moved into the second row, which I didn't initially enjoy, but I adjusted and I think it has been to my benefit, helped me in areas of the game I can put to use at number 8. Then came the injury that forced me to miss the 2003 World Cup which, if nothing else, made me realise how much being part of the Welsh set-up had come to mean.

Michael Owen's all-round skills have seen him likened to many of his illustrious predecessors in the number 8 jersey, Alun Pask not least among them. A presence around the field, his timing when offloading passes in the tackle, the options he offers at the tail of the lineout and not least a vision and ability to read the game, all these began to highlight his captaincy potential and in 2005 circumstances presented the opportunity for Michael Owen to captain Wales.

I'd always captained school and youth teams and I led the Dragons five or six times when Jason Forster was injured, but apart from that I had no other experience at senior level. Then at half-time in Paris I took over from Gareth Thomas. There are so many good players in the team, players who are leaders in their own right, and I'm just lucky enough to be the one honoured with the captaincy. Mike Ruddock is a great believer in players taking decisions, keeping the tempo of the game at a level we want, and I don't think things would have been different if Gareth had stayed on the field against France. We had a penalty, I decided to take a quick tap and when we were given a second one, the French not retreating, Martyn Williams tapped it and scored. That's the way Mike encourages us to play; he allows us that responsibility which makes the captain's role a lot more straightforward.

There is no doubt that number 8 is a good position to lead from. You are constantly involved and have a good feel for how the game is developing but I think that the man is more important than the position he plays, particularly in today's game. Many people would argue that full-back is not a good position to lead from, but Gareth brings so much to the job, personality, character and loads of enthusiasm which all rub off, but most importantly being made captain didn't change him. I could never be a Gareth Thomas, would never try and emulate him, the guy's mad, but I like to think being captain hasn't changed me. That is important; you have to be yourself and bring your own personal qualities to the role.

As had been the case during the 2005 Six Nations, the absence of Gareth Thomas from the squad saw Michael Owen again called upon to lead Wales. Toulouse had first claim on Thomas when Wales met Fiji in the autumn, and Owen presided over a nail-biting 11–10 victory in Cardiff before continuing in the role for the final three matches of the 2006 Six Nations. This was after Thomas bowed to medical advice and sat out the remainder of the season following a scan to investigate bouts of dizziness, which had led to the player collapsing at home, revealed an injury believed to have been sustained while playing for his club.

Wales struggled to recapture the heights of 12 months earlier, with several leading players joining Thomas on the injured list. A heavy defeat in Dublin, a fortunate draw with Italy in front of a despondent home crowd and a much-improved performance against France in front of the same supporters seven days later brought a mixed bag for the captain to add to his tally, which now reads three wins, a draw and two defeats in his six matches in charge.

* * *

Number 8 is a position perceived as being ideally suited to the role of captaincy, not only by those captains who have led from the middle of the back row but also by many players who are associated with other positions on the field. Three of the nine Grand Slams saw the team led by a number 8 and Michael Owen's contribution in 2005 should also be considered when making the argument.

Disregarding the importance of the position when selecting a captain, the second school of thought maintains that it is the calibre of the individual which above all else should be of prime importance. Strong cases can be built in favour of both arguments but at number 8 it is possible we have a position towards which men of suitable calibre naturally gravitate, resulting in the perfect balance.

Generalisation is a dangerous game, but of all the forward positions it is number 8 which stands out as the most suitable from which to captain the team. Just as the hooker dominates the front row, so does the eighth man dictate the back row but with a much greater vision of the game, greater communication with the backs. His is an ideal position from which to determine when the hard-won ball should be released, when to bring the backs into play – and it is time for these pages to do the same.

VI

THE PRESSURE POINT: SCRUM-HALF

'If' is a big word, the fact that they don't come much smaller a mere irrelevance: if Thomas Castaignede had converted a last-minute penalty; if Neil Jenkins had missed a last-minute conversion; if Argentina hadn't squandered a 23-point lead; and if the Springboks had, well, played like Springboks. If any of these instances had resulted in a different outcome then Wales's run of ten successive victories would never have occurred. But they didn't and it happened. And if the WRU had awarded caps for the pre-RWC fixture with the USA Eagles, then the record run of 11 consecutive victories would have been equalled – but they didn't. Yes, 'if' is a mighty word, but in reality it rarely means anything, leaning very much towards the hypothetical.

Happenstance aside, the events of 1999 are there for all to see. Wales won ten consecutive matches, the run starting in the Five Nations with victories over France and England, which sandwiched a meeting with Italy, who would join a new Six Nations in 2000. It continued in Argentina, where both Tests were won, followed by a first-ever victory over the Springboks at an unfinished Millennium Stadium, then, in the weeks leading up to the RWC two warm-up matches against Canada and France brought the run to eight, and the first two Group matches of the tournament against Argentina and Japan completed the romance. Welsh rugby was on a high and the man leading Wales at the time, ever present in the ten-match sequence, was scrum-half Robert Howley.

With 59 caps Rob Howley is Wales's most capped scrum-half and in

22 of his appearances he was captain. First capped at Twickenham in 1996 in what was a try-scoring debut, Howley decided to bring his international career to an end six years later following the Six Nations and in the summer completed a move to London Wasps, where the next two seasons saw some vintage performances help secure winners' medals in the Parker Pen Challenge Cup, the Zurich Championship and the Heineken Cup.

His rugby career began at Bridgend but he was attracted to the capital city and all that the self-styled 'Greatest Club' had to offer and won 53 of his caps while a Cardiff player. Two British Lions tours in 1997 and 2001 should have been among the high points in his career but injury denied Howley the opportunity to play Test rugby in South Africa and ruled him out of the final deciding Test in Australia four years later.

Indirectly, Howley's involvement with the Lions in the 1997 visit to South Africa opened the door for another scrum-half to experience the honour of leading Wales.

A tour to North America not only presented a rare opportunity for Paul John to play international rugby but also saw him called upon to lead the team against Canada, and in so doing become the only player from Pontypridd to captain Wales. The tour party was led by Gwyn Jones but after two victories against the USA injury forced him out of the final match, allowing John his opportunity. With many leading players absent this was a far from comfortable sojourn for a Welsh squad which included several new names, but all six matches were won and despite trailing by four points going into the final quarter at Fletcher's Field, Toronto, under John's guidance, Wales dug deep and kept their unbeaten record intact.

The unfortunate circumstances which brought Gwyn Jones's playing days to an end have been recorded but his misfortune inevitably led to an unexpected and unwelcome need to find a new leader. Paul John had to accept playing second string to Rob Howley in the Welsh set-up and in a championship warm-up match in February 1998 it was Howley who led the team out against Italy at Stradey Park, Llanelli, another of Wales's temporary venues while the Millennium Stadium was under construction.

The Cardiff–Swansea match was horrific: Gwyn's injury and Garin Jenkins's father suffering a heart attack on the terraces. The result and the game became insignificant, but it didn't go unnoticed that Gwyn was injured in the 13th minute on 13

December after running onto the pitch behind number thirteen! Over the Christmas period I began to come to terms with the impact of the situation, as did the whole of Welsh rugby. I visited Gwyn in hospital on Christmas Day but things hadn't really changed and yet there was an ongoing debate in the press about who was going to be the next Welsh captain. Unbeknown to me, coach Kevin Bowring had also been to see Gwyn and we met up shortly after and he offered me the captaincy. Eighteen months earlier I had been in a similar situation when Jon Humphreys was unavailable for the match against the USA, but I had declined the chance to captain Wales, knowing the time wasn't right, but now I felt ready and I also felt a certain responsibility to Gwyn who had suggested me as his replacement. My answer was yes, I was ready for that poisoned chalice.

Howley's first Five Nations in charge in 1998 saw record scores registered by England at Twickenham and France at Wembley, Wales conceding 60 and 51 points respectively. And barring injury Howley would have led Wales on that ill-fated day in Pretoria when a mammoth 96 points were scored by the rampant Springboks.

The first five matches under Kevin were difficult. We may have had a good team on paper but there was a great lack of self-belief and confidence among the players. We started well at Twickenham, Alan Bateman scored a couple of tries, and although the final score may not be a fair reflection on the game it's the 60 points that the supporters remember and the word humiliation comes to mind. We had to beat Scotland and performance went out of the window in our efforts to get the win and then we went to Lansdowne Road with a chance to get back some of our credibility. As captain, I found these circumstances difficult to cope with. I was very aware of the great expectation and became very insular, narrow-minded and blinkered to other things. The pressure of wanting to succeed overtook everything.

I felt that we achieved something in beating Ireland but had no idea what lay around the corner. The one thing that has haunted me is my decision making as captain during those early matches. Against England I was always looking to take the quick tapped penalty in an effort to speed the game up, to gain some ground, but I made a lot of poor decisions. In the French match I took on board judgements from senior players and decided not to take kicks at goal having fallen so far behind early on and I wish I had been more assertive in taking those decisions but when you are 30 or 40 points down, to kick at goal does seem somewhat unrealistic. Later on I would be looking to kick for position or take the points.

Was the partnership between Rob Howley and new coach Graham Henry one forged in heaven? Eleven of the sixteen matches which saw the coach and captain work together were won and in none of the defeats were Wales embarrassed by first-class opponents. The matches against South Africa at Wembley and Australia in the RWC were not without controversy, while Scotland and Ireland in the Five Nations seemed to catch Henry unprepared for the intensity of the competition, and it was only Samoa who perhaps showed up some unexpected deficiencies in the Welsh game plan when they were surprise winners in the Group stages of the World Cup.

Graham had a tremendous knowledge of the global game. We were familiar with a certain amount of analysis but he took the preparation to another level and that, coupled with the input of Steve Black's sheer enthusiasm and ability to instil a high level of confidence in the players, saw the mental hardness improve by 25 per cent.

Personally I felt very vulnerable when Graham arrived. The tour to South Africa had raised many questions and it was only later that I learnt that Mike Ruddock had been earmarked to take over from Kevin and that he had, in fact, sounded out Ieuan Evans with regard to taking over the captaincy. That didn't materialise and it was Dennis John who took over as caretaker coach, but there were so many things going on at the time that I began to doubt myself and it was only four days before we left for South Africa that it was confirmed I was captain, which was a great relief. I was very unsure of my future at that time and not at all convinced that Dennis wanted me.

When Graham came on board, I had just come back from honeymoon. I met him at the Copthorne Hotel and after a couple of hours I felt that we had hit it off. He told me that he wanted me to be his captain but that it would work within his planned structure. He talked about his experience with the Auckland Blues, where several senior players had taken an active role on the field and I think this was his way of saying that he was going to help me out. He brought Dai Young, Colin Charvis, Neil Jenkins and Scott Gibbs in as decision makers and within the traditional framework he took the team forward by introducing these new responsibilities, something none of us had experienced before.

They say that to enjoy the highs you have to experience the lows and for Rob Howley and his team, 1999 proved to be payback time. It all started in Paris where Wales had not tasted victory for 24 years, but Castaignede's missed penalty saw a memorable 34–33 win which was capped in the final match of the championship when Neil Jenkins's conversion of Scott Gibbs's try in the closing minutes at Wembley gave Wales a victory to savour. Improbable it certainly was, impossible the consensus of many, but against a mighty English pack and after spending most of the game on the back foot, Wales pulled off a result which is regarded with much affection by those privileged to be in north London on a balmy, spring Sunday afternoon. The records show that Wales won the match 32–31 but what they cannot describe is the atmosphere generated by the massive travelling support to one of Wales's best 'home' victories.

We showed great tenacity at Wembley; didn't give up until the final whistle and old twinkle toes Gibbs and Neil's brilliant goal kicking kept us in the game. If you look at the overall picture in terms of possession and dominance, England probably enjoyed 75 per cent of it but what it confirmed was how far we had come on as a team, how much our self-belief and confidence had improved under Graham and Steve.

Did England captain Lawrence Dallaglio make a mistake not asking Jonny Wilkinson to kick for goal at a crucial moment late on? Was there a touch of arrogance in the way he instructed Wilkinson to kick for position and give his forwards the chance to exploit the resultant lineout and confirm their supremacy? Maybe, but he didn't, which brings us back to that word 'if' again. To hell with it! Throw it out of the dictionary, the language; throw it into oblivion – if only.

Following the Five Nations we travelled to Argentina for two Tests. We went there full of confidence but come the first Test we found ourselves 23–7 down at half-time. Graham completely lost his rag, kicked the water bottles around, told us we didn't deserve to pull on the jersey, how poor we were playing. It was the first time we saw the other side of Graham Henry, but it worked. We pulled the game around in the second half and went on to win the second Test.

Howley and his men were on a roll and when South Africa turned up on 26 June 1999 to officially open the Millennium Stadium, albeit an unfinished one, Wales recorded their first victory over the Springboks in front of 27,000 people and were at last able to boast success against all opponents. This one ended 29–19 and Wales had gone some measurable distance towards cancelling out those three record defeats that had heralded the induction of Robert Howley as Welsh captain.

We were really on top of our game following the tour and the victory over South Africa. The training sessions were going well, our fitness levels were good and it was obvious that there was a huge amount of confidence among the squad, but I wonder if perhaps we didn't peak too early in 1999, something which is extremely difficult to measure. England just about got away with it in 2003.

The World Cup comes around every four years and many players only have one serious chance of winning it. For most of the Welsh team 1999 represented that chance and we were quietly optimistic about making the semi-finals, at which stage anything can happen. We missed a great opportunity when we lost to Australia in the quarter-final. Walking in at half-time 10–9 down we knew the game was still there to be won. Graham worked on the confidence, stressed how we had cut them up a couple of times, but not quite finished the moves off, but unfortunately, 40 minutes later, we were out of the tournament.

And then it all came to an unexpected end. Henry wanted a change and following the World Cup a new man was appointed as captain and the press was full of innuendo: why had Howley been relieved of his job?

There's no doubt that I didn't have a great World Cup. Any captain has to be certain of his place and in the months following the tournament various rumours were reported as coming from the management that I was under pressure. Those months were the most difficult I ever went through as a player. There was no clear communication with Graham. He didn't get in touch and tell me that he thought I wasn't playing well, that I had to buck my ideas up, nothing. Two weeks before the start of the Six Nations I got a call asking me to meet him at his house and deep down I knew what was coming.

Lynn Howells was already there and I thought that he wouldn't discuss the captaincy issue in front of somebody, so maybe it was going to be all right, but shortly after my arrival Lynn left and I feared the worst. Graham got to the point and said that he had to take the captaincy off me and that there were two ways of doing it. Either I could go to the press and say that I had resigned, which he would endorse, or he would have to tell them of his decision. I didn't want to go along with the resignation story. Nearly three months had passed since the World Cup and to suggest that I would wait until two weeks before the next match before making such an announcement was wrong – it would certainly have reflected badly on me. But that aside, I'm an honest individual and preferred to take it on the chin. Dai Young was appointed to take over as captain, but I have to say that I struggled to come to terms with what had happened.

Losing the captaincy took some getting over. I relished the responsibility and all that went with it. The relationship with the coach, the line of communication with the players, the chance to talk to them one to one, get them to ask questions about themselves. I found all that particularly interesting. On the field I wouldn't have described myself as an in-your-face, motivational type of captain, a Lawrence Dallaglio; more a Martin Johnson, quiet and unassuming, with the knowledge and understanding of the game to be able to tackle the problems as they present themselves. I never felt that players should need motivation; being involved is motivation enough.

Regarding scrum-half as a position to lead from, the advantages and disadvantages are fairly obvious. On the one hand you are constantly involved in the game and to a certain extent able to control the pace and direction it takes, while on the other it can be said that the scrum-half is too involved and that the added responsibility can have a detrimental effect on individual performance. I experienced a lot of criticism as captain largely from people who were of the opinion that I didn't play as well when I led the side and to a certain extent I have to agree. When he told me that I was losing the captaincy Graham Henry said that one day I would thank him, that in 18 months' time I would be first-choice scrum-half for the British Lions, and he was right.

Rob Howley's career took off at Twickenham with that try-scoring debut and eight years later it ended at the same venue with a most improbable injury-time try, which secured the Heineken Cup for London Wasps. While the ball bobbed about as rugby balls are prone to do and while Toulouse full-back Clement Poitrenaud watched on rather than kick it into touch, so Howley, who had put the ball deep into the Toulouse 22, continued his run up the touchline getting ever nearer, and nearer, and nearer, as 70,000 spectators held their breath in disbelief. Howley scored a remarkable try which proved to be a fitting climax to a career that was declared over less than six months later; surgery unable to repair a wrist which was trampled on during that Heineken Cup final.

* * *

Any connections between Welsh international rugby and the Wasps prior to Robert Howley are difficult to find and those that may exist are tenuous to say the least, but following a career path from Abertillery to London Welsh and Northampton, scrum-half and Welsh captain William 'Wick' Powell found himself at Sudbury, the home of the famous London club, albeit in the years following his retirement from international rugby.

It was as a London Welsh player that Wick Powell led Wales twice in 1927, an expected win against France and a defeat in Dublin, results which surprised nobody. These were dark days for Welsh rugby with victories in the championship proving difficult to come by and but for the presence of France, who were still struggling to come to terms with the competition, there was little to enthuse about for five years; even the French were about to reverse the trend with a welcome first victory over Wales in 1928. Powell was the 17th of 20 players to captain Wales in the 1920s, an unprecedented figure and, unlike in previous years which saw the captaincy passed around as a token of esteem among the senior players, this time the many candidates were more often than not found wanting, Wick Powell among them.

Wales's winning run of ten consecutive matches has only been bettered once, during 1907–10 when the sequence extended to eleven. Unlike in 1999 when five players started in each of the ten games which took place in a congested seven months, unsurprisingly there was no ever-present in the run of eleven which covered a period a little short of three years, but scrum-half Richard Owen, together with his club partner Richard Jones, appeared in eight of the matches.

Dickie Owen played international rugby for a decade during which he won 35 caps, a record for the time which would not be broken until 1955. He was first capped against Ireland in 1901 and played throughout two Grand Slam and four Triple Crown campaigns in addition to matches against the three major touring teams from the Southern hemisphere. Following the retirement of Gwyn Nicholls after the defeat by the Springboks in 1906, Owen was chosen to lead Wales for the opening championship match against England, played at his club ground in Swansea. Despite a resounding Welsh victory it was five years before Dickie Owen led his country again. This time he was given the honour on the event of his becoming Wales's most capped player and although the match at Twickenham ended in defeat Owen retained the captaincy for a return to St Helen's, which saw Scotland comprehensively beaten in what turned out to be the local player's final representative outing.

Dickie Owen's 35 caps were won during a period that saw Wales play a total of 40 matches. Richard David and William Morgan each played once and Tommy Vile featured in the other three. Vile's international career is one of the longest: having been first capped in January 1908, he made his final appearance thirteen years later in February 1921, during which time he won the surprisingly small number of eight caps. Even allowing for the war years and the latter part of the Dickie Owen era, Wales played thirty-seven matches during that period which saw four other scrum-halfs preferred to Vile at various times, but with two of them signing for rugby league clubs the selectors were fortunate to still be able to call on the experienced campaigner for international duty.

Tommy Vile first captained Wales against France in March 1912 and continued in the role when the South African tourists arrived to play Wales in December. Vile was joined in the Welsh team by four of his Newport colleagues who had helped the club defeat the Springboks earlier in the tour but, as is so often the case, Wales failed to replicate the success, losing an error-strewn encounter by a penalty goal to nil. When England won in Cardiff the following month Tommy Vile lost not only the captaincy but also his place in the team and when war broke out in 1914 there seemed little likelihood that he would gain any further international honours. It seems almost inconceivable but after a break of nine years the selectors once again went knocking on Vile's door for one final appearance in the red jersey and that as captain. When he led Wales onto the field against the Scots at Swansea on 5 February 1921 Tommy Vile was 38 years and 152 days old. One of seven players who represented Wales before and after the First World War, following his retirement Vile continued his involvement with rugby becoming an international referee, Wales's representative on the IRB and president of the WRU in 1955–56.

Where seven players had been capped either side of the First World War, only four could make a similar boast following the 1939–45 conflict, among them a scrum-half who spent the early part of his career with Swansea and after the enforced break the remainder of it at Cardiff.

Haydn Tanner was 18 when he made his international debut in the team that defeated the 1935 All Blacks and for the next 14 years he made the position his own with 13 consecutive appearances before war broke out and a further 12, all as captain, on the resumption of international rugby in 1947. The immediate post-war years failed to deliver the success that Wales so desperately sought after the long period of mediocrity of the 1920s and '30s, but under Tanner's guidance the side started to develop and the beginnings of what would become the successful Welsh team of the early 1950s first saw the light of day.

Haydn Tanner was undoubtedly one of Wales's finest scrum-halfs but unlike some of the other greats in his position he was unfortunate to play behind a pack often forced onto the back foot and also at a time when the Laws offered little or no protection against the marauding back-row forwards who made life so difficult for the link men at half-back. Pre-war, Tanner primarily partnered Cliff Jones and Willie Davies, his cousin, with whom he had debuted for Swansea, the pair still at school, while in the second half of his career Glyn Davies and Billy Cleaver were usually his targets and all enjoyed the best of services from a scrum-half intent on protecting his partner from receiving any indifferent possession.

Despite changes in the Laws which have seen the scrum and lineout rigorously addressed in efforts to create a more flowing and entertaining game the remit of the scrum-half is much as it always has been but for one glaring exception. A strong, fluid pass is and always has been a priority, as has the ability to tackle the much bigger men who now carry the ball from phase to phase, often seeking out the smaller opponents as a possible breach in any organised defence. But where once the ability to dictate play by kicking out of hand was essential to the make-up of both half-backs, no longer can the scrum-half control the pattern of the match by such repeated tactical kicking after every set piece. Possession is now the name of the game and it is only forfeited when either defences are stretched or much needed territorial gains are the order of the day. This is not to suggest that a scrum-half should go onto the field of play deficient in the kicking stakes, far from it, but kicking out of hand is now a skill in which all backs need to be competent, with the regular bouts of ping-pong often determining in which half of the field play should take place, but in the early '60s things were much different.

This was a time when three-quarters spent much of a game as spectators, often watching from afar as eight forwards and a pair of half-backs worked the touchlines with a vengeance; a time when many teams at club and international level were criticised for playing 'nine man rugby' – a time which saw the emergence of Daniel Clive Thomas Rowlands.

Clive 'Top Cat' Rowlands could justifiably lay claim to the title Mr Welsh Rugby. Player, captain, selector, coach, team manager, president – the complete package which few others, if any, can boast. Added to the above is his role as manager of the British Lions, champion of charitable causes, broadcaster, bon vivant, raconteur par excellence and lawmaker. And Clive Rowlands can talk. He talks passionately about the game of rugby, enthuses about it, is never less than positive about the game in Wales and most importantly he is extremely knowledgeable and never more so than when discussing the subject of captaincy.

A captain has to be a leader, one the players respect. He has to have the knowledge and confidence to see the job through and he has to be a communicator, a motivator who can get the best out of each individual. Those are the main points, but he also has to have players around him who he can depend on, senior players who lead in their own specialist areas of play. I was very lucky to have so many teachers in my teams, people who taught the game and were themselves leaders and communicators – Dewi Bebb, John Dawes, Grahame Hodgson, Alun Pask, Brian Price – a pattern which was replicated in the 1970s.

I believe the same qualities apply to both captain and coach. When I held the positions, I likened myself to the mother of a typical Welsh family because there were things in the attitude of a strong Welsh mother which influenced me. If her son did something bad, she told him so within the four walls, but if he did something really good, pass exams, whatever, she'd tell the world about it and that was a philosophy I took on board. I also placed great emphasis on off-the-field activities. When we travelled as a team, South Africa in 1964, for example, being Welsh we were expected to sing and so we practised as a choir. If they expected us to sing we would make sure we sang well, there's no point in getting up, singing badly and making fools of yourselves. We may not have had great voices but we sang well and the players used to look forward to it, which I think in turn made them better players, more confident players. It was nothing new, but I believed that if we were good at such off-field activities it was a way of developing a better team.

It almost seems that Clive Rowlands was born to captain Wales. At Cardiff College of Education it was Roy Bish who first identified qualities which Rowlands himself was unaware he possessed and it was these qualities which, when brought to the attention of the Welsh selectors, would persuade them not only to select him but to give him an unprecedented run of consecutive matches in charge.

When he was chosen to captain Wales against England in 1963, Rowlands's experience of leadership had been restricted to two seasons at college and a few months leading Pontypool. The match played at Cardiff on 19 January was under serious threat, Britain experiencing a particularly long, cold winter, and it probably should not have been played, but a mountain of straw and hundreds of volunteers helped avoid its postponement.

We weren't sure if the game would be played. I'm panicking, selected as captain and not certain that I'm even going to get to play for Wales. The format in those days was to train on the Friday, go home, meet at the Royal Hotel on the Saturday morning, have lunch and then following the after-match dinner go back home. The weather was so bad we didn't train on the Friday and when we got to the ground on Saturday, it was so cold the teams stayed in the changing-rooms while the anthems were played. Everything was frozen and they issued us with a pair of gloves, woollen vests and pants, and when we finally ran onto the field, the studs on the rock-hard ground sounded like a herd of cattle. They shouldn't have played it, but I'm glad they did because it was my first cap and I may not have got one if the selectors had been given a chance to change their minds. But I was lucky. Lucky in that I was definitely trained to be captain of Wales.

There have been many significant amendments to the Laws of rugby union, amendments which seek to improve both the safety of players in an increasingly physical arena and the enjoyment of spectators, who are essential to the future of any professional sport. Arguably the single most significant change to the Laws of the modern game was introduced in 1970 when it was determined that no longer would a player be able to kick the ball directly into touch out of hand from outside what was then the 25-yard, now the 22-metre line, penalty kicks excepted. Seven years earlier the Scotland–Wales match at Murrayfield had witnessed an unprecedented 111 lineouts, most at the instigation of Wales's scrum-half Clive Rowlands, who, rather like the Grand Old Duke of York, marched his forwards up and down the touchlines in search of a victory which was duly delivered, Wales winning the encounter 6–0. Pretty it certainly wasn't and the IRB experimented with the suggested improvement before finally introducing it into the Laws of the game.

Clive Rowlands suffered mixed fortunes in his first season as captain with only the victory in Edinburgh to show for his team's efforts. The fifth All Blacks were in uncompromising mood later in the year, committing Wales to defeat and Rowlands to the first-aid room with a serious back injury, but the 1964 championship saw Wales undefeated with victories over Scotland and Ireland, and the matches against England and France both drawn.

In the summer of 1964 Wales tested pastures new when Rowlands led a squad of twenty-three players on a four-match tour of South Africa, playing a match against East Africa in Nairobi en route. What would now be viewed as a normal summer tour was in 1964 anything but, the climate in particular an element that few of the tourists would have experienced before. Similarly, although the one Test was played at sea level in Durban, the tour finished on the high veldt with matches in Pretoria and Bloemfontein introducing the players to the problems that playing at high altitude present. That the Test was lost was not surprising, but what did surprise was the pace and level of fitness of the South Africans, who were obviously more comfortable playing in their home climate than the British winter that touring Springbok teams were forced to enjoy. Despite plenty of possession and a half-time 3–3 score, the second half exposed the visitors' fitness levels and South Africa romped home 24–3. Harsh as they may have been, lessons were learnt and Wales would be stronger for them come the start of the 1965 Five Nations.

It was also as a result of the visit to South Africa that the role of coaching started to be investigated by the WRU. Rowlands recalls:

Following the tour the recommendations of manager Dai Phillips were very strong, particularly with regard to coaching because the Southern hemisphere was certainly far ahead of us in that area. To be fair to the management they pushed and pushed to get this through and David Nash was eventually appointed as the first national coach in 1967 and I succeeded him in 1968.

What I always felt very strongly about, as Welsh captain and then as a coach and selector, was continuity. For example, when I was captain, John Dawes was a player, then during my time as coach, John became captain, and finally when I managed the Welsh team, he was the coach. That sort of continuity enables the people concerned to form a mutual understanding of what is required. When John took over from me as coach, he wanted Mervyn Davies as his captain. As a selector I was favouring Gareth, but it is essential that captain and coach are on the same wavelength and Mervyn was appointed. There is no point in the coach doing all the work off the field if the captain turns round and tries to do something else on it.

As a player and captain the selectors had shown a lot of faith in me, something I still believe very strongly about. If a player is seen as the best in a position and good enough to play today, if he has a bad game, he should still be good enough to play tomorrow. I remember when Jeff Squire was first capped. I didn't want him but I was outvoted. Jeff was chosen and he didn't play that well but where others wanted a change I nominated him for his second cap. At the selection meeting I insisted, 'If he was the best player two weeks ago, then he is the best player today.' So we gave him another chance and he was there a long time.

Whether the selectors were considering Rowlands's future role in the team when he was not selected to play in an uncapped match against Fiji in 1964 is uncertain, but despite a Welsh win in a free-flowing encounter he was called upon to lead the team once again when England visited Cardiff to kick off the new campaign, and he did not disappoint. Taking Wales forward from the previous season to win a tenth Triple Crown, and despite failure in Paris, the Clive Rowlands era has to be viewed as one which saw Wales improve through the three seasons during which he was involved. Welsh rugby may have been on the receiving end of some harsh lessons but they appear to have been taken on board.

Clive Rowlands heralds from west Wales, the road to Pontypool coming via his time at Cardiff College of Education and the presence of international scrum-half Onllwyn Brace at Llanelli, which denied him a regular first-team place. Brace was captain of the Scarlets between 1959 and 1961 and although Rowlands experienced some first-team rugby it was far from enough for a player looking to make his mark at the highest level, hence the move from Stradey Park to Pontypool Park. Brace had first played for Wales in 1956, winning five caps as a Newport player, and in his last two seasons in the game he made a further four international appearances, two as captain, both matches against Ireland, with Wales winning on each occasion.

In the 1950s there was little about rugby football which could be described as complex. It was a simple game, played in a straightforward fashion with particular attention placed on getting the basics right. That done, it was left to a dominant pack of forwards to win sufficient ball for the exciting backs which Wales had in abundance to show off their great flair and skill. Of all the captains who led Wales during the decade only John Gwilliam and Bleddyn Williams can be described as truly great thinkers on the game, men who were looking for that extra ingredient which often made the difference between success and failure, an observation their records support. Onllwyn Brace is one of several captains of the time who view captaincy as a position given to a leading player who had the ability to motivate, but he cannot recall much in the way of astute tactical decision making being done on the field by any of his contemporaries.

The old adage was that once the captain was selected all he had to do was toss a coin, decide which way to play and say a few words at the dinner, and by and large they weren't astute, strategic thinkers. All the selectors were looking for was someone to inspire and motivate others, and in that respect I think the job has gone full circle, with the coach now playing such a big part in the preparation and tactics.

We spent so little time together that the match itself was largely played off the cuff. When I was first capped, I partnered Cliff Morgan and through the three trial matches we only spent 40 minutes playing together. It was very much a case of we'll try this or that and nobody was there to point out if it was right or wrong. Nothing was rehearsed and at an early lineout in that first match I remember saying to the great Ken Jones as he was about to throw the ball in that if my right foot was in front of my left he was to throw it to the front jumper, left foot in front of right to the middle jumper and both feet together he should throw it to the back. He said 'I'll decide where to throw it,' and he did. In other words only Ken knew who the ball was going to be thrown to. For a young man up from Oxford University where attention was paid to such detail, it was a shock, laughable to a certain extent, and many people I speak to don't believe the story but that was the amateur approach.

Onllwyn Brace describes the five years between his first and last caps as a 'stagnant period' for Welsh rugby, a period which saw fifty-seven new caps introduced in the twenty-five matches played with as many as twenty of the players winning no more than one or two caps. There was little continuity and only twice was the same team fielded in consecutive matches, which brings the selection policies into question.

One cannot account for the vagaries of selection that were apparent at the end of the '50s and into the '60s. Carwyn James was a great footballer but he was an out and out fly-half, not a centre, where they decided to play him on one occasion. After we beat Ireland 9–0 in 1961 there were seven changes made. I was dropped together with Ken Richards, who had scored a try and kicked two penalties and it was no surprise when he joined Salford. The match was certainly pedestrian. Both sides were to blame for that, with Ireland kicking everything above the daisies, but we won and yet so many changes were made.

It is very rare that a winning combination is changed unless such changes are enforced but to make seven from a winning combination has to be viewed as extreme.

Scrum-half was the in-vogue position in 1960, with Dickie Jeeps of England and Ireland's Andy Mulligan providing much evidence of the advantages to be had by a team being led from the base of the scrum and so too did Onllwyn Brace strengthen the argument in Wales with his leadership of both club and country.

I particularly like the idea of scrum-half as captain. A lot of people think that you are so busy with your own game that you can't attend to general matters, but for a quick-thinking, darting scrum-half, captaincy is ideal because he is at least able to endorse his own decisions.

Inconsistent they may have been but the selectors did show some continuity when they chose Cardiff's Lloyd Williams to replace Brace at scrum-half and also appointed him as the next man to lead Wales. Lloyd Williams was one of eight brothers to play for Cardiff and although elder brother Bleddyn is undoubtedly the best known of the octet, Lloyd gets his due accolades ahead of him in this work as the chapters progress from the front row to full-back.

Lloyd Williams was introduced into the Welsh team against Scotland in 1957 and won the first seven of his thirteen caps in tandem with club partner Cliff Morgan. The selectors favoured club partnerships at half-back to such an extent that when Morgan withdrew from the team to play Australia in the following January and was replaced by Carwyn James they also replaced Williams with James's club partner Wynne Evans. A Welsh victory counted for naught when the team to play at Twickenham two weeks later was announced, with Morgan and Williams reinstated. The outside-half was nearing the end of his glittering career and those seven matches in partnership with Williams would be his last in the Welsh jersey, heralding a period of uncertainty which saw the selectors chop and change the half-backs in their search for the ideal pairing.

> Before I played my first game Cliff said 'You'll be coming off the field before you know it,' meaning that you went up two or three gears more than in a club match. The concentration required is higher, the game much quicker and that is why you are picked, because you are seen as able to do it, but I didn't appreciate the demands until I actually played international rugby.

Among seven new caps against England in the opening match of the 1959 Five Nations was Aberavon outside-half Cliff Ashton. He partnered Lloyd Williams in three matches before the pair were dropped, but not following a defeat, rather an exciting, hard-fought victory over Ireland. How close Wales came to winning a Triple Crown in 1959 is best described by Williams.

> The Arms Park was its usual mud bath in January when we played England, but Dewi Bebb defied the elements to score the match-winning try. After being 6–0 down we scored two tries to beat Ireland, but in between we lost to Scotland by a single point. Down 5–6 we had a scrum in a perfect position for Cliff Ashton to try a drop goal. I put the ball in and Bryn Meredith made a

perfect strike, but when it reached the back row John Faull put his foot on the ball, giving the Scottish back row the time to get at Cliff, forcing him to hurry the kick. We actually thought the ball had gone over but it just dropped under the crossbar and one match later they dropped Cliff and myself.

In the next nine matches the selectors tried six half-back partnerships before recalling Lloyd Williams to the side as captain for the final championship match of 1961 against France in Paris.

I was injured at Old Deer Park in December and didn't play again until February, returning for Cardiff against Aberavon the day Wales lost 3–0 at Murrayfield. I would have played for the Barbarians against the Springboks when Andy Mulligan cried off but the shoulder was still strapped up. It was Bleddyn who broke the news of my recall to the team and my elevation to the captaincy. He called at the house and asked if I had heard the news – 'What news?'

I was captain for three matches and what stands out is the fact that we didn't convert a try or kick a penalty in any of them. In a scoreless draw at Twickenham Kelvin Coslett missed five penalties, while Terry Davies and Ken Richards, who were kicking goals from all over the place for their clubs, missed penalties and two conversions in the 8–6 defeat in Paris, the only points coming from the boot, an Alan Rees drop goal against Scotland.

That match was played in atrocious conditions. Bryn Meredith had a try disallowed when the referee misinterpreted the Law regarding a tap penalty, for which he later apologised to me, but I knew that a Welsh defeat would cost me my place. I didn't think I played badly. I did my share of tackling and have got the aches and pains today to prove it but at the end of the day I was very pleased to have had the chance of captaining Wales, something I never expected. There is no doubt that the selectors were struggling to create any stability in the side during the period and when Cliff Morgan finished they certainly messed about with it far too much.

However, once they had selected the team their input into match preparation was nil, but away from that the players were treated like children. The biggest problem was that they were old-fashioned and didn't want to change. They were in charge and if they told you not to do something, you had better not do it. They didn't trust you and on away trips you often felt cooped up in the hotel. To go out for a stroll was not always acceptable because they probably feared a hidden agenda of some sort, though none of the players in my time would go on the binge the night before a match. I really don't think they knew how to treat us.

Between them, Onllwyn Brace and Lloyd Williams dominated the scrum-half position for six years and they leave no doubt that the 'vagaries' and 'old-fashioned' attitudes of the selectors had a negative effect on the team during the period. This would begin to change following the appointment of Clive Rowlands in 1963 when the Big Five finally began to show a tolerance and desire for stability that, apart from 1950–53, had been largely absent from their decision making since the concept of a selection committee was first introduced in 1924.

When looking at the successful periods in the history of Welsh rugby, it is clear that a level of stability and continuity exists but what may not be so obvious are the periods of learning which always preceded them; periods when faith and confidence in players may have been pushed to the limit by selectors and the public alike. Great players and teams don't arrive in neatly wrapped parcels with a bow on the top, they have to be carved from wood, sculpted from stone, nurtured and cared for before anything like the finished article sees the light of day. Brace and Williams together with many of their contemporaries did not benefit from such consideration, and neither had so many before them and even more since, but theirs are experiences to be learned from. There are times when it is necessary to step back, look at the bigger picture, have a little patience and not panic. What goes round comes round and the only thing those in charge of the situation have any control over is the size of the circle – how long it takes to rotate.

From the late 1940s to the mid-1950s Cardiff RFC could arguably boast one of the greatest club sides of all time. Despite being a seemingly constant source of first-class forwards the strength of the team was undoubtedly to be found in the backs, where Bleddyn Williams and Jack Matthews at centre, Frank Trott at full-back, and Gareth Griffiths, Gwyn Rowlands and Alun Thomas on the wing in turn spearheaded a remarkable three-quarter line, while at half-back, firstly Haydn Tanner and Billy Cleaver and latterly Rex Willis and Cliff Morgan were the instigators and exponents of rugby magic.

Rex Willis was ready and waiting in the wings when Tanner finally called it a day and not only did he step into Tanner's shoes at Cardiff but was also his immediate replacement on the international stage, making his debut in a Welsh victory at Twickenham in 1950. Ever present in Wales's Grand Slam season Willis was included in the British Lions team that toured Australia and New Zealand in the summer, winning two caps, but was another who fell victim to the 30-year age limit unofficially imposed on the 1955 tourists.

The first of Rex Willis's two outings as Welsh captain saw him stand in for the injured Rees Stephens. France were the visitors to Cardiff in March 1954 and long gone were the days when the fixture could be seen as providing a likely victory. However, on this occasion Wales ran out 19–13 winners of a finely balanced match which saw the teams separated by two penalty goals. Murrayfield 12 months later proved yet again to be the stumbling block of Welsh aspirations, a 14–8 defeat ruining any chance of Triple Crown and Grand Slam glory, and for Rex Willis it was an end to his involvement with the captaincy duties. His international career finished two matches later. He played a further three seasons with Cardiff, gradually conceding pole position to the up-and-coming Lloyd Williams, who took the club onwards into the 1960s, but with Tanner, Willis and Williams, Cardiff were rarely without an international scrum-half in the line-up during fifteen post-war seasons.

* * *

All Fools' Day 1967. Stade Colombes, Paris. Gareth Owen Edwards. It is said that any pranks and tricks pulled on 1 April must be executed before midday, but on a glorious spring afternoon in Europe's favourite city it is unlikely that the Welsh selectors were thinking of anything untoward when they launched the international career of Wales's finest thereby making the afternoon kick-off an irrelevance.

Nobody present in Paris or in the season's remaining fixture in Cardiff could have possibly predicted the heights to which the 19-year-old scrum-half would aspire. Here was another player at the start of his international career and whether it would culminate with a handful of caps or more only time would tell. In the case of Gareth Edwards it was more, many more: a total of 53 won over 12 seasons, a record haul at the time of his retirement. Not only a record, but an unbroken run of 53 matches – Edwards was never dropped and also had the good fortune to avoid any serious injury.

By common consent Gareth Edwards is recognised as Wales's greatest-ever player and many argue his standing as possibly the greatest rugby player of all time, accolades which are difficult to either dispute or concur with because, while great skill and prowess as a scrum-half can be measured against the ability of other scrum-halfs, how can Edwards's strengths be measured against those of a Colin Meads, for example? It's one for those boring coach trips or, more likely, the last hour before the friendly landlord calls time, but that Gareth Edwards was a truly great rugby player by any measurement is beyond question. However, does that automatically make him a great captain to be appointed at each and every opportunity, or should such talent be left to wreak havoc with the opposition without the added responsibilities that captaincy introduces? Edwards was appointed Welsh captain in his fifth match, ten months after his debut. He remains Wales's youngest captain at 20 years and 206 days of age. He led the team on thirteen occasions and the games can be broadly divided into two periods. The first between 1968 and 1970, the matches when he was still a relatively inexperienced player on the international stage, and the second 1973–74 when he was a seasoned player with 30 caps to his credit.

Gareth Edwards first led Wales on 3 February 1968. Scotland were the opponents at the Arms Park and a dreadful match saw Wales sneak a 5–0 victory following a try scored after a blatant forward pass that went unnoticed by the referee. Why Edwards was replaced as captain after leading a winning team only the selectors could say but defeat in Ireland under John Dawes saw the ball passed back to the scrum-half, so to speak, but another defeat, this time to France, brought a disappointing season to an end. The selectors recalled Brian Price for the 1969 Five Nations and he led with aplomb only to miss out on the final celebrations through injury. It was Edwards who led Wales against England in Cardiff to secure an 11th Triple Crown and the championship. By 1969 some of the greatest names in the history of Welsh rugby were beginning to feature regularly in the starting line-up, among them Edwards's half-back partner Barry John, and the two would soon gain rugby immortality.

The 1970 campaign started with a fortunate draw with the Springboks, the nearest Wales had come to victory in the fixture after seven meetings. Success against the Scots and English followed, which set up a Triple Crown match in Dublin, but at Lansdowne Road the dream came apart and Edwards yet again saw the captaincy passed on, John Dawes once more the recipient. It is difficult to assess the first seven matches under Gareth Edwards's captaincy because there is very little to criticise with four won and a best result gained against South Africa. But as is so often the case it was one result that prompted change, that in Dublin when the captain was perhaps exposed by a low level of tactical awareness which deteriorated as the game unfolded. Edwards's place in the team was never in question but it would be for others to lead and dictate tactics in the heat of battle – for a while anyway.

The following three years witnessed the legend that is Gareth Edwards gain a momentum that would stay with him for the remainder of his playing days. A magnificent Welsh Grand Slam in 1971 was followed by a record-breaking British Lions tour that saw the visitors win a first Test series in New Zealand. It was more of the same in 1972, only the IRA denying Wales an opportunity of back-to-back Grand Slams. Edwards was in tandem with Phil Bennett for the 1973–74 campaign and the partnership was every bit as explosive as Edwards and John had been, both based on an uncanny awareness created between two players who were able to instinctively play off each other. After three years during which Gareth Edwards had played such majestic rugby it was almost inevitable that the selectors would invite him once again to take over the reins as Welsh captain.

Edwards's second spell lasted for six consecutive matches, beginning with a defeat in Paris, followed by victories against Australia and Scotland, drawn matches with Ireland and France, and ending with a most controversial match at Twickenham which saw England win 16–12 after a disallowed 'try' by J.J. Williams, who claimed to have won the race for the touch down but was denied by referee John West, who, at some distance from play, was unsighted and gave the benefit of the doubt to the defending team. The scrum-half's worldwide reputation continued to grow in the summer of 1974 when he was a member of the unbeaten British Lions team in South Africa, the only country that may have still questioned his ability. Outstanding performances on tour dispelled such scepticism once and for all – Barry John may well have been the 'King' but Gareth Edwards was simply the greatest.

In considering Edwards's long reign one must spare a thought for Ebbw Vale's Glyn Turner, Maesteg's Ray Hopkins and Aberavon's Clive Shell, three fine scrum-halfs all consigned to the role of spectator as the genius that was Edwards dominated the international game. Hopkins and Shell were both capped as replacements and Hopkins's ability was recognised by his inclusion in the 1971 British Lions party but despite Welsh rugby being blessed with an abundance of talented players all vying for the number nine jersey there was only room for one player in it and the pretenders to the throne must have wished that their lot had been cast at another time or in another place.

It was much the same at Cardiff, where a talented Brynmor Williams, also a British Lion before playing for Wales due to the shadow cast by Edwards, finally decided in the summer of 1977 to move to Newport and the assurance of more regular first-team rugby. However, the blazers at the Arms Park had no cause for alarm, secure in the knowledge that further down the pecking order was yet another prodigious talent waiting to be let loose.

Terry Holmes was a product of Cardiff Youth and had been recognised at an early age as a player with a great future in the game. A big man for a scrum-half, Holmes had a very physical approach which led to him scoring over 120 tries for Cardiff in fewer than 200 appearances. He could boast a further nine for Wales in winning twenty-five caps, many of the tries scored from close range, Holmes taking on opposing back-row forwards with a relish that would eventually be his undoing in a career plagued by injury.

When Gareth Edwards finally called it a day, he was joined by half-back partner Phil Bennett, and the Welsh selectors had to find two players to fill some enormous shoes. A summer tour to Australia presented the first opportunity to look at the heirs apparent and included in the party at scrum-half were Brynmor Williams and Terry Holmes. Both made their debuts for Wales Down Under, Williams in the first Test, Holmes in the second and for the first match of the 1978–79 season it was Holmes who got the nod to face the All Blacks when the infamous Andy Haden dive cost Wales so dearly.

> We thought we were on our way to a famous victory when Gareth Davies made a clearance kick. I don't recollect any infringement problems with the lineout that day; there were no penalties awarded for pushing. The referee was fooled, and I've no respect for Haden and the others who conspired to do it. Sport is all about winning but the great All Blacks didn't need to do that. Quittenton was fooled and he ought to come out and admit it; the players have.

Injuries regularly disrupted Terry Holmes's appearances for Wales and, in addition to Brynmor Williams, the opportunity to impress was in turn handed to Gerald Williams, Ray Giles, Mark Douglas and David Bishop, but the selectors always returned to Holmes when he was fully fit.

> The first major problem occurred with the Lions in South Africa in 1980 when damaged knee ligaments put an end to my tour.

From then on there was a history of shoulder and knee problems. The shoulder was fine once it had healed, till the next time, but the knee was different, the surgery and reconstruction wasn't as advanced as it is today and I just had to learn to get on with it.

A shoulder dislocation playing against London Welsh ruled Holmes out of the 1981 championship and in 1982 there was more of the same when he had to leave the field at Twickenham. On tour with the Lions in 1983 it was the knee which once again limited his involvement and, although a double British Lion, his total number of appearances was restricted to eight.

In 1985 Holmes was handed the Welsh captaincy for the Five Nations opening match at Murrayfield and continued in the role throughout the campaign, Wales winning two and losing two of the four matches in a season that was largely representative of the 1980s.

Being chosen to lead Wales for the first time was a very proud moment for me, but I think I was picked on experience more than anything else. The way I played the game was a bit individualistic, so captaincy was something which didn't suit me 100 per cent. It is a huge honour to captain your country but I used to enjoy playing more without that burden because at scrum-half you already have a lot of responsibility. It is a good position to captain from but it is very much dependent on the individual. If you have an all-action type of player, then it is difficult to be captain, but somebody such as Jacques Fouroux would be very different, more of a controller.

The rumour mills were working overtime at the start of the following season and after leading Wales to a comfortable victory against Fiji in Cardiff on 9 November, Terry Holmes signed professional papers with Bradford Northern and was lost to the union game.

Obviously it was a financial decision to go north. Bradford made me an offer I couldn't turn down, and in hindsight I wish I had gone earlier, as league was a game I enjoyed and I think I could have achieved a lot. By 1985 my body was on its way out; in fact, the problem with the knee meant that I failed the medical at Bradford, but they were prepared to go ahead. If I had been fully fit, things could have been different but I was just about able to get on the pitch from one game to the next, basically playing on one leg.

Unfortunately, the injuries which had proved to be so disruptive in his career to date continued to plague him and two years after turning professional Terry Holmes was forced to hang up his boots before making any lasting impression on rugby league.

* * *

Unlucky 13. Thirteen scrum-halfs have led Wales and somebody has to be the 13th discussed in this record which chooses not to conform to a chronological pattern. Apologies, then, to Robert Jones, but perhaps of all Wales's scrum-half captains his really is the unluckiest of stories.

The immediate successor to Terry Holmes, Jones made his debut at Twickenham in a match which saw England outside-half Rob Andrew score all his side's 21 points, denying the visitors a deserved share of the spoils with an injury-time drop goal. This was the first of Jones's 54 caps, all won as a Swansea player, which saw him pass Gareth Edwards's 53, but with an appearance as a replacement on the wing he was jointly, with Edwards, Wales's most-capped scrum-half until the record was eventually broken by Robert Howley.

Robert Jones had all the necessary attributes to play international rugby at the base of the scrum: a pass second to none, a good rugby brain and the ability to tactically kick opponents into eventual submission whenever the conditions dictated. There was no better example of this than in Cardiff on 18 March 1989 when a much vaunted England were continually pushed back into defensive positions by the probing kicks launched by the scrum-half, one of which produced the match-winning try for centre Mike Hall.

The opportunity to captain one's country is the highest honour the sport can offer and it was Robert Jones whom the selectors invited to lead Wales against the visiting All Blacks in November 1989, the start of a five-match run which brought a sequence of results that tells its own story – New Zealand 34 Wales 9; France 29 Wales 19; England 34 Wales 6; Scotland 13 Wales 9; Ireland 14 Wales 8. Five matches, five defeats – never before had Wales lost five consecutive matches, a run which included a first-ever Five Nations whitewash, and it was forgivable if thirteen years later Jones afforded himself a wry smile as Wales embarked on a run of eight consecutive defeats among which was a first-ever Six Nations whitewash – the albatross could now be passed on.

There were many factors which played a part in the demise of Welsh rugby following the Triple Crown in 1988, the lure of rugby league not least among them, and we were certainly clutching at straws to field a side of top-quality international players but it doesn't hide the fact that ultimately we weren't good enough. There had been a change of coach in 1988 and probably for the first time we were told things in training which went against the general traditions and philosophy of Welsh rugby in terms of flair. Now we were told what we should do in each area, which meant that the pressure was on players to play by numbers rather than rely on instinct. Really, the whole game was in a state of turmoil which began after the success of 1988, but the last thing I wanted was to be involved in a first-ever whitewash, never mind captain the side through it.

The French game saw us reduced to 14 men when Kevin Moseley was sent off but it was the performance at Twickenham which summed up where we were and brought another change of coach, Ron Waldron coming in for the Scottish game, which we probably should have won, and the game in Dublin, where I had a kick charged down which brought about the decisive score. The change of coach halfway through the season didn't help because Ron had a totally different philosophy that he wanted to implement straight away. The idea wasn't just about the way we played, it involved the way we trained and our attitudes, and to try to introduce it in the two weeks between matches was difficult. There was little consistency during the season and it's only now that I can look back and clearly see all the mitigating factors which were involved.

Why Robert Jones was particularly unlucky is largely due to the fact that for much of his international career he played behind a beaten pack of forwards. No scrum-half likes to be on the back foot but this was where Jones very often found himself and it is to his great credit that when the opportunities to play at a higher level came he was not found wanting. The British Lions tour to Australia in 1989 probably saw the player at his best when he helped the tourists recover after losing the first Test to go on and win the three-match series, and five years later in Dublin he led the Barbarians to victory against a South African team which twelve months on would be crowned world champions.

TOP: Three Welsh captains appeared in the team that played Scotland in Cardiff in 1896. Seated from the left are Gwyn Nicholls, Billy Bancroft and matchday captain Arthur Gould. Between them they guided Wales into the first Golden Era – Gould was succeeded by Bancroft, who in turn passed the honour on to Nicholls.

BOTTOM: Six captains featured in the team which defeated England at St Helen's, Swansea, on 10 January 1903. In the back row on the left is Arthur 'Boxer' Harding, third from the left is George Travers and on the extreme right, Rhys Gabe. Tom Pearson is the captain (seated) and in front are, on the left, Dickie Owen and his half-back partner, G. Llewellyn Lloyd.

TOP: The Golden Era over, this is the line-up which faced Scotland in 1912. In addition to captain Dickie Owen, standing on the left is Glyn Stephens and second from the right Harry Uzzell, two players who continued their international careers after the First World War, and in the front on the left is Jack Bancroft together with Billy Trew.

ABOVE LEFT: The Revd. Alban Davies, who led Wales and his forwards, the 'Terrible Eight', in the 1914 championship. The photograph was taken at a retirement home in Los Angeles shortly before his death on 18 July 1976.

ABOVE RIGHT: The great Gareth Edwards led Wales seven times in the late 1960s and on a further six occasions during 1973–74. His record as captain includes six victories and three drawn matches, which compares favourably with most, but there was a general opinion that his unique talent was seen at its best without the added responsibilities that the captaincy brings.

(© Huw Evans Agency)

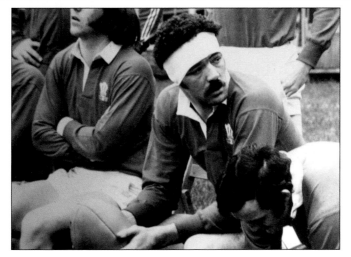

TOP LEFT: Gerald Davies touches down in an uncapped match against Argentina in 1976 while J.P.R. Williams watches on. Wales got out of jail on this occasion, an injury-time penalty by Phil Bennett securing a 20–19 victory, but such tries by the right wing regularly featured among the many highlights witnessed at the Arms Park during the 1970s. (© Huw Evans Agency)

TOP RIGHT: A man denied – John Lloyd didn't get his chance to join the elite band of captains who have led Wales to a Grand Slam, but as John Dawes's successor he kept the wins coming.

BOTTOM: The team photograph – J.P.R. sits ready and waiting, Bennett adjusts a bootlace and captain Mervyn Davies wishes they would just get on with it all. (© Huw Evans Agency)

TOP: It has been a while since 'Benny' hung up his boots but he is regularly seen around the grounds of Wales in his capacity as a radio and television commentator. For those who don't recall the outside-half in his heyday, this is what he looks like circa 2005 – not much different really. (© Huw Evans Agency)

BOTTOM: There had been five Triple Crowns in the 1970s but Wales had to wait until 1988 for the next, and it was centre Bleddyn Bowen, seen here making a break against Ireland, who was at the helm. (© Huw Evans Agency)

In the aftermath of the 1970s, rugby in Wales became the ultimate spectator sport (clockwise from the top left): Eddie Butler watches David Pickering's groundwork against France; Bob Norster watches 'Spike' Watkins, a man on a mission; Robert Jones is too late to stop French scrum-half Pierre Berbizier get the ball away as Bleddyn Bowen looks on from the centre; in the same season, Jonathan Davies supports Paul Thorburn against Scotland in the second leg of the 1988 Triple Crown. Eight captains who between them can certainly claim to have enjoyed the ups and downs of international rugby. (Top left, top right and bottom left © South Wales Argus)

TOP LEFT: When Wales travelled to New Zealand for the inaugural Rugby World Cup, it was second-row forward Richard Moriarty who had the honour of leading the squad to a third-place finish, the best performance in the five tournaments played to date. Moriarty led Wales on seven occasions, every time away from home, thereby missing out on leading the team onto the hallowed Arms Park turf. (© Huw Evans Agency)

TOP RIGHT: Ieuan Evans celebrates another try, this one against Italy in 1996. On his retirement Evans was Wales's most capped player, record try scorer and, with 28 appearances, had led his country on more occasions than any other. Players have now won more caps and Gareth Thomas has broken the try-scoring record but Evans's 28 matches in charge is yet to be bettered. (© Mark Lewis)

BOTTOM: Happy days! Welsh captain Rob Howley and coach Graham Henry celebrate Wales's first victory over South Africa. The new Millennium Stadium was unfinished and the match was played in front of only 27,500 spectators, the workmen contracted to get the job finished in time for the 1999 World Cup and no small amount of cranes and building equipment. From a record 96–13 defeat on 27 June 1998 to a 29–19 win on 26 June 1999 it was a remarkable turnaround – Welsh rugby was on a roll! (© South Wales Argus)

TOP: In his first match as captain Dai Young eludes the tackle of Christian Califano against France in Cardiff on 5 February 2000. In support are the other members of the front row, hooker Garin Jenkins on the left and prop Peter Rogers. (© South Wales Argus)

ABOVE: One year on and Colin Charvis puts the bitter memories of the 2003 defeat in Rome firmly behind him by leading Wales to a convincing 44–10 victory against the Italians in Cardiff in the 2004 campaign. Unfortunately, more controversy would dominate the headlines when Charvis led the Welsh squad to Argentina and South Africa in the summer. (© South Wales Argus)

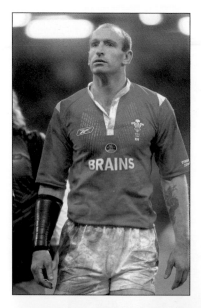

What a difference a point makes! Captain Gareth Thomas wonders what might have been after Wales were beaten 26–25 by New Zealand in November 2004 but things were about to get better, Wales winning a first Grand Slam for 28 years in 2005. Thomas, together with Michael Owen (below) led a rejuvenated Wales through a memorable season which saw the national team play the type of rugby for which it is famous wherever the game is played. Injury forced Thomas off the field at half-time in Paris, Owen taking over the captaincy and continuing in the role for the remaining matches against Scotland and Ireland. (Both © South Wales Argus)

I had experience of captaincy with Swansea and Bristol and I have come to the conclusion that the job is mostly about personality, experience and respect. I don't think that the position has much bearing on the captain's input and success. You pick the best man for the job regardless of where he plays, but what is important is that player's readiness to accept what captaincy involves. There is no point in picking a player to lead the team if it is going to have a bad effect on his performance, if he is going to worry about the responsibilities which go with the job, the relationship with the media or the formal speeches captains are expected to give.

When Alan Davies took over as coach he gave us a series of tests, questionnaires which would give him information about individual players regarding their suitability or otherwise for leadership. He would analyse the results, which told him which players liked responsibility, liked to dictate, and he used the information as the basis for selecting his captain and decision makers. No matter how small the responsibility, if it was going to affect performance then the player would be protected from it and the job was given to someone who would enjoy it. Responsibility affects different people in different ways but it must never be allowed to have a detrimental effect on overall performance.

Much of what was introduced during the late 1980s is no doubt now seen as fundamental to the modern game: coaching by numbers, in-depth analysis of each player's skills and mental attitude, their ability to accept a leadership role as part of the bigger picture. The period can also be identified as the time when traditional Welsh flair was suddenly shackled, put on a tight rein, where it would remain for the next 15 years before the backs would once again go onto the field with the total backing of a coach who was happy to let them take chances, express themselves.

* * *

There is a strong argument that scrum-half is one of the better positions on the field from which to captain the side. Several of the players interviewed drew comparisons with France who, though showing an overall leaning towards forwards as captain, have enjoyed enormous success under Jacques Fouroux, Pierre Berbizier and more recently Fabien Galthie. However, there is still the question regarding how performance is affected by the responsibility, particularly in a position which is so involved in all areas of play.

Those in favour of a number nine as leader will throw Nick Farr-Jones, George Gregan and Joost van der Westhuizen into the equation and there are others who come to mind, particularly in Scotland, where Gary Armstrong, Roy Laidlaw, Andy Nicol and Bryan Redpath are among the most recent. But elsewhere few have been given an extended run, which adds credibility to the opposite argument, that scrum-half is a sufficiently demanding position without any additional responsibility.

That one of Wales's finest was a scrum-half is beyond doubt, but only Gareth Edwards knows how much his game may have been affected by the role of captaincy. Clive Rowlands wished he had played a few games for Wales without the responsibility 'just to see what it would be like not having to think about those 14 other players'.

When Gregan retires, no major rugby-playing nation will have a scrum-half as captain, a situation which seems unlikely to change in the near future. So, perhaps they are best left to cajole and encourage forwards with appropriate slaps in appropriate places, left to pass, kick or run at will and let someone else look at the bigger picture. But no matter who is in charge on the field, one thing is for sure – you won't stop scrum-halfs grabbing the ball and taking those quick-tap penalties and looking for contact to get the extra ten metres!

VII

THE ENTERTAINERS: OUTSIDE-HALF

In the not so distant past, hundreds, even thousands, of schoolboys seeking to emulate their heroes on the rugby field kicked oval balls on park grounds, in the street or anywhere else where they could gather without upsetting the neighbours or the local constabulary. Before proceedings could commence, however, there was one issue to resolve – whose turn was it to be the Welsh outside-half, the number ten.

If this scenario took place in the 1950s, the lads would be Cliff Morgan, the 1960s saw little David Watkins running amok and in the 1970s 'King' Barry appeared on every park in the land. He in turn became Phil Bennett, who was followed by Gareth Davies, Jonathan Davies, Neil Jenkins and Stephen Jones. Why? Why does Wales and its rugby public have this fixation with one position above all others? Why is the outside-half such a huge part of Welsh rugby folklore? No other country spawns so many impish, mischievous youngsters who all want the same thing – the jersey with number ten on the back. Why? The general perception of the outside-half as seen through Welsh eyes was that of a playmaker, an orchestrator, even a Merlin-like figure, a weaver of magic, a wizard. Not any more. No longer is the individual flair that so many of the great entertainers possessed seen as an essential ingredient in the make-up of an outside-half. Tackling, distribution of the ball and positional kicking are the more required skills, with the template suggesting a much bigger player in the role – a sad indictment of a game that has become more concerned with defence than attack.

Does this mean that the will-o'-the-wisp number ten was too much of an individual to be accommodated in the structure of the modern game? Accepting that no other country placed such emphasis on the position, perhaps the time had arrived when Welsh rugby had to reassess the priorities needed by the pivotal player. After all, many of the great outside-halfs will confirm that they didn't know what they were going to do themselves before they were committed to the move, so how on earth could the players around them be expected to? This is best summed up by paraphrasing a conversation which allegedly took place between Lions captain Willie John McBride and his outside-half Phil Bennett in the changing-room before a Test in South Africa in 1974:

McBride: Phil, you remember all that jinking and sidestepping you did under the posts which ended with Edwards's try for the Baa-Baas?
Bennett (proudly): Yes, Bill.
McBride: Well, any of that nonsense today and you'll have me to answer to.

* * *

Willie John's comments would not have fallen on deaf ears but neither did they restrain the adventure with which Bennett played the game, yet they may have been a reflection of how the role of outside-half was seen elsewhere. Thirty years on it is tragic that the game has no place for the traditional Welsh number ten, as a search through its 125-year history reveals several enterprising outside-halfs who led Wales with distinction, among them a player listed simply as half-back by the game's early chroniclers but included here as the first outside-half to captain Wales.

Charles Henry Newman played in the first Welsh international at Richardson's Field and was one of four players from the team to be included against Ireland in Wales's second fixture. Full-back against England, one of two as was customary at the time, Newman was now selected at half-back from where he would eventually captain the side six times. And for half-back read outside-half, as his usual partner, W.H. Gwynn, is confirmed as having a good pass from the scrum, thereby giving no little credibility to the assumption.

Wales were new to international rugby, with England, Scotland and Ireland having stolen a march on them. Little surprise then that only five of the first twenty internationals played were won. It was Charlie Newman's misfortune to lead Wales during this development, which resulted in his record of four defeats and two drawn matches with Scotland in Glasgow and England at Llanelli, both matches ending scoreless.

Newman was a clergyman and at some time in his career moved to Durham and played both club and county rugby in the north of England. Described by Gwynn in *Football: The Rugby Union Game* (edited by Revd. F. Marshall) as 'thick set, short in stature, but powerful', he is also credited by the same source as being 'the first man in South Wales to introduce the passing game'. This can be interpreted to mean that he was one of the innovators of the link between forwards and three-quarters which would gradually evolve into half-back play as we now know it. Originally, it was not intended that half-backs should distribute the ball; their brief was to remain in contact with the forwards or kick for position, but Newman introduced the new concept, probably picked up at Cambridge University, which was taken further during the 1890s and early 1900s by successive half-backs, notably David and Evan James, Selwyn Biggs, Fred Parfitt, Dickie Owen and George Llewellyn Lloyd.

Llewellyn Lloyd was possibly the first archetypal Welsh outside-half – short, light in stature, dark haired and extremely quick off the mark. First capped in 1896 he made a further eleven appearances in the following seven seasons and had the misfortune to captain Wales in one of only a handful of matches lost during the first decade of the twentieth century. Scotland away has been the downfall of many Welsh sides of which great things were expected, and in 1903 the 6–0 defeat put paid to any ideas of back-to-back Triple Crowns.

In the years immediately following the Great War, Welsh rugby entered an enforced period of transition during which the team had to be virtually built from scratch. Outside-halfs Clem Lewis and Jack Wetter had played international rugby before the war and both were invited to captain Wales during the 1920s, Lewis as a seasoned 32 year old and Wetter, firstly shortly after his 33rd birthday and finally a few weeks before his 37th. Neither player enjoyed any success, Lewis experiencing two defeats and Wetter three, the last of which saw Wales heavily beaten by the invincible All Blacks in 1924. In appearance Clem Lewis conformed to what would become the quintessential Welsh outside-half but the same could not be said of Wetter, who was a balding figure in his later appearances for Wales and bore no resemblance to those who would wear the jersey in the second half of the century and beyond, the one obvious exception being the 'Ginger Monster', the points machine that was Neil Jenkins.

The classic persona of the Welsh outside-half as epitomised by Llewellyn Lloyd became recognised wherever rugby union was played. Then the game went big. From numbers one to fifteen, coaches were on the lookout for big, athletic individuals who were more reliant on brute force than natural guile, but in Wales the six-foot-six forward is a rare enough commodity, never mind the six-foot-plus backs. A noticeable gap between the haves and have nots started to open up with the distinct possibility that the position Welsh rugby had made its very own would become extinct, the outside-half factory close and the young lads have nobody to imitate.

* * *

On 2 November 2003 Wales met New Zealand in the last match in Pool D of the RWC at the Telstra Stadium, Sydney. Little, if anything, was at stake, both countries having already qualified for the knock-out stages, and when the Welsh coach, Kiwi Steve Hansen, selected what looked to be largely a second-string side, Wales appeared doomed, a case of damage limitation at best. Twelve months on, this defining game is seen as the day Welsh rugby once again realised where its strength lay and that the future had to be dependent on innovation not imitation. Wales lost to New Zealand and were knocked out of the tournament by England in the quarter-finals, but the manner of the two defeats triggered a serious rethink, which, 18 months later, bore fruit in the shape of a first Grand Slam for 27 years. What did Wales do against New Zealand and England, and continue to do with more confidence in subsequent matches? They ran the ball. They used it at every opportunity, maybe even overused it in the euphoria that was prevalent, but for the first time in more than 25 years a style of play could be seen, a style uniquely Welsh which would hopefully lead to the re-emergence of the outside-half as a potent attacking force.

Stephen Jones was the Welsh outside-half during this uplifting revival. For many years associated with Llanelli and subsequently the Scarlets regional team, at the start of the 2004–05 season Jones took his undoubted talent to France, signing for Clermont-Auvergne, a move which many saw as a golden opportunity to put the finishing touches to his game, playing outside the structure of the Welsh season which had started to become all too familiar.

Stephen Jones led Wales against England in a warm-up match before the 2003 RWC. It was not a happy afternoon for the new captain, England registering that country's biggest win in Wales, 43–9, a result that would have been expected at the hands of the pre-tournament favourites, but not from England's second string, which didn't include any player who was in the starting line-up at the final three months later. Jones is not recognised as a traditional Welsh outside-half, rather a player who conforms to the modern criteria: a fine tackler, distributor and kicker of the ball out of hand, who has accumulated a host of points with his accurate goal kicking. The return to a more recognised Welsh style of play brought with it a lifeline, an opportunity to reintroduce one of the special ingredients of a unique brand of rugby. It fell on the shoulders of Stephen Jones to be the first player presented with the opportunity to put the Welsh number ten back on the rugby map as an attacking force, a line breaker, an entertainer – a huge responsibility.

Body language tells the experienced analyst much about a person and on the rugby field the swagger and strut of a confident outside-half can be likened to a matador, a prizefighter or a model on the catwalk. What it says is: 'Look at me, I'm the star of this show.' If the outside-half can win the mind games, then there is every likelihood that the team will win the match. Jonathan Davies was a player who oozed confidence playing rugby union and took it to rugby league, where he made an even bigger impression. He commanded the respect of his peers, not only because of his undoubted ability but also his understanding of all aspects of both codes. Little surprise, then, that Davies captained Wales, perhaps not with any great distinction – that would come later as a rugby league player – but with great fervour and commitment coupled with a belief that attitudes within Welsh rugby had to change if the national team was to compete against the world's best. All of which may seem a little surprising when one considers Wales had recently celebrated a third-place finish in the 1987 RWC, followed by the Triple Crown in 1988, but these performances were really just papering over the cracks. The more astute observers could see that there were serious problems that needed to be addressed.

Jonathan Davies was introduced into the Welsh side in 1985. England were the visitors to the Arms Park and the build-up to the match was dominated by the selectors' apparent uncertainty regarding outside-half. When the team was announced, there was no number ten named, which led to the retirement of an ex-captain, and the baptism of a future one.

It was a strange introduction. I knew Gareth Davies, we went to the same school, but I didn't feel any pressure on me as a result of the controversy. I was a youngster coming through the system and just wanted to get out there and play my best. It didn't matter who they picked at number ten as long as it was J. Davies! It wasn't the best way to end Gareth's career, the way it was handled was poor, but I was over the moon.

It was as a Neath player that Jonathan Davies first led Wales to a comfortable victory over Canada in a Pool match in the 1987 RWC at Invercargill, that rugby outpost at the southernmost tip of New Zealand's South Island. Twelve months later, now with Llanelli, Davies led Wales in the second Test on a blighted tour of New Zealand, this time played at the other end of the country, at Eden Park, Auckland. A systematic hammering best describes the outcome and following the 52–3 defeat in the first Test, Wales now went down 54–9 but with the captain competing to the finish, scoring a late try at the end of a 70-metre dash for the line. It was following this tour, on which only two of the eight matches were won, that Davies offered to address the AGM of the WRU, but he wasn't even given the courtesy of a reply and it was clear that the administrators were not happy with much that Davies represented.

There was a lot of talent in the side. The World Cup and the Triple Crown had seen the confidence in the squad grow but what we needed was a less arduous tour to one of the developing countries, Canada or Japan, where we could have built on it. To go to New Zealand, which had the best team in the world at the time, was not what we needed. They were the best team I ever played against. We weren't able to mix it upfront, depending on a more open game which involved good ball-handling forwards, a style we needed to develop, and New Zealand wasn't the place to try and do that.

I enjoyed the tour, but it was a real eye opener. I always enjoyed training, looking after my fitness and preparation, but they were on a totally different level. Their players were endorsing products, getting sponsorship, not actually getting paid for playing but these were avenues which allowed them to concentrate on their rugby. That was the point of view Bob Norster and I wanted to put over to the union but they didn't want us to say anything; it was an opportunity missed. We weren't looking to highlight the problems in Wales, point the finger at the committee men, we simply wanted to advise them on what was happening elsewhere, but they didn't want to know. They preferred to look for a scapegoat and Tony Gray and Derek Quinnell got the chop, a typical knee-jerk reaction. I wouldn't suggest that John Ryan wasn't an able coach but Gray had established a style of play which was right for us and it was inevitable that a new face would see things differently. Then, ironically, ten years later they bring a New Zealand coach in.

Davies's departure from Neath had been particularly acrimonious, while in the media his name was continually being linked with rugby league clubs. Two disappointing performances in the autumn finally brought things to a head. Western Samoa were not expected to present Wales with any problems but a comfortable victory produced a far from convincing performance and consequently when Romania turned up four weeks later the pressure was on. Five years earlier, in 1983, Wales were comprehensively beaten in Bucharest and now history was about to repeat itself, this time at the Arms Park in front of 20,000 despondent supporters. The coach, captain and outside-half were the public's targets following defeat, meaning Jonathan Davies was found doubly culpable for his leadership and personal performance, and he willingly put his hand up on both counts, but what he was not prepared to accept was the apparent ostracism which came from within. The union officials were once again indifferent in their handling of the matter; nor was coach John Ryan looking to have a clear-the-air meeting with his captain. And in the background the rugby league clubs, Widnes in particular, were intent on getting their man.

Romania had a huge pack and a big-kicking outside-half, but I felt confident if we won sufficient ball we would be all right. There were some poor selections and in the end it didn't work out and I was the one who copped all the flak. I took it on the chin, feeling that even if the union and coach weren't going to publicly support me they would do so privately, give me the chance to say my piece, but unfortunately there was no communication. I was generally happy at the time, particularly enjoying my club rugby with Llanelli, and nothing gave me more pleasure than playing for Wales, but that lack of support got me thinking. Rugby league clubs had shown an interest in me when I was at Neath – Warrington and St Helens in particular. Now Widnes came knocking.

They were good businessmen, told me to weigh up the pros and cons, but at the end it was a decision made purely and simply on financial grounds, for the security of my family. Looking back maybe I went a little early. I missed the Lions tour in 1989, but now I had to prove myself in the other code, the hardest thing I've ever had to do, and I'm just pleased that I succeeded. I was one of several players who turned professional in the late '80s and what this exposed was the lack of strength in depth in Welsh rugby at the time. When the first-choice player was gone, usually from a key position, there was little seen to be coming through, something which the introduction of leagues highlighted.

Jonathan Davies won 32 Welsh caps. The record books list him as captain on four occasions but he sees this quite differently, bringing a fresh and thought-provoking argument to the table.

I always saw myself as captain, something I believe goes with the position. No matter where on the field the captain is, the number ten dominates the game. He's the link between forwards and backs, the player most aware of the way the game is unfolding, the controller, the eyes of the team, the eyes of the captain. Martin Johnson's England had Jonny Wilkinson and the great New Zealand side of the late '80s under Wayne Shelford had Grant Fox. Inspirational captains, but their number tens were the most important players and I don't see that has changed, even in the modern game, where four or five 'captains', each with designated responsibilities, has become the norm, outside-half among them.

The character of the individual is the most important aspect to consider when looking for a captain, the man recognised on the team sheet. There is no doubt that the front five is not the best place from which to gain an overall perspective on how the game is being played, and full-back is probably too far away, but while it is important to bear such points in mind, if the most suitable candidate is found in one of those positions, he should be selected. In today's game his decision making on the field is down to a minimum, the taking of penalties and so on, but he has the added responsibility of bringing together all the different parts of the team which come under the immediate remit of others and that is where strength of character is essential.

When Jonathan Davies signed for Widnes in January 1989, Wales lost another star to the professional game, but this was something it had become more than used to, having to sit back and watch as one by one its leading players were tempted by the lucrative financial offers northern league clubs would put on the table, a practice which would continue unabated until rugby union became a professional sport. Jonathan Davies was the incumbent Welsh captain at the time he signed for Widnes, as was Terry Holmes before him, but some 20 years earlier it was David Watkins who had led Wales in recent matches when he signed for Salford in October 1967. Watkins was the 75th player to captain Wales and when he turned professional became the first of the elite group to do so.

David Watkins was everything that a Welsh outside-half had come to represent: quick off the mark, often leaving opposing forwards grasping at thin air; an accurate kicker of the ball out of hand with either foot; and, most important of all, a player who could turn a game on its head in the blinking of an eye with some outrageous sleight of hand or dexterous dance work which he was able to introduce regardless of conditions – be the surface firm or a mud bath, David Watkins was in control.

First capped alongside Clive Rowlands against England in 1963, Watkins was put firmly in the frame when the time came to select the 30 players to tour Australia and New Zealand with the British Lions in the summer of 1966 after his run of 18 consecutive matches. He played in all six Test matches, leading the team twice against the All Blacks, but overall the tour was a disappointment, with eight matches lost in New Zealand, including all four Tests. The local media were far from complimentary in their summation of Watkins, claiming 'whatever nuisance value he was, was cancelled out by the nuisance he was with his individualism and his habit of losing contact with his supports'. What must be appreciated here is that in 1966 the British and New Zealand styles of play were poles apart, with the All Black approach much more forward orientated, and despite the success this brought, the Lions, particularly players like Watkins, had hit a nerve with their entertaining approach which left the New Zealand public wanting to see their own heroes playing a more expansive game.

When the fifth Wallabies arrived in Wales in the autumn, the pre-match build-up focused largely on whether the Welsh selectors should continue with Watkins or blood an exciting new talent, Llanelli's Barry John. They opted for the latter and for the first time in his international career David Watkins was not in the line-up, adding more fuel to the flames of the east–west divide that is ever present in Welsh rugby.

I returned from the Lions tour full of confidence, having led the team in two Tests. I played in the Welsh trials at Swansea and Cardiff and then found myself left out of the side to play Australia. What made the situation even more frustrating was that Cliff Jones, Glyn Morgan and Rees Stephens, three members of the Big Five, spoke to me individually and confirmed I'd had their vote, which of course didn't add up. I was bitterly disappointed. I lost out to a young lad from Llanelli called Barry John who kept his place in the team for the visit to Murrayfield.

Australia were clear underdogs going into the match but, as is so often the case, form counted for nothing and the tourists claimed a dramatic 14–11 first official win against Wales. Defeat in Edinburgh prompted the Big Five to not only recall David Watkins but also install him as captain for the season's remaining matches. Defeats against Ireland and France saw Wales looking at a first-ever Five Nations whitewash if England were successful in Cardiff but the selectors showed enormous faith and adventure when they gambled on playing an 18-year-old goal-kicking sensation out of position at full-back. The gamble paid off, Keith Jarrett scoring a record-equalling nineteen points in a dream debut which helped Wales avoid the ignominy of five consecutive defeats and that dreaded whitewash.

The selectors asked Newport to give Keith a run-out at full-back and we played him against Newbridge the Saturday before the England match. He had a nightmare, dropped everything, and at half-time I put him back in the centre. I apologised because I knew what I was doing but the selectors had made up their mind and he played full-back the following week. What followed was like something out of *Boy's Own*.

It was a swansong for the outside-half, Wales winning in front of the home crowd with some style, and a few months later David Watkins was on that road heading north to a second sporting career which in many ways, like that of Jonathan Davies some years later, eclipsed the first.

I'd no thoughts of playing rugby league but it came about as a result of a charity seven-a-side tournament in Manchester at the start of the season. Newport second row Bill Morris had entered a team based on the successful Newport sevens side, which he called the David Watkins Seven. The tournament was played on a Sunday, which the WRU didn't include in the rugby calendar, so the team couldn't be called Newport, but the timing caused a bit of a problem as Brian Price and myself were committed to playing for the Irish Wolfhounds in Galway on the same weekend. It was a bit of a rush, but the sponsors in Ireland agreed to fly us to Liverpool and we managed to play in both events.

Brian and I arrived in Manchester with minutes to spare before the first-round tie against Sale which we won before going on to win the tournament, beating Harlequins in the final. Among the crowd was Brian Snape, chairman of Salford, who was interested in signing me for the club. He contacted me in work the next day and made an offer of £10,000, which I declined, then over the next few weeks increased it to £12,000, £14,000 and finally £16,000, by which time it had become a serious issue. I played for Newport at Abertillery on a Wednesday night and on the Thursday travelled to Tewkesbury for a meeting with Salford officials. After four or five hours of negotiation and deliberation I signed the papers. There were some initial regrets, not being able to play for Wales again among them, but I soon took to league like a duck to water.

David Watkins captained Wales in union and league but suggests no difference in the role, captaincy dependent on the same criteria in both codes.

So much is said about captaincy but I believe most of it is fairly straightforward. You have to be seen by the players as a controlling influence and be able to get that bit extra out of them, particularly those who are perhaps not among the stars of the team and can be prone to a lack of confidence on the bigger stage; you have to be able to bring the best out of such players. During the match the decision making is fairly obvious but overall I think the job is clearly defined and if you have got quality players around you, it's not that difficult.

The half-backs are the hub of the side and have the advantage of on the one hand being close enough to grasp the commitment of the forwards and how they are faring, and on the other knowing the abilities and strengths of the backs outside them. They are good positions from where to decide when to utilise the one against the other, maintain the forward effort or get the ball away quickly to bring the three-quarters into play. It's very simple really, following the tempo of the game, and taking the appropriate options.

Where David Watkins in 1966 failed to convince the New Zealand media of the merit of an attacking outside-half who played the game off the cuff, in South Africa in 1955 an earlier model of the genre had no such problems. Cliff Morgan was introduced to international rugby in 1951 following in the footsteps of Glyn Davies and Billy Cleaver, who, between them, had dominated the outside-half position since the resumption of fixtures following the Second World War. A product of the Rhondda Valley, Morgan was born in Trebanog, a small village within spitting distance of Cilfynydd and Treorchy, where Davies and Cleaver had first seen the light of day, the middle of a hotbed of Welsh rugby that is now under serious threat following the demise of the Celtic Warriors and the lack of regional rugby. But it should be remembered that things were no different in 1950 when all roads led to Cardiff, the emergence of the Pontypridd club as a major force still some years distant.

Cardiff it was, then, for the young Morgan, the opportunity to play alongside Willis, Williams and Matthews too great an opportunity to miss, and it was at the Cardiff Arms Park that he showed the rugby world what Welsh outside-halfs were put on this planet to do – entertain.

Nowhere did Cliff Morgan entertain more than in South Africa with the British Lions in 1955. One of the game's everlasting images is of Morgan scoring in the first Test at Ellis Park, Johannesburg, in front of 90,000 spectators, having left the Springbok back row flat footed with a marvellous shimmy and outside break before scoring a try under the posts which set the Lions up for a sensational 23–22 victory. For the first time rugby union followers in the Southern hemisphere saw for themselves the unique skills and craft that were integral in the make-up of a Welsh outside-half. Here was the finished article others would aspire to, tweak to suit their own preference and redesign in general appearance, but it was a model which few would truly emulate.

For the 1956 championship the Welsh selectors appointed Cliff Morgan as captain. He played the season in tandem with new scrum-half Onllwyn Brace but for some inexplicable reason these two highly talented individuals didn't quite click and the partnership failed to deliver all that was expected of it, despite Wales winning three of Morgan's four matches in charge. Ireland spoiled the party with a typical forward onslaught in Dublin but could not prevent Wales claiming a fifth championship since the war.

In his autobiography *Beyond the Fields of Play* Cliff Morgan recalls his childhood in the Rhondda Valley with enormous affection: school, religion and music; the Welsh language that was, and is even more so today, under threat in the area; and the early influences on him as a rugby player. From his references to Glyn Davies and Billy Cleaver it is clear that these were early role models, Davies in particular impressing as 'probably the most naturally gifted player that I remember at outside-half'. Three great players all born within a short punt of each other, and an equally short punt in the opposite direction would see the ball land in the village of Porth, birthplace of yet another star who played no small part in creating the myth of the Welsh outside-half.

William Clifford Jones played his 13th and final game for Wales on his 24th birthday. At a particularly young age this product of Porth County School, Llandovery College and Clare College, Cambridge, brought his glittering playing career to a premature end following an exceptionally cruel run of injuries. A small man, even by half-back standards, Jones's name would be linked with Welsh rugby long after his playing days had finished, but it was on the field that he would first gain the plaudits.

He was one of the thirteen new caps in the disastrous England match of 1934 but was retained for the trip to Scotland and would keep the jersey for ten consecutive matches before injury put him out of contention in the 1936–37 season. His ability to beat a man off either foot saw him break many defences and together with Wilf Wooler and the veteran Claud Davey he formed a formidable Welsh midfield which thrived in the space created by Haydn Tanner's controlled passing.

It had been some years since Welsh rugby had boasted players who gripped the public imagination in the way this quartet did and the 13–12 victory over the third New Zealand All Blacks in 1935 ensured that Wales would play to full houses with crowds of 50,000, 60,000 and even an unofficial estimate of 70,000 flocking to watch the new generation. If injury had not forced Jones into retirement, the outbreak of war in 1939 would certainly have put his career on hold. However, in his last season he led Wales in a championship which saw victories over England and Ireland but defeat at Murrayfield, a late penalty deciding the outcome. What disappointed most was that the penalty in front of the posts was awarded against a player for lying on the ball, the referee unable to take into account the fact that he was barely conscious and could do little to extricate himself from the situation. Unfortunately it is on such issues that championships and silverware are so often won and lost.

Cliff Jones put much back into the cause of Welsh rugby. A selector for over 20 years, during which time Wales enjoyed the Golden Era of the 1970s, his huge contribution was recognised when he was elected president of the WRU for the 1980–81 centenary season, which saw the eyes of the rugby-playing world fully focused on the Principality.

* * *

It remains a sad fact but within the boundaries of South Wales there is an invisible line that is of equal importance to the local populace as the coastline facing the Irish Sea and the border with England. This line of division, while not so politically significant as the Berlin Wall or the 38th Parallel, divides South Wales into east and west factions that are separated primarily by language, the native tongue being more prominent west of the axis. Then there are the different cultures that are represented by the capital city and its closest rival, Swansea; the political divide which sees a much stronger nationalist movement in the west; and by the game of rugby where the divide is an amalgamation of all the above. The line can probably be located somewhere near Pyle, where the old A48 used to pass the tallest rugby posts in the country. Not surprising, then, that where there was a small pocket in the Rhondda producing mercurial number tens in the 1950s and earlier, so appeared a similar pocket of talent west of the Swansea Valley which in turn produced extraordinary outside-halfs destined to have as significant an impact on Welsh rugby as had Jones, Davies, Cleaver and Morgan before them.

West of the River Neath lies an area which locals will claim to have had a more prolific output of prodigious talent than that found in the upper reaches of the Rhondda. The names Cefneithen, Felinfoel, Laugharne, Trebanos and Trimsaron all alert the laptop computer that something is amiss, each entry highlighted by a wavy red underline; even Carmarthen suffers the same fate, one which Llanelli somehow avoids. Modern technology aside, each of the highlighted villages and towns can boast of being the birthplace of one of the great entertainers at number ten. But we can do even better than identify an area of some 500 square miles in our search for a focal point in the development of the west Wales version of the outside-half – we can locate a school playground and the fields that surround it which have an extraordinary claim to fame in Welsh rugby history. The playing fields of Gwendraeth Grammar School saw Carwyn James, Barry John, Gareth Davies and Jonathan Davies first kick the oval ball in earnest. The great mentor and his most famous prodigy never captained their country and we have already witnessed the fortunes of J. Davies, which leaves the talent that was William Gareth Davies.

* * *

The National Stadium, Cardiff Arms Park, complied, as do all other rugby stadia, with the regulations laid down by the IRB in that the field of play was not more than 100 metres long, excluding the dead-ball areas, and no more than 70 metres wide. Gareth Davies played those 7,000 square metres like nobody else, with a kick out of hand that was executed with slide-rule precision, time after time after time. Never was a ball simply booted out of play by this Oxford University Blue. Davies took to the field having weighed up the height and speed of the opposing back three, worked out the wind velocity, taken into consideration any likely change in the elements, and calculated the time it would take the players to turn and head for the destination of the ball. Then, in a split second, he was able to weigh up this abundance of data and place the thing a couple of inches beyond despairing hands with yet another perfect touch finder – or so it seemed.

Gareth Davies won the selectors' vote in their search for an outside-half to replace the retired Phil Bennett and made his debut on the 1978 summer tour to Australia, partnering Brynmor Williams in the first Test and club colleague Terry Holmes in the second, and it was the latter partnership which took the field on 17 of Davies's 21 appearances.

That Welsh rugby was at an all-time high at the end of the 1977–78 season is never questioned but unfortunately once such heights have been scaled there is only one way to go. Despite a disappointing summer tour the visit of the All Blacks in the autumn provided the opportunity to confirm to the Welsh public that although many kings were now 'dead' there were more waiting to be crowned. The controversial outcome of that match is discussed elsewhere, as is the Triple Crown that followed, but Welsh rugby and its stars were heading for a period of mediocrity and few would escape the inevitable recriminations and criticisms from a demanding public.

Gareth Davies won ten consecutive caps before injury brought the run to an end against Ireland in Cardiff on St David's Day 1980. The recurrence of a knee injury first picked up at a training session with Llanelli three years earlier now meant an extended break from the game which gave Davies the chance to fully recover in time to take his place on the British Lions tour to South Africa in the summer. The problem hadn't gone away, though, and during the second Test another knock saw him off the field and off the tour.

Following more enforced rest he was reunited with the Welsh jersey for the visit of New Zealand in November and carried on in the Five Nations, but there was nowhere to hide when the selectors dropped several leading players after a miserable performance at Murrayfield. A further recall was inevitable and when Australia arrived in December 1981, there was not only a recall but Davies was also chosen to captain the side. Following a successful debut he continued in the role for the 1982 championship which ended with another wooden spoon, the only victory gained over a poor French side which shared the dubious distinction of propping up the table.

We beat Australia and France but they were dour matches and as the season unfolded so my captaincy came under fire. I was injured in Dublin and had to be replaced by Gary Pearce at half-time. Then followed the French match, but the press got on my back after Twickenham, playing on the fact that I'd chosen to play into the wind in the first half, something I'd always do given the option. Against Scotland we were the better side early on but after knocking on the door for 15 minutes we suddenly found ourselves behind when Roger Baird scored a breakaway try, and while it wasn't quite a case of having to play catch-up rugby nothing went right after that. Instead of putting the foot on the brake, calming the boys down, I allowed us to get drawn into the game the Scots wanted to play and we just got worse. For the start of the next season there was a change of coach, John Bevan replacing John Lloyd, and someone close to Bevan had a word in my ear. I was told that Bevan wasn't a Gareth Davies fan and to watch my back, I was going to be struggling. Prophetic words.

Three years in the wilderness followed and it was a comprehensive home defeat by the Wallabies in 1984 which prompted the selectors to once again call on Davies.

I'm sure that during the period I was out of the national side I played the best rugby of my career. The pressure of playing for

Wales had gone which allowed me to totally focus on club rugby, and my eventual recall was a bit of a surprise because I never got on with Bevan, who clearly didn't like me. I didn't have any confidence in him and I'm sure I was only back in the side as a result of pressure from other people. I was a bit of a loose cannon at the time and when I dropped a goal in the first minute against Scotland the thought went through my mind to make the obvious gesture and walk off, a cynical way of proving a point, but you can't do that, it's not what the game is about.

That Welsh rugby lost its way in the immediate aftermath of the 1970s is beyond dispute and whether sufficient attention and preparation was given to the inevitable retirement of so many star players – retirements which all came within a few seasons – is doubtful. The early 1980s saw leading players openly criticise the way Welsh rugby was run, the management and selection policies were called into question and after two further appearances Gareth Davies finally walked away from the international arena when the selectors, in announcing the team to face England in the final match of the season, named A.N. Other at outside-half, electing to continue their deliberations a while longer.

I went to watch Cardiff play South Wales Police on the Wednesday night and somebody came up to me on the terraces and asked if I'd heard the Welsh team, specifically the fact that the selectors had left open the outside-half berth. I contacted Rod Morgan, chairman of selectors, and he told me that the coach wanted to wait until after the Cardiff–Swansea match due to be played on Saturday before deciding between myself and Malcolm Dacey. Bevan preferred Dacey's style of play and I suggested that that being the case they should go ahead and pick him rather than undermine my position. The upshot of it all was that I pulled out of the issue by telling Morgan that I was retiring from international rugby. I did things the right way. The press had got hold of the story but I wanted to tell the selectors before speaking to the media.

Come the Saturday, Cardiff thrashed Swansea. I played well, scored a lot of points, and Malcolm had an off day. I had a call in the evening asking me to reconsider but my mind was made up. Later there was another call, Rod explaining that they couldn't possibly select Dacey after such a poor performance, as good as asking what did I suggest. What did I think of Jonathan Davies?

I said there was no comparison between the two and Jonathan played against England.

Gareth Davies had a full season leading Wales. Five matches with mixed results but his was an experience he strongly advocates should be available to others.

To establish yourself as a leader takes time, you have to get the confidence and respect of the players and this takes more than a couple of matches. It's very different being a club captain because you have the time to allow the relationships to develop and I was pleased that Mike Ruddock, on naming Gareth Thomas as captain, suggested it was a long-term appointment. So much of the responsibility once associated with the captaincy has changed with the greater involvement of the coach but this has in no way diminished the overall importance of leading Wales. It is still a huge responsibility and an even greater honour.

When Gareth Davies stepped up for his first cap in Brisbane, he knew that the boots he was about to fill were big. The final match of the 1978 Five Nations Championship had brought unbeaten France to face an unbeaten Wales in Cardiff – one of those rare occasions which saw both teams with everything to play for. A game for the rugby aficionado, the connoisseur, it would test Wales's finest half-backs against a French back row still talked about with a reverence rarely equalled, never bettered. To watch Jean-Pierre Rives, Jean-Pierre Bastiat and Jean-Claude Skrela go in search of Edwards and Bennett was the stuff of legend. Elsewhere on the field, Faulkner, Windsor and Price took on Cholley, Paco and Paperemborde in the scrum, and in the lineout it was Martin and Wheel against Haget and Palmie. Every position saw personal confrontations of the highest order and inevitably the 30 players produced a match to remember. Welsh captain Phil Bennett celebrated his 29th and last cap with two tries and became the fifth player to lead Wales in each match of a Grand Slam season, joining Billy Trew, John Gwilliam, John Dawes and Mervyn Davies.

I wanted to go out at the top. I'd decided that France was going to be my last game for Wales and I was desperate to win. We had won a triple Triple Crown in Dublin two weeks earlier, but the Grand Slam would make a fitting finale. I didn't say anything beforehand because I didn't want to detract from the occasion but my mind was made up and when I shook Gareth's hand in the changing-room after the match and told him he said that it was his last game as well. I had no idea.

The time was right. I'd got to a point where packing my bags to go to an away match was becoming difficult. More time away from home, and while it is the greatest honour to play for Wales, something that I didn't want to abuse, I felt that by continuing I would be cheating people and I wasn't prepared to do it. The Irish match also played a part in the decision. It was one of the most vicious games I ever played in; it was a war. We had just won another Triple Crown but the changing-room was like a morgue. There was a lot of blood and I know that Gareth and Gerald were deeply affected by what had gone on. Great friends who had travelled the world together as British Lions had beaten each other up and while you can't take the physical side of the game away there is an unwritten law, a respect that went out the window that day. Hard man as he was, Scotland's Gordon Brown would never kick you on the floor, but that day at Lansdowne Road took away some of my faith and I asked myself how much more my body could take. I knew then that I had one match to go.

Phil Bennett left international rugby on his own terms and on a high note but it had all been so different in Paris in 1969 when he had the distinction of becoming Wales's first replacement in an international when he came on for the injured Gerald Davies in the centre. His second cap and first start saw him on the wing against South Africa in 1970 and then he was chosen in the centre before finally making his first appearance at outside-half in place of an injured Barry John. A two-year break finally ended when once again he was introduced as a replacement, this time for J.P.R. Williams at full-back, all of which meant that in his first five appearances Phil Bennett had played in four different positions. Little surprise, then, when he called his autobiography *Everywhere For Wales*, but with Barry John's early retirement the next twenty-four outings were all at number ten, culminating with eight matches as captain.

What happened to Mervyn Davies was tragic. He was in his prime, playing the best rugby of his life and he had established himself as a great Welsh captain. Quiet on the field but someone with a fine tactical brain and it was down to me to take over what was really Mervyn's team. When you talk about captaincy, the focus tends to be on either the position or the man, and I think Mervyn epitomised both, a man of enormous stature who had the utmost respect of his players, leading them from number 8, which gave him a good perspective on things. The outside-half enjoys similar benefits, standing ten metres from the set pieces with perhaps the added advantage of not having his head in the scrum or his back to the open field. The same can be said of inside centre, but I have my doubts about scrum-half. It's such a hard position and comes under such enormous pressure that I question whether the added responsibility of captaincy is a sensible choice. At outside-half you do get that second or two longer to weigh up the options and there's always a wing forward looking after you, certainly in my day.

When it became my turn to lead Wales, I was very aware of the wealth of experience I had at my disposal, not just experienced players but experienced captains, and I saw myself being there simply to make the right decisions. Everybody wanted the ball. I'd have Gerald moaning on the one wing, J.J. Williams on the other, with JPR going mental because he wanted to come into the line. Then you had Bobby Windsor, who had learnt so much in South Africa with the Lions in 1974. Sid Millar had the forwards scrummaging for days on end and they destroyed the Springboks. He brought all this to the Welsh pack, which became a formidable outfit, and every now and then I had to tell Bobby the forwards were playing well but to let the ball out. I had all this talent to try and balance but being surrounded by such players made it all quite simple really.

Phil Bennett was also a British Lion in South Africa in 1974 where, despite the threat of oblivion from the man from Ballymena, he danced his way across the country, leaving forlorn tacklers in his wake, and in 1977 was chosen to lead the tourists when they visited New Zealand, but the decision to accept the honour did not come easily.

For many years I hadn't enjoyed a complete summer break from rugby which was one of several reasons that gave me great reservations about the Lions tour in '77. A year earlier my wife and I lost a baby boy which truly put playing rugby in perspective and thankfully, we had recently been blessed with the birth of our son. I was aware that because of rugby and the training involved I was not really spending my time as I should. I'd drive to Afon

Lido on a Sunday to meet up with the Welsh squad and see the fathers taking their kids to the park, knowing that was what I should be doing. I didn't want another three months away from home, I wanted to be with my son, but when the captaincy was offered, after much discussion and soul searching we decided it was something I couldn't turn down.

I still had reservations and I know that I wasn't right mentally to go on that tour. When we got to New Zealand, the weather was atrocious, it rained virtually every day. I didn't play well and the All Blacks were desperate to win the series after a few recent disappointments. As the tour unfolded we started getting bad press back home, as a result of which we became insular as a group and I was very homesick. I was constantly questioning myself; it was the hardest thing I experienced as a captain.

Phil Bennett led Llanelli for six seasons, 1973–79, but it was in October 1972 that he enjoyed the club's finest hour and an example of leadership which he never forgot.

Llanelli beating the All Blacks 9–3 was the pinnacle of my career. Grand Slams, Triple Crowns, winning the Test series in South Africa with the Lions were all wonderful experiences, but that day at Stradey was for the town, the people I was brought up with, the people I worked with, my mother and father, who were staunch Scarlets supporters.

That day Delme Thomas gave the finest speech I have ever heard. Norman Gale, Ray Williams and Carwyn James had spoken to the team at the Ashburn Hotel in the morning and then Delme spoke to us about ten minutes before kick-off. He went around each player, looked them in the eye, talked about what it meant to us as Welshmen, as Llanelli men. He pitched it perfectly. Gravell was crying; JJ, never one to get carried away, was visibly moved. I think we were all emotionally affected and we burst onto the field perhaps knowing that something special was about to happen. That's leadership.

* * *

To entertain or not to entertain, that is the question. Whether there is room in the game that rugby union has become for the dashing cut and thrust of a Morgan, Watkins, Bennett or Davies is questionable. The set piece provided the platform from which their flair and unique talents blossomed, but there are fewer scrums in the modern game for outside-halfs to exploit, while the lineout has become a game within a game, the roll of the dice before the phases come into play. Phases which see props on the wing, second rows in the centre, full-backs on the floor at the bottom of rucks and outside-halfs frantically trying to join up the dots.

A position to lead from? In the days of the great entertainers certainly. Days which saw the simple version of what has become a far too complex game, one which could be controlled with ease by the man at number ten who one ex-captain observed was 'always the captain'. But things have changed. In ten years of professional rugby the major rugby-playing nations have all but neglected three positions in their search for a captain: prop forward is a banker with wing three-quarter also a good bet, but few would guess that outside-half would be the third.

VIII

THE CONTROL CENTRE:
CENTRE THREE-QUARTER

More captains have led Wales from the position of centre three-quarter than anywhere else on the field. A total of twenty-five, added to which are two, classed as three-quarter backs, but who played the game more as a modern-day centre than wing three-quarter. Centre is the position that dominates the story of the Welsh captaincy, contributing more than twice the number of any other; claims that it is ideally situated for the purpose cannot be ignored.

The history of rugby union offers a fascinating pursuit for those with the time and the inclination to dig deep, its origins and how it evolved being of particular interest. From games between villages where the number of players was an irrelevance, rugby football had seen teams conform to 20 players by the time England and Scotland met in the first international in 1871. When Wales entered the arena ten years later, this had been reduced to the fifteen players that now take the field, but the number allowed in a team did not actually become Law until 1892, and even then there was inadequate wording which was not clarified until 1926. Despite this, rugby union was a 15-man game in 1880 and where our interest now leads is to the way in which those 15 players were variously dispersed; not all countries have been uniform in their approach to how the players should be distributed.

For that first match under the captaincy of James Bevan, the Welsh team fielded two full-backs, two three-quarter backs (Bevan among them), two half-backs and nine forwards, but for the next match the three-quarter backs had been increased to three at the expense of the forwards, who now numbered eight. Two matches later one full-back, two three-quarter backs, two half-backs and ten forwards took the field before the selectors finally settled on a full-back, three three-quarters, two half-backs and nine forwards. Then a young man from Somerset turned the game on its head with a revolutionary formation behind the scrum which is still in universal use.

Frank Hancock joined Cardiff in 1883 and such was his impact that the club decided to change the established six backs and nine forwards format to accommodate his talent and, more importantly, his revolutionary thinking on the art of three-quarter play. This was achieved by introducing a fourth three-quarter at the expense of a forward and the game as we now know it was seen for the first time. Cardiff benefited from the system and in 1885–86 under Hancock's captaincy won all but one of the twenty-seven matches played. It was in 1886 that those responsible for selecting the Welsh team decided to introduce the four three-quarter system to the national side and, not surprisingly, it was Hancock who was elected as captain. What had proved a great success at club level was not immediately transferred to the international stage and defeat at the hands of a Scottish side still playing with nine forwards brought a quick end to the experiment which would not be tried by Wales again until 1888 from when it became the accepted formation.

His four three-quarter concept viewed as a failure by the Welsh selectors, Frank Hancock never played for his country again. Most of the criticism came from within, Newport's Arthur Gould prominent among the system's detractors, although his opinions were seen as being based on envy rather than constructive criticism, the Cardiff–Newport rivalry being well established by the late 1880s. However, time would prevail; here was one piece of forward-thinking that was not going to go away.

Few Welsh rugby players have had as many column inches devoted to them as Arthur Joseph Gould. Much written about this first 'superstar' relates to the end of his playing career and the gift of the deeds of his house in Newport presented to him by an adoring public. The money had been raised by subscription to a testimonial organised by a local businessman in conjunction with the town's local newspaper but the gesture was deemed to be in direct contravention of the amateur status of the game. The Welsh Football Union, the Newport club and all associated parties who had supported the campaign fell foul of the

English and Scottish unions and although there had been much support from outside Wales, Gould attempted to defuse the highly contentious issue by announcing his retirement. Despite this, international rugby suffered the repercussions when Ireland and Scotland withdrew from fixtures with Wales in 1897 as the controversy gathered momentum. Scotland continued the break in relations the following season before normal service was resumed in 1899. Significant as Gould's testimonial may have been, occurring as it did in the immediate aftermath of the formation of the Northern Union and professional rugby league, it was Arthur Gould the player and Arthur Gould the captain who dominated the game in Wales at the end of the nineteenth century.

The arrival of 18-year-old Arthur Gould into the Newport team on 18 November 1882 heralded the start of a rugby-playing career that would eventually take the game into the lives of people who had previously shown little but a passing interest in what was still a fledgling spectator sport in the early 1880s. Gould represented everything the quintessential Victorian gentleman was perceived to be: he was an extraordinarily handsome man who cut a fine figure; he was a distinguished athlete; his presence was much sought after in social circles; but above all he was a rugby player of enormous ability, among the first who could claim to put 'bums on seats' wherever he appeared.

First capped by Wales in 1885, Gould played two matches at full-back before moving into the centre, where he won the remainder of his 27 caps. One of six brothers who played for Newport, he appeared for Wales with firstly Bob, a forward, and latterly Bert with whom he formed a centre partnership on three occasions. Business interests interrupted his international career, with Gould absent for the whole of the 1890–91 season, and but for this and the occasional injury it is unlikely he would have missed a match in the 13 seasons during which he represented Wales. In 1889 he made his debut as Welsh captain in a match that saw Ireland gain a first victory on Welsh soil, prompting the selectors to revert to forward Frank Hill for the next match. Another defeat provided a second opportunity for the young centre to show his leadership qualities, against England in a match played at Dewsbury on 15 February 1890.

Wales were now totally committed to using the four three-quarter system and against England's nine-man pack of forwards gained a first-ever victory over the old enemy. How important a victory this was should never be understated and one only has to consider the anticipation with which the annual fixture is still greeted to grasp some understanding of the impact the result had on a nation finding its feet in a rapidly expanding commercial and industrial world, one that saw the neighbouring English very much to the fore.

Arthur Gould led Wales 18 times, a record which stood for a century, but was he a great captain or simply a great player whom the selectors automatically chose to lead the team? What we should remember is that at the time of his introduction Wales had played seven matches, winning only twice, and in Gould's first six appearances failed to add to that total. Despite a successful club structure which was producing many talented individuals, transferring this to the higher demands of the international game was proving difficult and, great player though he undoubtedly was, Gould could only boast eight victories in his term as Welsh captain. The teams he led included many leading lights of the first 20 years of Welsh rugby, but by 1897 many were at the end of their playing days, particularly the forwards, where a completely new pack would soon be in place. Behind the scrum Billy Bancroft, Gwyn Nicholls and Selwyn Biggs had arrived and would take Wales into the new century and a decade of rugby supremacy. And it is to this that we should look in measuring the legacy left by Arthur Gould.

First and foremost he was a charismatic personality who reached way beyond the playing fields in his impact on Wales and its people. He was revered by a nation in the throes of a huge industrial revolution which saw men working at the hardest of tasks to make ends meet, and the rest cure provided by the heroes of the day, such as Gould, was readily grasped. Frank Hancock may have devised it for Arthur Gould to initially reject but it was the latter who finally took the revolutionary concept of four three-quarters and built Welsh back play around it, others eventually reaping the benefit in the first Golden Era of Welsh rugby, the period between 1900 and 1910. In his eighteen matches as Welsh captain Arthur Gould had seven partners in the centre, but it was the player who joined him for the last three who became a natural successor in every way: classical player, esteemed leader, people's champion.

Erith Gwyn Nicholls was born in Westbury-on-Severn, Gloucestershire, on 15 July 1874 but by 1880 the family had moved to Cardiff. Their arrival in Wales coincided with the formation of the Welsh Football Union and that infamous defeat at Richardson's Field, and it is not surprising that the young man, undoubtedly influenced by the game's prominence in the city, made his debut for the Cardiff club in 1893, following seasons with two of the city's junior teams, Cardiff Stars and Cardiff Harlequins.

From his first cap in 1896, Gwyn Nicholls's place in the Welsh team was virtually assured and, as with Gould, only injury and unavailability due to business interrupted his run of appearances. Following Gould's retirement the captaincy had been the responsibility of full-back Billy Bancroft and when he called an end to his playing days, the selectors chose Nicholls to take over the mantle and he first led Wales against England at Blackheath in 1902. Forever associated with Cardiff RFC – elaborate ironwork gates were erected at the entrance to the club in his honour in 1949 – Gwyn Nicholls was actually a Newport player in 1902, having joined the club as a matter of convenience when his laundry business opened new premises in the town, and although his stay at the club was short – he played only ten matches, none of which was lost – the captain of Wales during their third successful Triple Crown campaign was a Newport player.

In 1905 Gwyn Nicholls was undoubtedly a Cardiff player and it was on 16 December that he led Wales to that finest of victories against New Zealand, the only defeat suffered by the tourists in the 35 matches played. Wales had won four Triple Crowns by December 1905 and long gone were the days when the other home nations held the upper hand, but for many it was this stunning victory over one of the game's greatest teams that firmly put Welsh rugby on the map. A record crowd of 47,000 saw Wales score the game's only points, a try instigated by a dummy attack from a set scrum and a reverse pass, and they witnessed great controversy. Did Bob Deans score what would have been a match-saving try for the tourists? The referee said no, citing a double movement, and the flame which ignited the great rivalry between the two countries that still exists 100 years later was lit.

Gwyn Nicholls was a British Isles tourist in 1899, won twenty-four Welsh caps, led his country ten times, including a Triple Crown, and captained Cardiff in four seasons, but it is as Welsh captain on 16 December 1905 that he is best remembered. The 1906 championship saw Wales fall at the final hurdle, Ireland gaining a convincing victory in Belfast, and Nicholls announced his retirement from international rugby with that last defeat the only blemish on a record which showed seven games won and a draw with England.

But it didn't end there. The Springboks were scheduled to play Wales on 1 December and despite a lack of rugby in the early part of the season, Nicholls found himself under enormous pressure from colleagues, friends and a demanding Welsh public to once again lead Wales into battle. He finally acquiesced to the many demands by taking his place in the team, again as captain, but it was a mistake, Wales losing 11–0 with a miserable performance that was as forgettable as the match played 12 months earlier had been memorable.

Arthur Gould had laid the foundations for the first Golden Era of Welsh rugby, Gwyn Nicholls had continued the work leading Wales to the first Triple Crown of the twentieth century and the victory over New Zealand, and it was another centre, this time from Swansea, who played throughout the decade and beyond, firstly influencing and finally captaining Wales to unsurpassed glory.

It is an undeniable fact that the name William James Trew is not viewed with the same reverence in Welsh rugby circles as that of Gould and Nicholls, but it is an equally undeniable fact that it should be. His 29 caps bettered both and his 14 appearances as captain saw Wales win 12 times, again a better record than his illustrious predecessors could lay claim to. At club level, where Gould had led Newport during two seasons and Nicholls set a record when he captained the Arms Park club for a fourth term, Billy Trew led Swansea through five consecutive seasons, 1906–11 and again in 1912–13.

First capped as a wing three-quarter against England in 1900, Trew won six caps in the position before converting to outside-half, the position from which he first led Wales. The match against Scotland in Edinburgh ended in defeat but was followed by a run of 11 successive victories, which has never been equalled. But for a matter of principle Trew would have appeared in all 11 but he withdrew from the first in protest against a decision by the WFU to suspend Swansea player Fred Scrine for verbally abusing a referee in a club match, Trew viewing the punishment meted out as excessive.

His absence gave Cardiff centre Rhys Gabe the opportunity to lead Wales against Ireland in the first match of the record-breaking run. Originally a wing with Llanelli it was at London Welsh that he converted to the centre and later, on joining Cardiff, formed one of that club's and Wales's outstanding centre partnerships with Nicholls. Two points of reference are worth recording with regard to Gabe. First, he passed the ball for Teddy Morgan to score the winning try against New Zealand in 1905 and in the same match helped to pull down Bob Deans short of the line. Second, in an unexplained suggestion of dual allegiance, Gabe, now a Cardiff player, took his place on the wing for Llanelli against the Springboks on 29 December 1906 and three days later appeared in the centre for Cardiff against the same opponents.

Trew immediately returned to the Welsh team following his protest but this time in his preferred position of centre. He was reunited with the captaincy in the 1908–09 season when Wales defeated the first

Australian tourists and proceeded to win a second consecutive Grand Slam. Wales had commenced fixtures with France in 1908 and in defeating the new opponents together with the three home countries won a first Grand Slam, a feat now repeated, with Wales led in each of the four matches by William Trew. Two years later, in what would be the last season of Welsh dominance for many years, a third was won, Trew again leading the side but from outside-half and in only three of the matches, the captaincy being given to wing three-quarter John Williams for the visit to Paris.

There were two more appearances as captain, matches which saw Trew back in the centre, but a career that had begun at Kingsholm, Gloucester, in 1900 finally came to an end in Paris in 1913. A severe groin injury meant that the selectors had to find a new captain for the season's final match, the visit of Ireland to Swansea, and they looked no further than Trew's centre partner. Welsh electoral registers are full of the name Jones which can easily lead to confusion and in the case of Trew's successor particular care must be taken if a case of mistaken identity is to be avoided.

There were three brothers born in Pontypool in the 1880s, David 'Ponty' Phillips Jones, James 'Tuan' Phillips Jones and John 'Jack' Phillips Jones. All three represented Wales, 'Ponty' Jones on the wing against Ireland in 1907 and 'Tuan' partnered Trew in the centre against Scotland in 1913, both brothers scoring tries in their only appearances. However, it was the youngest of the trio, 'Jack', who became the most familiar to Welsh followers, winning a total of 14 caps either side of the Great War, and it was 'Jack' who led Wales against Ireland following the retirement of Billy Trew.

'Jack' Jones was in his third season as captain of Pontypool and at twenty-seven years of age was something of a veteran, having been on two overseas tours, the Anglo-Welsh visit to Australia and New Zealand in 1908 and two years later to South Africa with the British Isles team. His six Test appearances included one as captain in South Africa, and it was therefore into safe hands that the selectors placed their trust after Trew's injury. Jones did not disappoint, Wales winning a close match 16–13, the captain scoring his sixth international try.

His appearance as captain on 8 March 1913 brought to an end an extraordinary run of matches which had started on 6 January 1900, when Billy Trew first played for Wales. In the 13-year period Wales played a total of 52 matches and in 50 of them were captained by a back, the only exceptions being Boxer Harding and Twyber Travers, who were both handed the honour in recognition of services rendered.

While 1914 would see the emergence of the Revd. Alban Davies and the 'Terrible Eight', and the immediate post-war seasons would continue to see Wales led from the front, such dominance by either of the two collectives that make up a team has not been repeated.

* * *

The first centre to captain Wales following the First World War was Llanelli's Albert Jenkins, almost ten years to the day after 'Jack' Jones, and against the same opponents, Ireland. Where Jones celebrated victory at Swansea in 1913, it was the taste of defeat for Jenkins in Dublin. Exactly five years later he was asked to lead Wales for a second time but it was more of the same in Cardiff when the Irish once more spoilt what could have been two memorable parties, both matches played on 10 March, the captain celebrating his birthday on the 11th. The five years in between (1923–28) saw the new selection panel in a continual state of confusion over the captaincy. Under the leadership of 13 captains Wales lost 13 of the 20 matches played, statistics which speak for themselves, and those favoured with the captaincy during this unproductive period could do little to lift the gloom which had descended.

Four centres were among them, three Cardiff players who each captained the club together with Newport's Jack Wetter, whose recall at thirty-six years of age, three years after his last appearance, confirms the parlous state of Welsh rugby at the time. In two matches Arthur Cornish led the team – to victory over the French and defeat against Scotland. Bobby Delahay also led a winning team against France and in 1927, much as Jeff Squire would fifty-three years later, Ruel 'Lou' Turnbull led fourteen men for most of the match at Twickenham only to see his team lose by a couple of points, despite Wales outscoring England two tries to one.

The second half of the inter-war era saw a significant improvement and if fixtures with France had not been cancelled from 1931 it would probably read even better. The cessation of fixtures was due to the home unions' belief that French rugby was not being run on a strictly amateur basis; neither were they happy with the on-field violence seen in recent matches, and relations were not resumed until after the Second World War.

During the 1930s one could be forgiven for thinking that in rugby terms there were two roads leading out of Wales, one to the north of England and the other out to the famous cities of academia – Oxford and Cambridge. Fortunately there was some return to be had from the latter and between 1929 and 1938 four centres captained Wales, all of whom had won Blues playing for Cambridge University in the annual Varsity match – Harry Bowcott, William Guy Morgan, Idwal Rees and Wilfred Wooler.

Guy Morgan was the first of the quartet to be called upon and his first match as captain came as a revelation after all that had gone before, Wales scoring four tries in beating Scotland at Swansea. Less entertaining matches followed but Wales continued the rebuilding process, defeating France and gaining a draw in Belfast. Injury prevented Morgan playing against England and the captaincy was taken over by fellow centre Harry Bowcott. Another of those rare players with the perfect rugby CV, Harry Bowcott was a schoolboy international; a Cambridge Blue; a player for Cardiff, London Welsh, the Barbarians, Wales and the British Lions; a Welsh selector; president of the WRU in 1974–75; and a Welsh captain, but, alas, not a winning one: England were the victors at Cardiff in the first match of the 1930s.

Guy Morgan returned to lead the team in Paris in a match noted for its sheer brutality, which no doubt had some bearing on the decision taken in the following year. Another victory gave Morgan a record of three games won and a fourth drawn, making him one of only four players who have led Wales on three or more occasions and never experienced defeat: Tom Parker, with six wins and a draw; Bleddyn Williams, five wins out of five; and John Lloyd, three out of three, making up the numbers.

Following the selectors' speculative gamble of fielding thirteen new caps against England in 1934 four players shared the captaincy during the remainder of the decade. Outside-half Cliff Jones was another Cambridge graduate and his three matches have been recorded, but again it was to the centre that the selectors focused their attention.

Claud Davey, Idwal Rees and Wilfred Wooler were fine players who presented the selectors with the sort of problem they relished – which of the three to leave out of the team. With fewer options open to them on the wing the Big Five often included all three, Rees and Wooler equally at home in either position. Idwal Rees, in fact, led Wales from the right wing in the second of his three outings as captain, a victory against Ireland, added to which was a scoreless draw with England and a defeat by Scotland, the captain paired in the centre with Wooler on both occasions.

For the final match of the 1937 season the selectors gave Wilf Wooler his first taste of international captaincy but Wales were well beaten in Belfast, the backs playing with some uncertainty behind a dominant pack. The following year was Cliff Jones's season, with Wooler again leading the team in 1939, in what proved to be the last three matches for seven years. As he was only 26 years of age when he led Wales for the final time one is left wondering what the prodigious talent that was Wilfred Wooler would have gone on to achieve in the remainder of a rugby career suddenly brought to a premature end.

An accomplished all-round sportsman he found post-war fame as a cricketer. When the championship resumed on 18 January 1947, Wilf Wooler was 34 years of age and although older men had represented Wales it was Glamorgan County Cricket Club who benefited from his services for the next 30 years, firstly as captain – Wooler leading the county to a first championship in 1948 – and then secretary.

***

On 21 December 1935, Wales defeated New Zealand for the second time. There was no controversial issue to raise doubt (in contrast to 1905), just a wonderful team effort which saw Wales snatch victory with a late try after being reduced to fourteen men for the final ten minutes following an injury to hooker Don Tarr, who broke his neck on his debut and was never called on again. Cambridge men Vivian Jenkins, Idwal Rees, Wilf Wooler and Cliff Jones were joined in the backs by Geoffrey Rees-Jones, an Oxford Blue who scored two of Wales's three tries, the schoolboy scrum-half Haydn Tanner, and in the centre with Rees, captain Claud Davey, scorer of the third Welsh try. That the forwards, who included three new caps in their number, did what forwards are there to do goes without saying, and a great effort produced Wales's best victory of the inter-war years, a match which saw a boy become a man and a captain pass into the folklore of Welsh rugby.

Claud Davey was introduced to international rugby in 1930 at the battleground that was the Stade Colombes, Paris. Unlike his contemporaries who found solace among the dreaming spires of Oxford and Cambridge, Davey continued his studies at Swansea University and debuted for the Swansea club in 1928, making an immediate impact with his strong tackling and direct approach in attack. It was Claud Davey the selectors turned to after the failed introduction of 13 new caps and against Scotland he repaid their faith, leading Wales to victory at Murrayfield. He continued with wins over Ireland and another at the expense of the Scots, which sandwiched a draw at Twickenham, before Ireland brought the resurgent Welsh XV back to earth in Belfast in the final championship match of 1935. Then it was the All Blacks followed by yet another victory over Scotland and a disappointing defeat at Twickenham to a Triple Crown-winning England which ended the now London Welsh-based Claud Davey's term as captain.

For Claud Davey in the 1930s read Scott Gibbs in the 1990s: big tackler, an attacking force from inside centre who regularly punched holes in defences for others to exploit, and another Swansea star, although his career began a few miles up the road at Neath. Scott Gibbs had three distinctly separate phases to his playing days – amateur union player, professional league player and professional union player. Alan Bateman, Jonathan Davies, Scott Quinnell and David Young all benefited from the decision to make rugby union a professional sport and returned from rugby league to once again represent Wales; so too Scott Gibbs, who, after three seasons with St Helens RLFC, became the first of the ex-union stars to return to Welsh colours.

Before signing a professional contract Gibbs had won 20 caps and on his return in 1996 won a further 33, making him Wales's most-capped centre. Not only was he the first league convert to return to the national team when he was called up to face Italy in Rome, but three matches later he was captain when Wales played the USA, standing in for the suspended Jonathan Humphreys.

He would add three British Lions tours to his Welsh caps, league honours and great days with both Neath and Swansea but against England at Wembley Stadium on a glorious, unforgettable Sunday in April 1999 Scott Gibbs produced a defining moment, something which former international John Taylor once referred to when writing about the Welsh team of the 1970s in a Sunday newspaper as 'sheer bloody magic'. John Billot in his majestic *History of Welsh International Rugby* wrote: 'This was the assault on the Kashmir Gate, Badajoz and the Taku Forts rolled into one. Five tacklers failed to stop this glory boy as he strode down the Valley of Peril with breathtaking swerve and verve. Who will ever forget his try in the second minute of injury-time?' Who indeed!

* * *

Two months before Wales were due to compete in the 1995 RWC the game in the Principality was once again in chaos. A second whitewash in the Five Nations was not seen as ideal preparation for the upcoming tournament and questions were being asked, principally of those in charge behind the scenes, the coaching team and management. En bloc, coach Alan Davies, his assistant Gareth Jenkins and team manager Bob Norster tendered resignations that were accepted by the WRU, which now found itself with a matter of weeks, if not days, to find suitable replacements prepared to take over at such short notice.

The coach at Cardiff was Australian Alex Evans and it was to him the WRU turned in its hour of need, Pontypridd and Swansea coaches Dennis John and Mike Ruddock joining him in the new, albeit temporary, regime. With such little time for preparation, Evans went for players he knew and selected 11 from Cardiff in the squad of 26, but it was his choice of captain that made the old adage 'a new broom sweeps clean' totally inadequate. Ieuan Evans had led Wales a record 28 times and although included in the party, coach Alex Evans handed the responsibility to Cardiff's Mike Hall.

First capped as a replacement on the tour to New Zealand in 1988, Mike Hall was called onto the field when Wales were already 40 points down – 'welcome to international rugby'. A bad week in December saw him win a second Blue in a beaten Cambridge team and five days later he took his place in the Welsh side which suffered an ignominious defeat against Romania in Cardiff. The 1989 Five Nations was threatening a first-ever whitewash for Wales when the team found some inner strength in the final match, Mike Hall producing nothing remotely like the 'Hand of God' to help dispatch England but the home nations' selectors had seen enough to include him in the British Lions team which toured Australia in the summer, Hall playing in the first Test.

Ever present during Wales's 1994 Five Nations Championship-winning team it is not surprising that Mike Hall, like so many other players, views the silverware with some caution.

I still think that as a player the things you chase are the mythical titles, the Triple Crown and the Grand Slam. Even though I didn't get on the field, to be involved with the squad in 1988 when we won the Triple Crown was fantastic. Winning the championship at Twickenham in 1994 was a strange experience, Ieuan being presented with the trophy after we had just been beaten. The expectation on that occasion was far too high. People were making Grand Slam ties and sweaters and the team got caught up in it. I think it is the job of the coach to protect the players from the media hype such an occasion generates.

Twelve months later, with thirty-nine caps to his credit, Mike Hall was invited to lead Wales in search of more silverware, gold, in fact, in the shape of the Webb Ellis Cup.

I can see very similar parallels with what happened when Ron Waldron took over as coach in 1990 and Alex Evans in 1995. Both men were good coaches, men who I have the greatest respect for, and where Waldron introduced the Neath way to the Welsh team all the players at Cardiff had similarly bought into Evans's philosophy which saw 11 players from the club included in the squad. However, what both experiences prove is that you cannot impose the imprint of a club onto the national team, especially where the coach is as close to his club players as Ron and Alex clearly were. It was the relationship I had with Alex that prompted him to make me captain. He had very little time at his disposal which he felt would prevent him building up the relationship he wanted unless the player was one he knew well and it was because of this that he decided to appoint me in place of Ieuan.

On the basis of recent results Wales's opening match against Japan was ideal preparation for what lay ahead and Hall got off to a winning start but, as expected, things were very different in the second Group match against New Zealand – a 34–9 defeat – which meant Wales had to beat Ireland in their final match to progress in the tournament. A final score of 24–23, one which included five tries, suggests great rugby, but this was far from the reality of the situation, certainly for Welsh supporters, who watched their team lose with great naivety and little passion.

I think Alex as a caretaker coach was very much influenced on selection by Mike Ruddock and Dennis John, and I felt there were a few players who shouldn't have played against Ireland, that we would probably have been better going with the tried and tested, what worked at Cardiff. What annoys me is that the 1995 campaign is slated because we didn't get to a quarter-final. We lost to Ireland by a point and I actually think that if we had won and the team had spent another week with Alex then we may have given the French a run for their money. Apart from selection, the real problem which had reared its head was the split in the squad; there were a few players who became a disruptive influence because they were not getting the games they thought they should. Alex had called for a total ban on alcohol during the tournament which was observed by the Cardiff players and others in the Test team, but those who may have felt they were not involved were out every night and it all became very divisive – exactly the same as in 1991. As captain, I found this very difficult. At Cardiff everybody bought into the system and I was able to delegate responsibilities to players who I knew I could trust and if a player wasn't prepared to buy into what we were doing, he was gone. With Wales it was very different. There were some players who I just couldn't get on board, especially in such a short period of time.

The 1995 RWC will be remembered as much for the off-field events as for the exciting play that took place on it. Some years earlier it was cricket that had attracted the interest of Australian media mogul Kerry Packer, and now it was the turn of rugby. There was talk of a rugby circus, teams based in strategic cities throughout the world, but to achieve such an ambitious plan it was essential that the international captains be included because it was through them that the organisers hoped to enrol the players.

There was also an undercurrent at the time which involved Kerry Packer. Two weeks before the World Cup was due to begin I was invited to a meeting with his representative in Cardiff and told what was going on. You had to listen because the game was right at the cusp with huge demands being made on players, some of whom were also struggling with employers, while there was little in return. In South Africa all sixteen captains met with Packer's agents and in the three weeks after the World Cup I signed fifty players on conditional contracts which were lodged with a large firm of solicitors in Cardiff. I thought it was going to happen and it came within a whisker of doing so, but the IRB stepped in and the rest we know, but it certainly was an interesting time, very exciting.

As was the case with Paul Thorburn four years earlier, Mike Hall had no intention of retiring from international rugby, but following the bad experiences of 1995 he became totally disillusioned and after winning forty-two caps called it a day. There was much still to be enjoyed in club rugby, with the introduction in 1996 of a new European tournament which for Hall more than compensated for the international arena, one he surprisingly found he didn't miss. On captaincy, like so many others of his position, Mike Hall is quite clear.

> At centre you are in the middle of all the action, one removed from outside-half, who is obviously your main decision maker, but to make him captain puts more pressure on what is already a critical position. Centres are also integral in defence and I would say that they have probably got more in common with the forwards than the other positions among the backs.

> To have somebody like Ieuan Evans leading the team also has great benefits, someone who leads by example and encourages others to do likewise. When you went on the field with Ieuan you knew you were following a world-class player who immediately commanded respect but at the same time was dedicated and very personable, and all these things tend to rub off, particularly at club level where there is more time for a captain to make an impression, develop team spirit. There is no doubt that the role has diminished in recent years but it is still vitally important. The way they lead the team on the field, the example they set in training, the discipline around the hotel and putting into action what a coach wants. Gareth Thomas is proving to be a great captain, although I was a little disappointed in the New Zealand match [November 2004] when he wasn't aware of the time left on the clock, but he'll learn; he's good.

* * *

With skipper David Young injured for the autumn series of internationals in 2000 it was Mark Taylor who led Wales against Samoa and the USA in two matches both comfortably won. Wales were embroiled in yet another issue over who should wear the number ten jersey, Neil Jenkins or Arwel Thomas, and it was the latter who completed an all-Swansea midfield trio with Taylor and Gibbs.

The introduction of regional rugby saw Taylor move to Stradey Park, but after a season playing for Swansea's traditional arch-rivals, it was English Premiership outfit Sale who secured his services, and in 2005 he became the first player from the club to captain Wales. The British Lions tour to New Zealand saw several of the Welsh players who had won the Grand Slam selected, and Mike Ruddock opted to take a relatively inexperienced squad on the two-match tour of North

America. This made it all the more important that a man of experience and one who the players would respect was chosen to lead the team, and it was to Mark Taylor that the coach turned. Two comfortable victories enabled some of the stars of the future to shine on the international stage under Taylor's guidance, and the centre can now boast four victories in his four appearances as captain of Wales.

Something of a visionary in the new age of professional rugby, Mark Taylor is a qualified chartered accountant and his is an example which aspiring youngsters would do well to follow, there being little doubt that a longer career is to be had sitting behind a desk than the rough and tumble of modern rugby can ever promise.

On joining the Scarlets, following the introduction of regional rugby, Mark Taylor came under the watchful eye of assistant coach Nigel Davies, another international centre with 29 caps who captained Wales in one of those matches outside the normal fixture list which are viewed by a sceptical public as money-making exercises by a greedy union. France were the opponents in Cardiff on a Wednesday night in September 1996 which saw the stadium half-full, a crowd of 25,000 paying to watch a 'friendly' that was anything but, and the visitors ran out 40–33 winners.

* * *

If in 2000 Graham Henry had a problem deciding which of two players to include at outside-half imagine the dilemma which coach Tony Gray faced in 1988 when four suitable candidates had their hand up for the job. Gray's answer to the problem was quite simple – he included them all and in doing so produced a team brimming over with players of great craft and invention which took the Five Nations by the scruff of the neck at Twickenham in the opening match and didn't let go until the final whistle in Cardiff six weeks later, when France denied Wales the ultimate prize by a single point. Included in the starting line-up at Twickenham were Llanelli's Jonathan Davies at number ten, Swansea's Anthony Clement at full-back and from Pontypool the outrageous maverick that was Mark Ring, who partnered captain Bleddyn Bowen of the South Wales Police in the centre. Bowen had led Wales in the first match following the 1987 RWC against the USA in Cardiff, but from outside-half; now, with the revolutionary plans to include the other great playmakers of the Welsh club scene, he moved to the centre for the championship.

The team selected to play at Twickenham gave a good insight into Tony Gray's mind. How he wanted to play the game: expansive, 15-man rugby. With Ieuan Evans and Adrian Hadley on the wing, two players who were devastating in open and broken play, he wanted them brought into the game as much as possible, and we were given free rein to express ourselves. We got Adrian over for two tries at Twickenham, the first following a counter-attack by Tony Clement from deep in our own half and the second when Jonathan Davies switched direction to start a similar move. It is so important to win the first match of the championship and that result against England set us up for the visit of Scotland to Cardiff.

Finlay Calder scored an early try and shortly into the second half we were trailing 20–10, but it was a match in which the great players in the team really did stand up. Bob Norster produced some good lineout ball from which Jonathan dropped two late goals to put us 25–20 in front and it was also the match in which Ieuan scored one of his better tries, a jinking forty-yard run which saw him beat six or seven players.

Footage of the 1988 Five Nations confirms the almost reckless abandon with which Wales were playing the game. The ball handling of forwards and backs alike was of the highest quality and the spectators were treated to some high-octane rugby which produced the added bonus of matches won. After England and Scotland all roads led to Dublin, to be followed by the visit of the French to Cardiff – a nation held its breath.

The match against Ireland mentally tested me more than the previous two. The pressure on us to win a first Triple Crown since 1979 was enormous and having beaten England and Scotland playing such expansive rugby more of the same was expected. There's something different about Lansdowne Road. You just don't seem to find much room, it's almost as if there are 30 Irishmen on the field, and on the day they were certainly up for it and wanted to spoil the party. It was a much tighter match and I watched the expressions on the Welsh players' faces as the game unfolded, could see what it meant to them to win. They didn't have the smiles that were there at Twickenham and in Cardiff. It was a must-win game, the pressure really told and it took a Paul Thorburn penalty in injury-time to win the match 12–9 and the Triple Crown.

As a sportsman playing the game at the highest level those are the moments you look for, when there is a lot of pressure, the result so important, when so much is at stake. Next there was a Grand Slam to play for but France beat us 10–9. I'd played against them twice before, in 1984 and 1986, when we were lucky to come second, but I felt that we should have won in 1988. A couple of things went wrong on the day, but that's sport; I'm a big believer in fate and that was how it was meant to be.

On the back of a successful Five Nations, which ended with Wales and France sharing the title, Bleddyn Bowen led a party of twenty-five on an eight-match tour to New Zealand. Though his tour was cut short by injury after only two matches the Welsh captain still saw enough to convince him how big a task Welsh rugby faced if it was to consistently compete at the very highest level.

If you play rugby, you want to play against the best players in the world and I believe New Zealand at that time was the best team I have ever seen. They were a formidable outfit, almost professional, while we were still very much an amateur side that might have had some great individual players but collectively just couldn't compete – they were absolutely fantastic. It was unfortunate we had to play them during that era because when we came home there was a lot of disenchantment with the coaching and the performance of the team, then the rugby league clubs came in and cherry-picked the best players, five or six of them going north, which broke the heart and structure of the squad.

Bleddyn Bowen is the only player from the South Wales Police to lead Wales and his five matches produced four victories with only that one-point defeat by France spoiling a perfect record. Yet, leading his country was not something he had ever entertained.

When I was a young lad being brought up in Trebanos, rugby was my life and I always wanted to play for Wales but I never dreamt of becoming captain. I'd had some experience of captaincy, leading a very successful police team which included other Welsh internationals, Martyn Morris, Phil Davies and Steve Sutton, but this was from outside-half where I played most of my club rugby. It was Welsh coach John Bevan who moved me into the centre in 1984 and although I played at ten when I first captained Wales that was largely down to Jonathan Davies being injured.

I felt quite comfortable leading the side from the centre, knowing that in Bob Norster I had a great pack leader. Making the decisions behind the scrum was a straightforward application with so many great players around me and I felt perfectly at ease with the responsibility. Having done both, I personally think that centre is a better position to captain the team from because you do get a chance to sit back and look at what is going on while at outside-half you tend to be that much more involved with the game.

What Welsh rugby let slip through its fingers at the end of the 1980s we can only hypothesise over. A coach with an adventurous approach to the game who allowed his players to express themselves and, more importantly, enjoy themselves, was sacked and a tour on which no other European country would have fared any better was seen as a gauge and allowed to quickly lay to rest the great success of a few short months earlier. And we know that little consideration was given to the fact that in New Zealand they were playing the game under a different set of rules, rules which were in place to ensure that players were given every opportunity to develop to the best of their potential.

What Bleddyn Bowen experienced in 1988 was a mirror image of events 19 years earlier when Brian Price also led Wales to Triple Crown success immediately followed by a summer tour which included two Tests against New Zealand. On both occasions Welsh rugby was brought back down to earth by a New Zealand team which was found to be clinical and uncompromising in its approach, with Wales convincingly beaten in all four Tests, but the similarity between the two periods ends there. In 1988 it was coach Tony Gray who carried the can for the team's performances in New Zealand but in 1969 Clive Rowlands was under no such pressure and the difference in tolerance was highlighted in the seasons that followed which, respectively, saw Wales suffer a first-ever Five Nations whitewash in 1990 compared with a Grand Slam in 1971. Other factors came into play, not least among them the loss of players to rugby league in the late 1980s, but what comparing the two periods does confirm is the change in attitudes. One generation was prepared to show patience and allow the team to evolve while the other demanded an instant fix to all the problems and in doing so created an environment which put Welsh rugby in a must-win situation every time the team took the field and created unwanted pressure under which the players and coaches would have to work for several years to come.

It is unfair and unrealistic to compare teams from different eras, a habit which has gone on far too long in Wales, with constant reference to the 1970s something the players in the twenty-first century have had to put up with, which is ridiculous when few of them were even born when Gareth etc. were performing their deeds. The class of 2005 will have gone some way to exorcising those ghosts but it cannot be forgotten that in 1971 Wales had a great team, one of the greatest.

Before the final match of the championship in Paris 11 players had been selected to tour Australia and New Zealand with the British Lions, and Welsh captain John Dawes had also been chosen to lead the party, the first Welshman to captain a Lions squad fully representative of the four home unions. Dawes first led Wales in 1968 during a season when the selectors were undecided about the young Gareth Edwards's readiness for the responsibility, and two years later he resumed the captaincy, again at the expense of Edwards, following defeat in Dublin. The final match of the 1970 campaign produced a home victory against France and then came the 1971 Five Nations which saw Wales play high-intensity rugby and push the measurement of excellence a long way down the road in an ongoing search for perfection. The success was based on very simple criteria which coach Clive Rowlands instilled in the team at the training sessions and which were supervised on the field of play by John Dawes.

The winning of the ball is paramount and in training we concentrated on the lineout and scrum, realising that if they went well then the opportunities would be there for the backs to exploit. When the backs clicked, it worked but many times, by leaving it to the backs, they showed a little bit of disarray and this is where the early days of coaching differ from what you see today. They were much more player orientated and player controlled; much of it was off the cuff.

Where a lineout took place would determine whether the ball was thrown long or short and we would have practised a few options regarding what we did with the ball, whether to move it to the wing, try something in the centre which involved the full-back, or bring the blind-side wing into play. The only times we varied this was either by kicking for position or using a variety of kicks aimed at putting the opposition under pressure, an up-and-under aimed at the posts, for example. After that it was spontaneous, the game was that simple.

The transferring of the ball to the wing following a set piece is all but absent from the modern game. Rather than try and create space by deft handling and passing of the ball the players would rather create a maul or a ruck and I think this reflects the rugby league influence which has come into the game, one that I object to. The only way that you are going to get rid of it is when a team shows that the other system works. The players have to prove this to themselves before it is taken on board, they have to realise that it can be done. Take Shane Williams as an example. He thrives in open space, but in confined space I don't think he is that threatening, he doesn't operate. You have to create that space for him and this can be done in the centre where someone like Gavin Henson, a big man, can be used to good effect. Shane is an instinctive player, not in the same way as Barry John, who had the knack of being seen to do the right thing at the right time, but he has the threat of it and that's enough; that is Wales's forte.

We know England are big enough and strong enough to keep going through the phases, but we can't afford to do that, so we have to strike much earlier and in space. We can do it because we have this inherent skill of ball using but to succeed we have to re-establish our game, get back to the instinctive outside-half who will try all ways to break down the opposition, be it by running the ball or by using a variety of tactical kicks, by making them hesitate, by out-thinking them. You don't achieve that throwing aimless, long passes for the sake of it. There have to be better ways of using the ball.

Part of the problem stems from having New Zealanders as coaches. They don't understand the Welsh attitude to rugby, the movement of the ball and creation of space. They are not used to that, don't know how to coach it, don't know how to use it. Which is why I am pleased that we now have a Welsh coach in charge and already there are signs that we will return to our traditional strengths.

That Dawes was surrounded by enormously talented players in every department must in no way be allowed to undermine the importance of his captaincy skills. It is easy to fall into a misguided sense of judgement by thinking that with such a star-studded team Wales couldn't fail, to be forgiven for suggesting that, with such talent available, who needs a captain? Wales did, and in a desperately close match at Murrayfield, decided by a touchline conversion after great adventure among the backs, and again in a classic encounter in the Parisian sun it was John Dawes who steadied the ship, calmed, cajoled, guided and even reprimanded that abundance of talent. As would be the case with John Lloyd 12 months later, it is not unfair to suggest that it was one of Wales's unsung heroes who directed the great entertainment that was on offer whenever Wales played in the early 1970s.

I have no doubt that centre is the best position to captain the team from, with the proviso that the man has to be suitable. He has to be worth his place and someone the players will respect. When I became national coach, there were two new centres so I couldn't put this philosophy into practice; I had to look elsewhere. Gareth was the most recent captain but I wanted to take the responsibility away from him, so whoever I appointed had to be able to wear the mantle of taking over from the world's greatest scrum-half. Gareth was an instinctive player who performed at a level few could ever aspire to, but if things were going wrong he took it upon himself as captain to put it right whereas the answer may have been to use other people; he couldn't always see that. My choice had to be someone Gareth would respect and that person was Mervyn Davies. I also felt that if there wasn't a suitable candidate in the centre then the back row was the next best option. The half-backs tend to be too near the game, they need to be free and instinctive, but in the centre and back row you have a bit more time.

A simple, basic skill which all rugby players should possess, particularly those who elect to play among the backs, is the ability to both give and take a pass accurately and at pace. This may be stating the obvious but a season spent watching the modern game will prove that for many players, even those at the highest level, it is a skill which still has to be mastered. Sitting in a room with video footage of John Dawes should form part of a player's rugby education, as he would see a master craftsman at work. This was Dawes's great skill and, coupled with an exceptional rugby brain, he was able to use it to release those around him with devastating effect.

John Dawes led the 1971 British Lions in New Zealand with great distinction and repeated the feat against the same opponents for the Barbarians, historic landmarks in the history of British rugby which tend to lead people into remembering John Dawes as a long-term Welsh captain, something which is far from the case. Six matches spread over three years which culminated in the 1971 Grand Slam were followed by the Lions tour in the summer of what was a vintage year, but how much more would there be?

I hadn't given retirement any thought. The London Welsh boys in the Lions party didn't resume playing until November but when I started training again I quickly realised that I wasn't enjoying it. I always had to work at my training because I wasn't that gifted, always had to train a little bit harder and a little more often than other people. International rugby is very demanding and the training sessions meant a long journey from London and on principle we were never late, but once that enthusiasm goes you have to consider the situation and I knew that if I had lost the enjoyment of training, I wasn't going to perform to the required level. Once those feelings ebb a little you shouldn't be in the international arena because you'll be found out. I hadn't discussed it with anyone until Clive came to London Welsh and asked if I was OK for the coming championship. I told him how I felt and he accepted it, didn't put any pressure on me to reconsider, just respected my decision. There were no regrets.

I'd started coaching at London Welsh and thought that I might get the opportunity to take this further, in due course expecting Carwyn James to take over from Clive as national coach and stay in the job for ten years. Based in London I had no idea of the politics which were at work in Wales, Carwyn's demands to be sole selector and his Plaid Cymru associations, but he was successful and at the bottom of it all was jealousy. It was a Welsh trait. If you knew Carwyn, you appreciated that he was a listener and always took on board other people's opinions, and I believe that, for whatever reason, he was misinterpreted and once again Welsh rugby shot itself in the foot. He was quite distraught by it all. It was very sad but the outcome for me was a much quicker return to the international game than I ever expected.

There was a return to New Zealand in 1977 as coach of the British Lions, a tour which he feels would have been successful but for the weather: it rained virtually every day for three months. John Dawes left his mark on Welsh rugby as player, coach and administrator and went on to become coaching adviser to the WRU in 1980, a position he held for ten years.

Circa 2005 he has all but given up trying to influence the way the game is played at Old Deer Park, his touchline comments regarding the search for space largely falling on deaf ears, and it is as a chorister that he now seeks his active pleasures. Nevertheless his legacy to Welsh rugby is monumental and it is doubtful that there have been any players better qualified to captain Wales than John Dawes.

* * *

Partnering Dawes in the centre in three of the Five Nations matches of 1971 was Ebbw Vale's Arthur Lewis. Very much in the same mould, Lewis became the first player from the club to captain Wales when two seasons later he led winning sides against England and Ireland but suffered a 10–9 reversal in Edinburgh. There is no doubt that following the defeat Wales performed much better to beat Ireland, which made the decision to drop the captain for the final match of the season all the more strange, as rarely are winning captains removed during the championship.

> I know I wasn't a favourite with selector Harry Bowcott in particular and I later learned that he never voted for me. He was a London Welsh man and naturally pushed for the club's players to be selected but I felt some of them were found wanting, only included in the team on the back of the great London Welsh players who were representing Wales at the time. One of the good things about the current set-up is that players are picked on form, the issue of which club you play for no longer coming into it, but that never used to be the case and I'm sure there would have been more caps if I had played for one of the more fashionable clubs. Not long after I joined Ebbw Vale there was a chance to go to Newport coupled with the promise of a Welsh trial but I was happy where I was and possibly suffered as a result of that. I was 28 when I won my first cap and maybe if I had moved I would have been capped earlier, but I've no regrets, I got there in the end.

Arthur Lewis was originally selected to lead Wales against the All Blacks in December 1972 but a hamstring injury forced his withdrawal and it was Delme Thomas who captained the team to a controversial defeat. The injury, which became an ongoing problem, first occurred in 1971 when it forced him to miss the visit to Murrayfield. He picked it up in club training the week before the match and his first reaction was not to report it to the selectors, but the following day with the help of Gerry Lewis, Wales's physiotherapist, he concocted the story that it was done 'running for a bus'. He explains, 'I never really shook it off and it recurred a couple of times on the '71 Lions tour preventing me from making any serious challenge for a Test place.'

Captaincy holds little fear for the men appointed to lead Wales but where many are in agreement is on the fearsome matter of the captain's speech given at the after-match function. The build-up to the match and events on the field are nothing compared with the ordeal that, win or lose, waits in store.

I'd always been a captain, at school, at Crumlin and at Ebbw Vale, and I felt no pressure from the playing side of the role but the one thing I feared, if that is the right word, was the after-match speaking. I used to dread that. As a rugby player it wasn't something you were used to, you do a lot of it once you finish playing but not before and I was a little bit uncomfortable with it.

Clive Rowlands would give a team talk at the hotel before we left for the ground which left little more to be said. For half an hour he would be there whipping up a storm and the boys would feel ten feet tall but it was quite comical really, some of the older players were so laid-back. Dai Morris would have his little portable on listening to the racing.

Injury denied Arthur Lewis his opportunity to lead Wales against New Zealand in what was the first of two controversial matches played between the countries during the 1970s. When they met next as part of the WRU's centenary celebrations in 1980 there was nothing remotely controversial about the outcome, the All Blacks spoiling both the party and another centre's introduction to the Welsh captaincy.

Steve Fenwick was one of the new faces who blazed a trail in the famous Welsh victory at the Parc des Princes in 1975. A prodigious goal kicker, Fenwick scored a total of 152 points in his 30 appearances, the last 3 of them as captain. It being the season which celebrated 100 years of Welsh international rugby the union naturally had high hopes that 1980–81 would be remembered for some on-the-field success, a Grand Slam or at least a Triple Crown. The All Blacks had already scotched any dreams of an unbeaten season by the time Bridgend's Steve Fenwick led Wales into the Five Nations Championship, which began with a steal against England, a teasing dummy from the base of a scrum enticing the over-keen Clive Woodward to encroach offside in front of the English posts. Fenwick kicked the winning penalty but there followed a lacklustre display against Scotland which ended in defeat, heralding the end of two notable international careers, those of J.P.R. Williams and captain Steve Fenwick himself.

Like John Dawes and Arthur Lewis before him Fenwick was a

British Lion, touring New Zealand in 1977, and four years later, following the Welsh centenary season, he turned professional but not with one of the better-known league clubs based in the north of England. Fenwick joined the newly formed Cardiff City RLFC along with several other experienced union players nearing the ends of their careers. The venture was another attempt to introduce the 13-man code in South Wales, but like so many before, the club could not compete with the established union game and folded after a couple of seasons.

* * *

The final episode in the story of the centres who have captained Wales takes us back to the 1950s, a period which saw three distinguished players suffer mixed fortunes in their time as Welsh captain.

Newport's Malcolm Thomas was an instructor sub-lieutenant with the Royal Navy stationed in Portsmouth when he was selected for his first cap in 1949, one month short of his 20th birthday. Reading the *News Chronicle* he saw the headline 'Changes in the Welsh team to face France' and on closer perusal found he was one of four new caps included following consecutive defeats by Scotland and Ireland. Whether in the centre or on the wing Thomas played in every Welsh match through the next three seasons and toured Australia and New Zealand with the British Lions in 1950, returning nine years later, but a broken leg ruled him out of contention for the visit to South Africa in 1955.

It was in the Royal Navy that Malcolm Thomas was first introduced to the art of captaincy. He led their team to victory in the Inter Services Championship at Twickenham and also captained Devonport Services in 1950–51. Three consecutive seasons as captain at Newport followed later and in 1957 he was asked to lead Wales against England in the opening match of the Five Nations. Malcolm Thomas is convinced that the team selection for both his outings as captain was flawed and the two narrow defeats, 3–0 to England and 9–6 in Scotland, could possibly have been avoided. One example was the recall of Ken Jones, who played at Murrayfield.

Ken was not at his best in 1957 but he was very difficult to leave out because he was so quick and such a valued player, and I can understand why he accepted the invitation to play. A similar situation happened to me when I returned from the 1959 tour. Dai Jones, one of the selectors, wanted me to play against England at Twickenham but I had decided to finish and turned it down, and I am sure it was the right decision. I played in the Jubilee match at Twickenham in October and I was through a gap with the line at my mercy, deciding where to put the ball down, when David Hewitt caught me from behind and took my legs from under me. I decided immediately after the match that the time had come to call it a day.

In an international career spanning a decade Malcolm Thomas won twenty-seven caps, went on two British Lions tours and gained invaluable experience as a club captain. On the subject of international captaincy he is very forthright.

Captain of Wales is such an important position he needs to have input into team selection but in our day this was far from the case. You were simply told that you were the captain and left to get on with it, which was far from satisfactory. We travelled to Edinburgh by train, a particularly long journey, and I asked the selectors when we were having our pre-match run-out. We were allocated 2 p.m. on Friday, shortly after our arrival, which proved far from suitable. Nobody wanted to knuckle down and I remember Bryn Meredith telling me that the forwards had had enough despite the fact that they were not binding together, something which had been apparent against England, but I was unable to impose my views and disciplines, and come the match there didn't appear to be any clarity of thought as to how we were going to beat sides. I wasn't going to suggest what should be done in the scrum or the lineout but felt what should be instilled in the team was the pattern of play we were going to adopt and this is where somebody like John Gwilliam was strong. He made sure everybody knew what was expected of them within a certain framework.

At Twickenham in 1950 I remember Jack Matthews telling me to get the ball out to the wing at the first opportunity. The ball was won. Willis to Cleaver to Jack on to me and a pass out to Ken, which was intercepted, and we suddenly found ourselves five points down. I knew that to kick for position was the better option, which would also have been part of the game plan, but I followed Jack's instruction. Gwilliam took me aside, had a quiet word and told me next time to put the ball in the stand. He was quite clear what he wanted and was able to explain it to us, which was his great strength – communication, that and the ability to pull people together and get them to do great things.

Thomas was injured at Murrayfield in 1957 and unable to take his place against Ireland, a match Wales won, prompting the selectors to make just one change for the visit to Paris, which saw another win bring the season to a satisfactory conclusion. When the Australian Wallabies were beaten two weeks before the start of the 1958 Five Nations, there seemed little reason for change but what had not gone unnoticed was the lack of stability in the centre – three different pairings had appeared in the run of success. And when the team to play at Twickenham was announced there was a recall for Malcolm Thomas who went on to win a further four caps before the right time to finish presented itself.

* * *

Cardiff Station, 19 January 1952. Two friends meet to catch the train to London, destination Twickenham. Dai has a confession to make – he has left the match tickets at home. Gwyn, being the more fleet of foot, makes the dash to Dai's Grangetown home, returning with minutes to spare. Settled in their seats on the train Gwyn has some bad news for Dai. While picking up the tickets he caught Dai's 'missus' and the lodger in bed together. Dai ponders this information before telling Gwyn that he too is the bearer of bad news – 'Bleddyn isn't playing!'

Bleddyn Williams was one of eight brothers to play for Cardiff either side of the Second World War. First capped against England in 1947 after playing in seven of the uncapped Victory Internationals, Williams was joined in the Welsh team by several future stars, Jack Matthews among them. To talk about Williams to the exclusion of Matthews or vice versa is impossible. Like Laurel and Hardy, Tom and Jerry, fish and chips, in rugby parlance the names Matthews and Williams are synonymous. With Cardiff, Wales and the British Lions the pair were among the dominant names in the game during the years immediately following the war. They were a potent centre partnership for Cardiff, but an abundance of midfield talent was at the Welsh selectors' disposal with Billy Cleaver, Lewis Jones, and Malcolm Thomas in particular giving them plenty of options which they fully exploited. Jack Matthews played three matches on the wing in an attempt to squeeze a pint into a half-pint glass and, in fact, only paired up with Williams in the centre for Wales on five occasions, a figure matched on the 1950 British Lions tour to Australia and New Zealand when the partnership was selected in five of the six Tests.

Jack Matthews won the last of 17 caps in Paris in 1951 when the selectors chose him to lead the team in place of an out-of-favour John Gwilliam and he became the 60th player to captain Wales in what was its 200th capped match. Like Bleddyn Williams, Matthews featured prominently in the post-war series of Victory Internationals and also played in two Red Cross Internationals, organised as fundraising events, partnering Wilf Wooler in the centre.

Bleddyn Williams had an early taste of what captaining an international team entailed when he was selected to lead Wales in the uncapped match against the Kiwis in 1947 in place of Haydn Tanner, who was with the army in Italy and unable to get home. Two weeks later he won a first cap when England were the visitors to the Arms Park, but at outside-half. Against Scotland he was picked in the centre where he remained until injuries started to have an impact on his burgeoning rugby career. He was chosen to lead the team at Twickenham in 1950, again as replacement for Tanner who had retired, but injury saw his late withdrawal from a side that went on to win the Grand Slam under John Gwilliam.

> I was injured in the final trial, tore all the ligaments in my knee, but the selectors decided to include me in the team as captain, hoping the injury would clear up, but following a club game at Swansea it was obvious that I wouldn't be able to play at Twickenham and a couple of days before the match I was replaced. By this time I had given my player's ticket to my mother, a great follower of the game, but when I approached the WRU about another they refused and but for Wilf Wooler, who managed to get me one through contacts in England, the originally selected Welsh captain would not have seen the match. Looking back it really is extraordinary what the players had to put up with.

Williams missed the whole of the Grand Slam campaign but such was his reputation he was given a chance to prove his fitness before the British Lions side to tour in the summer was selected. 'When Wales were playing France for the Grand Slam, I played for Cardiff at Bath and came through the match with no recurrence of the injury which prompted the selectors to include me in the tour party.' Two years later it was a bout of influenza which forced him to once again pull out of the team at Twickenham, an occasion which Jack Matthews reluctantly recalls.

I had never played at Bath. The Cardiff fixture always fell on an international weekend and as I was dropped from the Welsh team I was expecting to put this right. At midnight on the Friday I got a telephone call from Bryce Jenkins, secretary of Cardiff, who said that Bleddyn had cried off and that I was playing, which was stupid because Alun Thomas was a reserve with the team in London, but he insisted that I was playing and told me to be on the train in the morning. The Welsh team were having their pre-match lunch at the Winning Post in Twickenham and as soon as I arrived Enoch Rees, chairman of the Big Five, confirmed my selection but not before I had told him how stupid it was bringing me all the way to London when they had Alun at their disposal. A quarter of an hour before kick-off the selectors came into the dressing-room, called captain John Gwilliam out and then sent him back to tell me that I wasn't going to play after all. I made my feelings known in no uncertain terms and told the selectors that they should never call on me to play for Wales again.

Jack Matthews was taken at his word and was never invited back. In 1953, following a poor home performance against England, the Big Five once again turned to Williams to lead Wales and this time he made the kick-off at Murrayfield and scored two tries in a convincing Welsh win. A home victory against Ireland at St Helen's and another in Paris brought the season to an end – next up it was the fourth New Zealand All Blacks.

Wales were 2–1 up in the series when the teams took the field on 19 December 1953. Two hours later Wales led 3–1, an outrageous cross-kick by a back-row forward, the luck of the bounce and an international sprinter securing a 13-8 victory in the last quarter of a fiercely contested encounter. It was Bleddyn Williams who became the third Welsh captain to taste victory against the Southern hemisphere juggernaut that is New Zealand rugby.

The only time we gave any particular attention to preparation was when we played New Zealand. Following the Lions tour in 1950 many of the team had a lot of experience playing against the All Blacks and before Cardiff were due to meet them some players – Rex Willis, Cliff Morgan and myself among them – went to Bristol and Llanelli to watch the tourists, following which we had an idea of what our game plan should be. We were much better behind the scrum but they had a very good back row, who broke out quickly, so we felt that on our put-in to the lineout we should throw the ball long and tie them up. Cardiff won a great victory and with so many of the team involved with Wales it was a case of the same again, but it must be said that these were certainly tactics which the players themselves had identified, with absolutely no input whatsoever from the selectors.

Yet again, come the start of the 1954 Five Nations Championship Williams was unavailable for selection and he missed the first three matches, only returning for the home defeat of Scotland. The following season saw his final appearance for Wales, once again reunited with the captaincy, appropriately at Cardiff, and once again he led a winning side. The mud and generally poor conditions at the Arms Park were not to Williams's liking and despite leading Wales to a 3–0 victory over England he had won his last cap, but the result brought his total to five wins out of five matches in charge – England, France, Ireland, Scotland and New Zealand the vanquished.

* * *

Of the 25 centres to captain Wales several can lay claim to being among the finest: from Arthur Gould, Gwyn Nicholls and Billy Trew in the early years, Claud Davey and signs of a revival in the 1930s, and Bleddyn Williams and John Dawes in the post-war era. Six players who go some way to explaining why there has been a preference for Welsh selectors to vest the captaincy in those found in the middle of the field, a preference not seen in any other country. Six players who between them led Wales fifty-seven times from the centre, thirty-nine of the matches won with a total of a hundred and twenty-five tries scored – figures significantly higher than the national average. They also led three Grand Slam-winning teams but perhaps more significantly, in Nicholls, Davey and Williams we have the three captains who, by the end of the 2005–06 season, had led Wales to their only victories against New Zealand.

How much should be read into such facts and figures? Statistics can often be massaged and manufactured to produce the required information, not necessarily produced to give a complete picture, rather to support an argument. But that would not appear to be the case here. Billy Trew and John Dawes did lead Wales to three Grand Slams and Wales were led from the centre each time the All Blacks were beaten – fact. Centre also produced some of the most influential captains of the

Golden Eras – again, fact. There are those who would look to question such information, suggest that there are other mitigating factors which should not be overlooked – the quality of the other players, even the quality of the opposition. And they may well have a point but there are times when coincidence has to be ignored and the bottom line studied more closely. This is one such time and it will be left to the final analysis to weigh up all the information and draw some conclusions but they will be based on fact and in the case of the centre the facts do appear to speak for themselves.

IX

A SPLENDID ISOLATION: WING THREE-QUARTER

The prerequisite of a wing three-quarter is the ability to score tries. Wings are not measured by the number of tackles they make, the number of drop goals they convert, the number of points they accumulate from place kicks or their ability to kick out of hand – they are measured quite simply by the number of tries they score.

> The ball must travel from the base of the scrum, via the scrum-half, the stand-off half and two centres to the wing, so quickly that a wing forward, starting from the base of the scrum at the same time, cannot reach the corner flag before the wing gets there.

Rugby football at its most simplistic, written by Rowe Harding in his *Rugby: Reminiscences and Opinions*, published in 1929. Times have changed. Rarely in the modern game is the ball transferred from the set piece to the wing in such workmanlike fashion and yet despite the many changes rugby union has witnessed since 1929 surely this should still be prioritised as a means of crossing the try-line – but it isn't. Too often the ball is carried back into the contact area to create second, third, fourth, fifth and even more phases of play before there is the remotest likelihood of the wing receiving a pass. Regularly, forwards who should be elsewhere are seen interfering with the movement of the ball, often losing it in the tackle and forfeiting an attacking opportunity that was so glaringly obvious to everybody watching on. Rugby union has arrived at a stage in its development which sees wings having to go in search of the ball if they want to get their hands on it and in doing so often leaving gaping holes in the defence for the opposition to exploit if it can secure turnover possession. Despite the game evolving in such a manner, with the influence of rugby league prominent in defensive strategies in particular, what remains unclear is whether defences are, in fact, that good or attacks that bad.

Plenty of splendid tries are scored to satisfy the casual supporter and the armchair spectator and even those who have a long association with the sport can't help but be impressed with the overall fitness and physical presence of players in the top flight, but rugby union in the professional era has changed beyond recognition. The reasons why are not that obvious, as the lawmakers at the IRB have to be immediately absolved of any implication, with no significant amendments to the Laws in recent years which can be held responsible for the new strategies. The television moguls are the more likely instigators of the modern game. Having laid out enormous sums to lay claim to the sport, they understandably wanted a product which would appeal to a new audience. It had to be attractive to watch, end-to-end stuff with an abundance of tries, hence the Super 12 which shows an apparent disregard for the minor Laws of the game with referees regularly allowing play to continue after obvious handling errors, forward passes, etc.

Can it really be that there are too many tries in the union game? They are actively encouraged, after all, with bonus points awarded for crossing the line, but familiarity if not exactly breeding contempt does introduce a certain laissez-faire when try after try is being run in. The Laws of Association Football haven't been tweaked to ensure the 7–6 or 10–3 scoreline but there is more interest in the round ball than ever before so why quantity is now preferable to quality among rugby union followers is a mystery – the game is in danger of selling its very soul.

The scoring of so many tries doesn't immediately answer the question of whether defences are that good or attacks that bad – in fact, it contradicts it, suggesting it be turned around. However, the vast majority of tries are now scored after a multitude of phases in a sport in which the turnover reigns supreme, taking the ball off the opposition in the tackle area and then quickly putting it to good use before the defensive patterns can be put in place. As a result of this new approach to a more open, less interrupted game what has been overlooked is the increase in penalty awards and the sin bin being used more than ever before, all of which has been brought about as the contact area lends itself to an abundance of offences which the more simplistic earlier version of the game avoided.

And the player most affected by this revolutionary new concept of what rugby union is all about? – the wing three-quarter. Not quite finding himself in such splendid isolation as in earlier days, he is nevertheless more likely to receive possession as a result of some wayward kicking by the opposition than by any constructive move made by his own team. And yet wings still score the tries, but how many more would the quickest men on the field get if they were used properly? It's astonishing the number of times a frustrated wing is seen head in hands after a clear overlap has been abused by a forward intent on taking the ball back into the contact zone. For goodness sake, these guys are quick, they know where the try-line is, and they know how to get there. Give them the ball!

* * *

The list of players who have led Wales from the wing includes some of the best-known names in Welsh rugby but it is for their try-scoring ability rather than their captaincy skills that the majority of them are remembered, only Willie Llewellyn and Ieuan Evans able to claim recognition in both departments. Six of their number arrived at the captaincy without ever actively seeking it, a variety of circumstances leading to their names being added to the roll of honour. Injuries to incumbents will always play a part in the game's fortunes and misfortunes, added to which can be the recognition of a job well done, the equalling of records set and even the ability to speak a foreign language. And if any player thinks his international days are behind him, there is some comfort to be had from the story leading up to Tom Pearson's 25 minutes as Welsh captain – surely in itself a record of sorts?

Tom Pearson was used to creating records. In 170 appearances for Cardiff during the seasons 1889–95 he scored 128 tries, 40 in 1893–94, which stood as a club record for over 50 years, until it was eventually broken by Bleddyn Williams in the 1947–48 season. He played with distinction for Wales, winning twelve caps between 1891 and 1898, the last three as a Newport player, before announcing his retirement, but there was more to come. One year on, Newport persuaded Pearson, still only twenty-seven, to resume his playing career and he made a further forty appearances for the club over the next four years and in his final months in the game, at St Helen's, Swansea, on 10 January 1903 Tom Pearson led Wales against England for twenty-five minutes before injury forced him to leave the field. Having scored a try he then watched his replacement, Jehoida Hodges, who was taken out of the scrum, score a hat-trick in a comprehensive 21–5 victory. What might have been for Tom Pearson had already been achieved by Willie Llewellyn against the same opponents at the same ground four years earlier. In an even more convincing 26–3 victory Llewellyn scored four tries in a devastating debut, setting the tone for an international career which saw him cross the line sixteen times in twenty appearances.

First capped from Lwynypia, Willie Llewellyn represented London Welsh and Newport before winning his final cap against New Zealand in 1905 as a Penygraig player. In a sequence of five matches between 1904 and 1905 he led Wales to victory over Scotland and a narrow defeat in Belfast before becoming the fourth captain to enjoy a Triple Crown. Later in the year victory over the All Blacks brought Willie Llewellyn's rugby career to a fitting end, one which had lasted barely six years and concluded a couple of weeks short of his 28th birthday. Certainly young, but unlike Tom Pearson, Llewellyn was not destined to return.

In 1904 he toured Australia and New Zealand with the British Isles team, scoring four tries in the three-match series with Australia, but failing to add to his total in the first-ever match between a British touring team and New Zealand, played at Wellington on 13 August. Another Welsh wing to play in the four matches was Edward 'Teddy' Morgan of London Welsh, who had won the first of 16 caps in 1902 and scored 14 tries for Wales including the most famous of them all.

Thirty minutes into the match at Cardiff, Wales heeled from a scrum in the middle of the field ten yards into their opponents' half. A reverse pass from Dickie Owen was picked up by Cliff Pritchard, who feigned to move infield before transferring the ball to Teddy Morgan, who rounded his opposite number before beating the full-back to score in the corner. A try like so many others: quick transferring of the ball, a little bit of craft, three points. But Teddy Morgan's try was different. Teddy Morgan's try was special. Teddy Morgan's try beat the 1905 All Blacks. Forget Bob Deans and the hoohah which has surrounded his disallowed effort ever since that December day 100 years ago, the 'did he, didn't he' nonsense that rears its head every time the two nations meet. Rather, remember that Teddy Morgan did score a try on the day, one which has gone into the game's folklore. An undisputed try which, together with Dean's effort, sowed the seeds for the great fixture that Wales against New Zealand has become.

Nobody in 1905 could have anticipated the impact one match would have on Welsh rugby or the reverence in which Teddy Morgan's name would be held a century later but on his final appearance in the red jersey he was handed the captaincy in recognition of services rendered and no player was more deserving. Morgan led Wales on 2 March 1908 against France, the first meeting between the two countries. A comfortable Welsh victory saw the captain end his career scoring two of his team's nine tries but it was over on the right wing that Cardiff's Reg Gibbs stared immortality in the face and then turned his back on it.

Nine years earlier Willie Llewellyn had created a Welsh record with his four tries against England, a record that several players have since equalled but, against France, Gibbs had the opportunity to stand alone as the scorer of most tries in a match. With four already to his credit he crossed the line for a fifth but decided to place the ball under the posts only to be tackled by a French player and lose possession.

Reg Gibbs was first capped in 1906 in the aftermath of the New Zealand victory which had seen Wales field seven forwards and eight backs for the first time. The selectors deliberated over the new and more recognised format of eight forwards and seven backs through the next six matches and Gibbs's inclusion in the team was very much dependent on which option they elected to use. Initially, he was chosen as an outside-half or extra back but when the selection committee finally found in favour of the traditional formation still in use today, Percy Bush, Richard Jones and Billy Trew were the serious contenders for the outside-half role and if the speedy Gibbs was to be included it had to be elsewhere. After scoring one try in four matches he won a further twelve caps on the wing from where he ran in another sixteen, ending his career having scored more international tries than the number of caps won. Another player to captain Wales because of injury – Billy Trew the unfortunate victim – Gibbs led the side to a comfortable victory over Ireland in Dublin. Despite scoring what had by now become an almost customary try Gibbs had to play second fiddle to Cardiff colleague John Williams, who ran in a hat-trick from the opposite wing.

Williams was another prolific try scorer. Where Gibbs had scored ninety in 130 appearances for the Blue and Blacks, Williams scored 150 tries in 199 matches. For eight seasons the pair dominated the scoring at Cardiff and the fact that only thirty-six matches out of the 257 played were lost confirms the strength of the club in the first decade of the twentieth century. Like Gibbs, John Williams took his try-scoring ability onto the international arena, crossing for 17 in 17 matches, but when it became his turn to lead Wales at the Parc des Princes it was for an entirely different reason than those which had seen Gibbs, and many others who led Wales only once, appointed. John Williams was fluent in French and would be comfortable with the expected captain's speech at the after-match dinner – *Très bien!*

What, if anything, is there to be learnt from the five players who captained Wales from the wing in the early 1900s? How much should be placed on the fact that between them they led Wales to eight victories in nine matches? Some would argue that during this first Golden Era any of the 15 players would have led such a talented team to success after success but that is far from certain. What must be remembered is that in its formative years rugby football was very much a forward-dominated game with a kick-and-rush style of play which usually resulted in the dominant pack securing victory. The arrival of Frank Hancock and his then revolutionary three-quarter formation made up of four players may have taken a while to become accepted but Wales showed total commitment to the system from 1888 onwards, with only a brief period of doubt following the New Zealand tour of 1905 when a variation was introduced to counteract the tourists' inclusion of a 'roving' forward.

Wales fully adopted the four three-quarter line-up five years before England, Ireland and Scotland and while it had no immediate effect on results it was through the next generation of players that its impact was fully realised. The stars of the Golden Era knew no other system and it was on their elevation into the Welsh team that the benefit gleaned from those five years during which Wales had stolen a march on her rivals really began to come through and reflect in the results. It now made sense that an experienced player in the three-quarter line would be in a good position to dictate the pattern of play and so it proved, with only two forwards chosen to lead the team during that first decade of the twentieth century – Harding and Travers.

For the first time Welsh rugby had led the way and with such devastating success it was inevitable that other countries would follow the lead, more confirmation that innovation is infinitely better than imitation.

* * *

Enough has already been written about the gloom and doom that surrounded Welsh rugby during the 1920s and, while opposing the argument that any player could have led Wales during the early 1900s, it is difficult not to concur that no player in any position could have led Welsh rugby out of the mire in which it found itself. Following Tom Parker's impressive record during 1921–23, the next seven seasons saw Wales play thirty matches under seventeen different captains and introduce ninety-nine new caps, and it is an unfortunate fact that at no other time have so few players whose names are now recognised wherever the game is played pulled on the red jersey.

Few in number they may have been but among them are to be found some fine individuals and there is no doubting the pedigree of Swansea wing three-quarter Rowe Harding. First capped at the age of 21, a year later on the occasion of his sixth cap he led Wales for the first time in the 1923–24 season's final match in Paris. He was then a member of the British Isles team which toured South Africa in the following summer, playing in three of the Tests. Cambridge University followed, where four Blues were won and during which time he took his number of international appearances to seventeen, but the poor Welsh performances of the time are highlighted by the fact that Rowe Harding scored only five tries for his country. His final game in 1928, the fourth as captain, was played at his club ground and England were the visitors. An unforced error on the slippery surface saw Harding beaten by his opposite number who crossed for what proved to be the decisive score, and but for this he could have boasted an unbeaten record as Welsh captain following the win in Paris, a draw with England and victory over the Irish in 1926.

Rowe Harding enjoyed a glittering public life. First a County Court judge, he later took his seat on the Circuit Court, all the while assuming responsible positions in a variety of fields. Politics, charitable organisations and distinguished Welsh institutions invited him to represent them, including the WRU on which he served as vice-president. His book *Rugby: Reminiscences and Opinions* touched on many controversial topics, not least among them the limitations imposed on the game by its strictly amateur ethos – the unavailability of many of the best players to undertake extended overseas tours due to work commitments, compared with the 'professional' attitude at Cambridge in the build-up to the Varsity match when all else was put on hold. He wrote of grants being made available to tourists to ensure they were not out of pocket, which would enable the leading players to travel, of public subscriptions being allowed and how he saw the game being more in the domain of the legislators than the players: 'If rugby is a game for the players, surely they should be consulted in matters which directly concern them.' Rowe Harding was certainly outspoken at a time when the impact of rugby league was taking its toll on the game in Wales and his comments were not particularly well received by those in authority, but the passage of time has shown that a visionary he certainly was.

* * *

The 1948 Olympic Games which opened in London on 14 August are best remembered for the exploits of Emil Zatopek and Fanny Blankers-Koen. There were only three gold medals – in rowing and yachting – for the host nation to celebrate but among the minor medals won on the track was a silver in the men's 4 x 100 yards relay. In 41.3 seconds John Archer, John Gregory, Ken Jones and Alistair McCorquodale carried the baton around the Wembley track to finish in second place behind the USA. The Great Britain squad was presented with gold medals following the disqualification of the Americans but these had to be returned the following day after an appeal was successfully upheld.

The athletic achievements of Kenneth Jeffrey Jones are best recorded elsewhere but suffice to say he could run. To be fast on a running track is one thing but to be able to take that speed and transfer it to the less than favourable surfaces found on rugby pitches is something else. That Ken Jones won 43 consecutive caps for Wales breaking all records for the time, not only in Wales but among the other home unions, is confirmation enough that the finely tuned sprinter could take his speed to the rugby field and put it to devastating effect. This, without any allowances being made for the fact that even out on the wing there were times when there was nowhere to hide and the physicality of the sport had to be coped with. Ken Jones coped – and how.

I was very fortunate to avoid any serious injuries and was always available for selection although following the war I did break my wrist twice while a student at Loughborough. I'm sure that my athletics training helped me escape the normal strains and pulls and I remember taking fitness sessions at Newport in an attempt to introduce some of this experience to rugby.

For ten consecutive seasons Ken Jones's name must have been the first the selectors wrote on the team sheet. He played in all forty Five

Nations matches between 1947–56 and scored eight tries in the two Grand Slam years of 1950 and 1952. In addition to championship matches Jones represented Wales against the three major touring sides and scored the winning try in the 1953 victory over New Zealand, a rugby nation which needed no reminding of his great skill.

> Ken Jones may be an Olympic runner, but he brings far more than mere speed to the rugby field. His determination, grand handling whilst going at top, ability to make the best of every opportunity and general all-round aptitude made him a class rugby winger. Well-built and strong, Jones thrilled the crowds with his pace and beautiful style. Altogether he registered 16 tries in the 16 matches in which he took part, and a number were classics.

It would be impossible to better summarise Ken Jones in so few words than this, from the 1951 *Rugby Almanack of New Zealand* which included him as one of its five players of the year. There would have been no surprise across the North and South Islands when news was received that Ken Jones had broken Kiwi hearts in Cardiff.

Rather than wait for him to beat it, on his equalling Dickie Owen's record number of caps in 1954 the selectors decided to honour Ken Jones with the Welsh captaincy.

> The match had been postponed earlier in the season and was the last championship match to be played at St Helen's but apart from the usual formalities and the after-dinner speech I don't remember any other notable incidents other than it being a great honour to captain the team. I was happy leading from the wing where you have a good perspective of the game. I can understand why the position has its detractors but look at Ieuan Evans.

Ken Jones led a winning team but was not among the four try scorers and although he won a further nine caps what was not appreciated at the time was that the try against the All Blacks would be his last for Wales. 'That was something I hadn't realised – the centres must have all been more comfortable passing to their left!'

Considering his magnificent career one is left wondering if perhaps the selectors were right to recall Ken Jones after omitting him for the opening match in 1957. He had won 43 consecutive caps, breaking all records in the process. He'd had an unblemished ten years of international rugby which had ended with a Welsh win in Cardiff and then, following defeat by England and now thirty-five years old, he was included in a losing side at Murrayfield in his 44th and final appearance. For those who like their packages neatly tied it was a match too far, but for Ken Jones it was another opportunity to play for his country and he was never going to let Wales down.

* * *

Baseball star Ty Cobb, in Grantland Rice's *The Tumult and the Shouting*, is credited with stating that 'Speed is a great asset; but it's greater when it's combined with quickness – and there's a big difference.' In rugby terms we can go some way to understanding this distinction by comparing Ken Jones with another who set Welsh hearts beating with his dashes down the right wing – Thomas Gerald Reames Davies. There is no doubt that over a hundred metres on a running track there would be only one winner but on a rugby field the contest would be much closer, and it is this quickness which was Gerald Davies's great gift rather than the out-and-out speed as demonstrated by Ken Jones. Of course Davies was fast, the footage of his many memorable tries gives ample evidence of that, but where perhaps opponents knew that Jones was going to take the shortest route to the line, relying almost totally on his electrifying speed, with Gerald Davies there were many more options to consider when trying to defend against such a talent.

That Davies won his first 11 caps as a centre confirms an ability to work the more confined space of the midfield, but it was on the right wing that he established his legendary status in the world game, a conversion which then Welsh coach Clive Rowlands insists on taking all the credit for.

He's probably right. In New Zealand in 1969 two of the three wings in the party were injured and as a matter of necessity Clive moved me from the centre to the right wing. I wasn't happy at all. I liked centre, liked to be involved, but Clive persuaded me that I could put whatever skills I had to better use in the extra space found on the wing, that more gaps would be created for me out there, but no, I wasn't happy.

There followed a self-imposed sabbatical which saw Davies devote a year to his studies at Cambridge with only the university XV enjoying the benefit of his extraordinary talent as a centre, but in his final year he did lead the team in the Varsity match from the wing before reappearing in the Welsh jersey against England in 1971 in the position he would make his own.

The history of rugby football is full of myths, stories that through the passage of time have been exaggerated in an effort to improve their constant telling and retelling. At Pontypool Park in January 1978 one such myth first saw the light of day, one so outrageous that no subsequent attempts have been made to embellish it. A disbelieving 15,000 spectators saw the indestructible Pontypool beaten in the third round of the Schweppes Challenge Cup by a Cardiff side which spent virtually all the match in its own 22. The final score of 16–11 gives no indication of the dominance established by the home forwards and but for Cardiff captain Gerald Davies, it would have been 'Pooler' who progressed to the next round. What did Davies do? Well, myth has it that he only touched the ball on four occasions and scored four tries and, of course, like all good myths, it is true.

That's the story. It was my favourite game as captain of Cardiff, bringing everything that I had been aiming for in a team together: the team spirit, the character and personalities of the players, the balance of players. We really had to dig out a win in a match in which, by and large, we were overwhelmed but it was good to captain a team who believed they were not going to leave Pontypool Park empty handed. They were terrific and confirmed to me what a captain is for and that, over a period of time, he can garner that spirit in the players, which carries them through to such a victory.

Elsewhere there were also tries aplenty. In forty-six appearances for Wales Gerald Davies scored twenty tries, eighteen of them in his thirty-five outings on the wing with seven during the three Grand Slam years of 1971, 1976 and 1978 in which he played in all but one of the twelve matches.

I missed the final Grand Slam match in 1978 due to injury. Between the Ireland and France matches Cardiff were playing Orrell for the first time in their history and as club captain I felt a sense of duty, an obligation to play. I pulled a hamstring and was forced to withdraw, which goes to show that there is a lot to be said for picking and choosing your games.

A triple Cambridge Blue, he was a member of the outstanding London

Welsh sides of the early 1970s before joining Cardiff, captaining the club in the three seasons 1975–78 with the chance to continue in the role, but events determined otherwise.

> I accepted a fourth term of captaincy at Cardiff knowing perhaps that I might not play but I was at a stage where I couldn't consider playing for the club without being captain. As things turned out I didn't lead the club again because come the start of the season I knew the time had arrived to call it a day.

British Lions tours in 1968 and 1971 meant all that was missing as retirement approached was the honour of captaining his country and it was in winning his 46th and final cap that this omission was corrected. Gerald Davies was first capped against Australia in 1966 and in the summer of 1978 ended his career against the same opponents at Sydney Sports Ground. Wales had undertaken a difficult tour and come the final match were a weary, injury-hit squad and it was Gerald Davies whom manager Clive Rowlands announced to the press would lead the team.

> Terry Cobner was the tour captain but he was among several players unavailable for selection through injury. By the end of the tour we were a tired, beaten team and unfortunately the best 15 did not take the field. Nonetheless, it was a match we should have won, there were some strange refereeing decisions, but I was glad of the opportunity to captain Wales.
>
> I enjoyed captaincy, loved it. Working out the next move, not a tactical move but one away from the field which would make the team better, take it forward. There were people who felt that I didn't have the captaincy earlier because generally I tend to be a quiet person. I'm not a flamboyant extrovert in any way, a quality some believe you must have to be a captain. I think it is a misconception many hold that a captain has to be this loud, blustering, forceful character and I certainly don't agree with it. To me, the main quality of a captain is how you manage the other players, your relationship with them. That's the critical thing, to get the conviction of the players through your own sense of leadership.
>
> There's a similar prejudice as to where the captain should be in relation to a certain position, again one I don't go along with. The captaincy depends on personality, knowledge, understanding, how he responds to others. The wing is supposed to be too far from the

action, the prop too close, but I don't believe that. It doesn't matter where you are. You're leading men and should be measured on your strength of character, how you manage the players and how you convey your ideas to them, not whether you are a second row, number 8, centre, full-back. But regardless of position the role of captain is vital, even today when so much has changed and so many other factors come into play.

What had started with defeat against the Wallabies in Cardiff ended 12 years later in similar vein in Sydney but in between there was much to cherish, moments which defy description, the stuff of legend, the stuff of myth.

* * *

It was not a good vintage for the rugby aficionados of Wales, 1991, more a *vin ordinaire* and a bad one at that. Cooking wine is probably the best a sommelier would say about it. A poor Five Nations, only a draw with Ireland avoiding back-to-back whitewashes, followed by an embarrassing tour to Australia, was not ideal preparation for the second Rugby World Cup, which would see Wales's Pool matches played in Cardiff. Before that tournament could get under way there was one chance to put the show back on the road, a midweek match with France to officially switch on the new floodlights that were now in place at the National Stadium.

Victory was unlikely against a team that had swamped Wales in Paris six months earlier but a level of respectability was hoped for and to a certain extent this was achieved, which must have come as a great relief to new captain Ieuan Evans. Evans won his 24th cap on that floodlit night in Cardiff and the next 27 would see him lead the team with only injury and British Lions duty interrupting the extended run that broke Arthur Gould's record, which had stood for almost a century before Evans finally improved on it in 1994.

Other than at school I hadn't any previous experience of captaincy and then I was presented with this wonderful opportunity. Wales had gone through a torrid three years, poor results and poor performances, which made it an onerous task but it was a responsibility that I held dear, one which may have intimidated a bit at first but one which also inspired me.

The new coaching team of Alan Davies and Bob Norster

wanted a new start which meant a new captain. They basically took a blank sheet of paper, put the names of the players virtually guaranteed their place in the team on it and took it from there. I was a bit of a dark horse because the media were focusing on other players with previous experience of the job at club level. When it came, I was pretty emotional about the appointment, being given the chance to lead the team onto that field of dreams which my heroes before me had graced. I was extremely grateful to Alan and Bob; they took a gamble in putting my name forward at a crucial time, to a certain extent basing their futures on my ability to lead from the right wing, which isn't an ideal position for a captain. It wouldn't be so much of an issue these days because the role has been marginalised, no longer the pivotal appointment that it used to be due to the impact of off-the-field personnel.

Many coaches have become control freaks, denying the players any freedom of thought during the game. I was delighted to see Mike Ruddock make a positive move away from that philosophy, allow players the opportunity to make spontaneous decisions rather than pursue pre-programmed, preordained and structured game plans, which is how it should be. Why pick a player on the basis of his talent, his expertise and experience and then ignore those qualities? Whether that is the coach trying to justify his role, I'm not sure, but it is to the detriment of the game, detracts from what people pay good money to go and watch – the players.

A record run of matches as Welsh captain allowed Ieuan Evans the opportunity to consider the role from every viewpoint, think about all its nuances and the obvious problems that such a responsibility brings with it.

There isn't a particular template that works. Mike Brearley, for example, was a great intellect, a captain who could keep the outrageous talents of an Ian Botham in check, while Martin Johnson would inspire through his belligerence, his sheer bloody-mindedness and his physical presence. Such apparently contradictory characteristics need to be balanced; there is a need to be passionate but it is equally essential to keep a cool head, remain detached. The one ideal you must stand by is to be yourself, a powerful ethos which should never be forgotten. People saw something which led them to make me captain, what that was I'm not sure but if it had influenced them, then why look for other influences which may put that quality at risk? Circumstances will change, you can consider matters in a new light, but through it all you have to be the constant which will galvanise the players. You evolve as a captain, mature into the job and learn to carry the responsibility, but as long as you retain your individual personality, that inner core, you're OK.

The changing-room presents a challenge. As a player you have your own way of preparing for the match, a favourite peg, a certain routine, but there comes a point where as captain you have to put the individual complexities aside, bring the team together as one. You know which players need that bit of reassurance and the ones who like to be shouted at, and the captain's job at this time is to help get the juices flowing, bring them to the boil but I do not view that as motivation. If any player has trained diligently for years in the pursuit of a dream, he shouldn't need motivating. If he does, then I would suggest it is time to start looking for something else, it isn't for them. We are talking about the most unforgiving environment in the world and that is the addictive part of it. We are masochists; all sportsmen are, rugby players doubly so. You only have to look at our medical files for confirmation of that. International rugby is the most potent of drugs, intoxicating, and you just want more of it. Anybody who is not ready for that encounter can find something else to do.

Ieuan Evans experienced the highs and lows of the game and accepted both with grace. His injury problems leave one questioning how he could still manage to achieve so much. A horrific ankle injury, dislocated shoulders and the run-of-the mill pulls and strains that haunt the fast men out wide were a constant worry and yet at Llanelli, with Wales, the British Lions and later at Bath he took the knocks but always bounced back clearly intent on leaving the game on his own terms when the time eventually arrived.

You can probably put it down to a lack of intellect but coming back from injury was never a problem, going into the tackle, into contact, which is the true test. I came back from the injuries mentally stronger even if on occasions a bit too soon. I dislocated my ankle at the end of October and was playing again in January, but wasn't ready and should have taken a few more weeks. Recovering from injury can be a dark time but it helps your resolve, makes you a stronger person and puts a better perspective on the good times. Life is a balance and these things help you to appreciate it more.

The highs? Well there were too many to acknowledge in these pages but ask Rory Underwood about that kick and chase in 1993 and David Campese what on earth he was doing behind the Australian goal line in the deciding Test in 1989 with one of the game's great predators breathing down his neck. Or ask any one of five or six Scots if they even laid a finger on Ieuan Evans as he scored one of the great individual tries of the modern game at Cardiff in 1988. And remember the 1994 championship when he became the first Welsh captain to actually lift some silverware, a trophy now in place for the undisputed champions. Then there are the three British Lions tours which saw Evans appear in seven of the nine Tests, numerous championship and cup titles won at Llanelli and lifting the Heineken Cup as a Bath player, a fitting swansong.

I really enjoyed my rugby on the Lions tours and found them a liberating experience. To be able to perform with the best against the Southern hemisphere countries on a level playing field was something which I wasn't able to do during much of my career and I particularly enjoyed New Zealand in 1993 which is always the benchmark tour. We lost the Test series 2–1, a series which we should have won comfortably, but we let ourselves down as a touring party mainly due to a lack of competition for Test places, something which the successful Lions teams have always enjoyed.

For the happiest and most rewarding time of my career I go back to 1988. The Welsh team was full of young men who Tony Gray and Derek Quinnell encouraged to go out and express themselves. They gave us total freedom and we had a ball. We could have won a Grand Slam that year but lost to France on a muddy Arms Park on a day when we couldn't get our hands on the ball. It sounds a daft thing to say but we would have beaten France in dry weather on a good surface because at the time we were running everybody off the park but we just couldn't get our hands on the ball. We were a young, cocky, arrogant side and we loved it out there but following the New Zealand tour people who didn't know what they were doing began to meddle. We lost the coaches, which affected us badly; we were a developing group of players which simply had the wind taken out of its sails and within a year the side had disintegrated. Nobody was looking at the bigger

picture and it was a long time before we pulled it around – proof
that a little knowledge is a dangerous thing.

Injuries aside, such high points are unfortunately compensated for by
some forgettable lows: as captain during the disappointing 1991 RWC;
a first Canadian victory, one achieved on Welsh soil to add to the
misery; and a second Five Nations whitewash which presaged the
biggest disappointment of them all.

In 1991 Ieuan Evans had been the beneficiary when he was
appointed Welsh captain for the final match before the RWC
following a disappointing sequence of results, and four years later he
was the unfortunate victim when the need to find a new coach at the
11th hour saw Alex Evans stamp his mark on the team by appointing
Mike Hall as the new captain.

We had just gone through a difficult season for which there were
a number of valid reasons but the year before we had been
champions and I felt that what was needed going into the '95
World Cup was continuity. It wasn't like 1991 when, following
three dreadful years, there was a need for change, something new,
a fresh approach. It was an awful decision to change the coach in
1995, particularly for what we knew was only going to be a stop-
gap measure. All of a sudden we had to change everything else, it
was disastrous. Though I didn't understand the appointment of
Alex Evans I could see where he was coming from, wanting to
bring in a number of players from Cardiff, players he was familiar
with, and wanting his own man as captain, but it was very
disruptive and led to an unhappy time. It should have been
handled better, put in place at the start of the new season, but not
at that juncture in time.

I wasn't happy but life deals these blows and you just have to get
on with it. As far as I was concerned captaining your country was
the pinnacle, not something I ever expected but something which
I aspired to, and then to find it's gone was a hammer blow. I
suppose it's human nature but I did start to question myself, my
strengths and abilities, which had obviously been called in doubt.
In international sport you constantly do this because it is such a
challenging environment, but when someone else does it you
begin to wonder if it is still the right environment to be in, but if
I had reacted any other way I would have started to question my
commitment, I'd have had to ask myself if I still wanted it.

Coming back from so many injuries I was used to picking myself up and getting on with things and thankfully I was able to do so this time.

Following his retirement Ieuan Evans remains involved with the game through his media work. Acknowledging that in 2005 Mike Ruddock guided Welsh rugby away from what was in danger of becoming a formatted, global bore by starting to reinvent the game, encouraging the players to think for themselves and detaching himself from the genre of control-mad coaches, Evans still holds grave reservations about where rugby is going in the twenty-first century.

I find it incredible that coaches are planning 80 minutes of rugby a week in advance, programming the players as to what they should or shouldn't do instead of accepting that in the heat of the moment the player is best positioned to determine the pattern of play. There are so many limitations placed on the game now that are unsustainable if it is to be allowed to develop, which I find quite worrying. It smacks of insecurity from the coach, something we have become familiar with throughout the world game, but thankfully Wales have started to show that there is another way, they are beginning to plough their own furrow which might not be right for other teams but that doesn't matter. It might suit Australian rugby to play a game which mirrors rugby league but it doesn't suit Wales. I want to be surprised and astonished when I watch a game of rugby, I don't want to know what happens next – I can watch the soaps or a re-run for that.

What Ieuan Evans is really suggesting here is that the game should be returned to the players.

The Parc des Princes was one of my favourite grounds. I had my first cap there and all I can remember was running out into this cacophony of sound and colour. Fireworks, bands in the crowd, chickens and cockerels on the pitch; the game started and it finished and I couldn't remember a second of it but I knew I wanted the experience again. The ground was special, as was the National Stadium and many other venues. They still are but the pitch should belong to the players and officials – thirty players and three officials; nobody else should be allowed near it. People dream of treading that pitch and now you've got every man and his dog out there, trainers, water carriers whatever; it's for the players and, barring those attending injuries, get the rest off.

The legacy left by Ieuan Evans is huge. He is Wales's longest-serving captain with very good reason. One of only a handful of players guaranteed his place in the team and one of an even smaller number of truly world-class stars to grace Welsh rugby in the 1990s he had the utmost respect of not only those he led but every player involved in the game. Both during his playing career and after his retirement, Ieuan Evans has been one of Wales's finest rugby ambassadors, respected by the commercial world, the media and followers of the game whatever their tribal allegiance. A rugby diplomat who together with fellow wings Willie Llewellyn, Teddy Morgan, Ken Jones and Gerald Davies represents the best of Welsh rugby throughout its 125-year history, but despite these players all being performers of the highest calibre our search for the outstanding Welsh captains and the best positions to lead from will unfortunately, like so much quality ball, probably not end up on the wing.

X

FROM DEFENCE TO ATTACK:
FULL-BACK

It had taken 53 years and it would be another 33 before it happened again. With an infrequency which rivalled the 75-year cycle of Halley's Comet, Vivian Jenkins was the first Welsh full-back to score an international try when he crossed the line against Ireland on 10 March 1934 and Keith Jarrett became the second in his record-breaking debut against England on 15 April 1967. Neither were Wales alone in this. Excepting two tries in the 1870s, it was England's Bob Hiller in 1971 who followed Tom Kiernan in 1961 and Ian Smith in 1969, the first full-backs to score for Ireland and Scotland respectively. In France it was Michel Vannier in 1957; Australia waited until 1961, New Zealand until 1959 and South Africa after an early effort in 1910 didn't see another Springbok full-back score a try until 1955. All of which tells us a lot about the role of the full-back in the first 100 years of international rugby.

He was there to defend; included in the team for his tackling ability, his unfailing bravery when required to fall on the ball in the face of the forward rushes which once so dominated the game, and his ability to kick the ball some distance up the field. And if he could kick goals, that was considered a bonus. The full-back would spend much of the match standing well back from the action, somewhere in midfield, which would enable him to respond quickly to any threat from either flank. His was a solitary existence which in winter months would see him doing all manner of exercises to keep warm and having little verbal contact with his colleagues. Not quite a spectator, nor in many people's opinions a position from which to lead a team, but some did and to date 12 Welsh captains have led from the back.

That April day in 1967 was, if not the defining moment, certainly the day from which selectors and coaches, players and spectators, began to realise that the full-back could add a new dimension to the attacking options available. When young Jarrett collected the bouncing ball inside the Welsh half and ran up the touchline to finish off a memorable afternoon, he unwittingly changed the perception which saw the full-back solely as a defender. Now he would be viewed as a counter-attacker and eventually become an additional component of three-quarter play.

Things have certainly changed on the scoring front with the international full-back regularly running in tries, but the attitude towards the suitability of the position as regards the role of captain still leans very much towards the negative. Recent years have seen Serge Blanco and Gavin Hastings as two notable exceptions, not only prolific try scorers but players who carried the responsibility of captaincy well; however, few others come to mind and the fact that New Zealand has never been led by a full-back in a capped match should not pass unnoticed. Among the number to captain Wales are: two brothers; two players who are their club's only international captains; the first captain to lead Wales to victory; a player disciplined and sent home by the WRU en route to Paris; the 100th Welsh captain; a true legend and one-time record cap holder; and a player who has in no small way helped return Wales to the forefront of the game.

* * *

Following the disastrous introduction to international rugby at Richardson's Field it was almost 12 months before Wales played their second match. Another away trip, this time to Dublin, saw 11 changes in the team with fewer players from Oxford and Cambridge included, the selectors relying more on the talent that was playing regularly for Wales-based clubs thereby avoiding the criticism which had followed that first defeat. Wales won in Dublin under the captaincy of Charles Prytherch Lewis, a product of Llandovery who became the club's first and only Welsh captain, and he was invited to carry on in the first match to be played on Welsh soil at Swansea in December 1882 and retained for the first visit to Scotland in the following month. Both matches were lost and next season the selectors were looking for the third man (after Bevan and Lewis) to lead Wales, but after an alarming introduction to the game at its highest level, Wales, under the leadership of Charles Lewis, had started to find its way and the great journey had begun.

We have already paid tribute to the years that led up to the first Golden Era of Welsh rugby – the important contribution made by Arthur Gould and his contemporaries in laying the foundation for the triumphs which would earn Gwyn Nicholls and his generation of players rugby immortality – but there is one final link between Gould and Nicholls yet to be acknowledged and that link comes in the shape of Swansea full-back Billy Bancroft.

The first of 33 consecutive caps was won against Scotland in 1890 and for 12 seasons Bancroft was a permanent fixture in the Welsh team. He played in Wales's first victory over England and its first Triple Crown in 1893, and after 22 appearances took over the captaincy from Arthur Gould in 1898. Eleven matches later he handed it on to Nicholls but not before leading Wales to a second Triple Crown in 1900. Future Welsh captains Willie Llewellyn, Billy Trew, Rhys Gabe and Dickie Owen all made their debuts under Bancroft and it would be for Gwyn Nicholls to guide these great talents through the next stage in their development as international rugby footballers.

Billy Bancroft scored 60 international points, a record which stood for 11 years before a young pretender broke it in only his 14th match and then went on to finish his career with 88 points to his credit in 18 appearances. The new record holder was Jack Bancroft, eight years his brother's junior; come the outbreak of the First World War, Wales had played 102 internationals with a Bancroft at full-back in exactly half of them. The eight-year age difference was sufficient to ensure that their international careers didn't overlap, nor did the brothers ever have to be accommodated in the same Swansea line-up: Billy retired at the end of 1902–03 and Jack made his debut during the invincible 1904–05 season.

Captaincy appears to have lain comfortably on the shoulders of Billy, who led the club for six seasons, while Jack's name is absent from the club's honours board: Billy Trew was the regular captain for much of the younger Bancroft's playing days. The age difference also represented the period between Billy's last cap and Jack's first. Llanelli's John Strand Jones played five consecutive matches but it was the next in line, Bert Winfield, who dominated the position during those eight years, playing in fifteen matches before the arrival of Jack Bancroft in 1909.

Bert Winfield was the brother-in-law of Gwyn Nicholls but the pair were not only related by marriage: they both played for Cardiff and were partners in a thriving laundry business, the expansion of which had taken Nicholls to Newport for a short period in 1902. Between them they captained Cardiff for six seasons, 1898–1904, and when Winfield won his first cap, Nicholls was Welsh captain. Full-back in the Welsh team which defeated New Zealand, Bert Winfield, together with three other heroes of the day, led Wales once during the 1908 Grand Slam. All four were coming to the end of their careers and after Boxer Harding, George Travers and Teddy Morgan had led winning teams against England, Scotland and France respectively the selectors gave the captaincy to Bert Winfield for the trip to Belfast. They may have made hard work of it but Wales got the victory which secured the Triple Crown and that first Grand Slam.

The selectors were spoilt with several options at full-back and the day that the young Bancroft would play for Wales was fast approaching, but they decided to put his first cap on hold, picking Winfield to play against the first Australian touring side when they visited Cardiff in December 1908. Wales won the toughest of matches 9–6, one very much dictated by the forwards, but it allowed Bert Winfield to bring his career to a fitting end when he kicked a penalty goal which proved to be the decisive score. He was selected in the team to face England in 1909 but injury forced his withdrawal and Jack Bancroft was called up with no little sense of déjà vu as Billy had also been first capped under similar circumstances.

Not blessed with the same injury-free career as his brother, Jack Bancroft was forced to miss several matches, but it would be wrong to suggest that the outbreak of war restricted his international appearances as he was in his 35th year in 1914 and there were already signs that his career was coming to an end. Where all of Billy Bancroft's caps had been won against England, Ireland and Scotland, Jack benefited from the inclusion of France in the championship and in four meetings with Les Bleus he registered over half his international points, including eight conversions and one penalty on New Year's Day 1910, a haul of 19 points equalled only by Jarrett in 1967 and Phil Bennett in 1976 before finally being bettered by Paul Thorburn in 1990.

The 1912 championship saw scrum-half Dickie Owen become the most capped Welsh player and in recognition of the achievement he was appointed captain for the visit to Twickenham. It would not have passed the Welsh full-back's attention that it was his elder brother's record which was now consigned to the history books and a final 35th cap for the scrum-half saw the goal for future players increased. But after two matches of the campaign Owen and half-back partner Billy Trew decided to concentrate on club rugby, preferring to go on tour with Swansea, which left the selectors searching for a new captain and against Ireland they passed the responsibility to Jack Bancroft, possibly the only time he ever led a team onto the field and to a 12–5 defeat.

After victory over Scotland in February 1912 the selectors presented Bancroft with a team which included seven new caps, a strange selection even allowing for the absence of the half-backs. Five were in the forwards but it was the more experienced backs who let Wales down on the day, squandering several try-scoring opportunities. His conversion of the only Welsh try saw Jack Bancroft create a new Welsh points-scoring record and in the space of six weeks brother Billy had seen his records as the holder of most caps and scorer of most points broken, although one did stay in the family.

It is not unusual for young lads on the terraces to watch their heroes with the hope that one day they may be able to emulate them, acquire the necessary skills and be given the chance to put them into practice, and naturally the desire to play in the same position will follow. Consider then the impact that the Bancroft brothers would have had on the lads who stood on the terraces at St Helen's dreaming of the day when they would be the Swansea full-back, the Welsh full-back.

Joe Rees may well have been influenced in such a way. It would have been Jack Bancroft whom Rees watched from the terraces at St Helen's and on the resumption of play after the First World War it was Joe Rees who replaced him in the Swansea team and a year later followed in his footsteps to that higher plane when he made his debut for Wales on his home ground. One of nine new caps introduced to the side after the defeat by the New Zealand Army, Rees won a total of twelve caps and led the team in his final match, played at St Helen's, four years later. Unlike the Bancrofts, Joe Rees rarely bothered the match scorer, his sum total for Wales two conversions and a penalty goal. The reason quite simply was that on his debut, Jerry Shea stole the limelight with 16 of Wales's 19 points, and in the remainder of his career it was Albert Jenkins who took on the goal-kicking duties.

Jack Bancroft's record number of points in an international stood the test of time longer than most, equalled twice but not beaten for 80 years when Neath full-back Paul Thorburn finally improved on it with a 21-point haul against the Barbarians in 1990. Whether caps should have been awarded for the match which celebrated the centenary of the famous club without a home became the subject of great debate, the dissenters arguing that the cap had been devalued. The practice was repeated when the teams next met in 1996 but all subsequent meetings have not been granted international status by the WRU and the awarding of caps in this particular fixture has ceased. None of which has any bearing on 1990 when Thorburn scored a try, then valued at four points, converted it and kicked five penalties, creating a record which four players have since bettered – Neil Jenkins, the current holder with thirty points, on no fewer than twelve occasions.

Paul Thorburn arrived on the international rugby stage with a reputation as a sound full-back but more importantly as a goal kicker of exceptional ability. He joined Neath at the start of the 1984–85 season and come its end had amassed 438 points, shattering the previous club record in the process, an achievement which had not gone unnoticed by the national selectors. Bad weather had delayed the start of the Five Nations until March and when Wales went down to eventual Triple Crown winners Ireland in a disappointing home defeat, full-back Mark Wyatt, following a particularly poor day with the boot, was one of a surprisingly small number of casualties, making way for Thorburn to win a first cap in Paris.

That forwards win matches and the backs decide by how much is readily acknowledged by all and it is amplified by the fact that the goal-kicking responsibilities usually lie with a back. To go onto the field with an experienced goal kicker in the ranks guarantees nothing, but to do so without one indicates foolishness in the extreme. Boring as watching the routines of the goal-kicking machines undoubtedly is, the sigh of relief when the ball bisects the uprights or the groans of dismay when it doesn't are a big part of the game and the fact that the many attempts to devalue the penalty kick have not been adopted indicates that it still has a major part to play in the outcome of most matches.

In 1986 Paul Thorburn lined up a penalty attempt at the National Stadium which was both speculative and audacious. With Wales hanging on to a slender 16–15 lead against a menacing Scottish team the kick would at least hold up the match for a minute or so which could only be to the home side's advantage, and with a strong wind in favour of the kicker there was always the chance that three points could be scored. Nobody would have put much money on the latter, the ball placed approximately sixty-four metres from the posts – one metre beyond the ten-metre line on the left-hand side of the field at about the fifteen-metre line running parallel with touch – a long way from the target. Thorburn kicked his way into the record books with a hoof that was later measured at seventy yards and eight and a half inches from where the ball left the ground to where it landed and, of course, on the way it pierced the uprights above the crossbar with something to spare. Minutes later he secured the Welsh victory with a further penalty, this a tap from one metre inside the Scottish half.

> The wind was gusting and if you look at the video of the match, you will see the flags on the far touchline blowing against the kick but on the near side they were blowing the other way, suggesting a swirling wind. I was always more consistent with the long kicks and, in fact, I think the second of the two was the better. It certainly made the crossbar with much more to spare.

The calls for the devaluing of the penalty had raged for many years and with Scotland outscoring the home side by three tries to one they gained further momentum but it was seven years before the problem was eventually addressed by the IRB and not in the way most anticipated. Rather than devalue the penalty kick the value of the try was increased to five points.

The next memorable kick from the boot of Thorburn came in the third-place play-off against Australia in the 1987 RWC. This was an injury-time conversion way out on the left touchline which sneaked Wales a 22–21 victory.

> That was certainly a pressure kick but of them all the most pressure came in Ireland in 1988 where so much was at stake with a Triple Crown to be won. It was a particularly blustery day and I hadn't kicked well, but the late penalty which put us in front ensured Wales won, which was all that really mattered.

Ten months later, after showing a high level of consistency for both club and country, Paul Thorburn became the 100th player to captain Wales but the euphoria of 1987 and the Triple Crown that followed in 1988 had been quickly dissipated by two ceremonial annihilations in New Zealand and a home defeat by Romania. The new captain had to lead his team well: there was a mountain to climb.

It's all in the wrist, you see. And if you didn't understand the deft up and down movement of the half-closed grip, there was the mouthed comment which the poorest lip reader the world over could translate. Paul Thorburn, Welsh captain, was seen by millions of television viewers venting his spleen on the press box as he left the field after

Wales's 12–9 victory over England had avoided an expected Five Nations whitewash in 1989. The *Sunday Times*'s rugby correspondent, Stephen Jones, had been severely critical of Welsh rugby in the build-up to the match and suggested drastic action would be necessary if England won in Cardiff. The victory saw the Welsh captain in vitriolic mood at the after-match dinner, taking his immediate post-match reaction further with pointed comments made in his captain's speech referring to the journalist in question as 'the scum of the earth', an unsavoury and unsuitable remark from the captain, which brought the appropriate apologies.

> I had been thinking about what I was going to say for an hour and undoubtedly if I had enjoyed the benefit of a media manager, I would probably have been taken to one side and told to calm down and events would have turned out differently, but unfortunately the back-up enjoyed by today's players wasn't in place. That aside, I certainly got the feeling that some representatives of the union seemed quite pleased that I'd stood up to the media, although I did cause some regrettable embarrassment, particularly at the dinner, but I probably said what a lot wanted to. The incident potentially cost me a Lions place; the team was announced two days later and I have subsequently heard I was in with a good shout.

Missing out on the Lions tour to Australia, Thorburn led Wales on a six-match development tour to Canada, where five matches were won, the sixth drawn. Yet for the 1989–90 season the selectors decided to introduce a new captain and Thorburn, though retaining his place in the team, was replaced by Robert Jones.

> In the final tour match against British Columbia we were winning 21–3 but let them back into it in the last five or ten minutes to salvage a draw. Coach John Ryan was a straight talker and following this he decided that we needed a captain upfront who would possibly control matters better; consequently I had the captaincy taken off me.

He was eventually reinstated as captain against the Barbarians in October 1990, the match in which he broke Jack Bancroft's points record, and continued in the role in the 1991 Five Nations, which saw England register a first win in Cardiff since 1963, Scotland and France comfortably win at home and only a draw with Ireland prevent a second consecutive whitewash and more Welsh blushes – but these weren't long in coming.

In the summer of 1991 there were Welsh blushes in abundance both on and off the field when Thorburn led Wales on a six-match tour of Australia. Wales suffered a horrendous mauling by New South Wales, losing 71–8, and it was more of the same against Australia in the final match, the 63–6 score confirming what everyone already knew: that there was much to be done before the RWC later in the year if Wales were to avoid an unceremonious early exit from the tournament.

Off the field things were arguably worse. The Welsh players embarrassed themselves with a display of ill-mannered posturing and infighting which ended in scuffles and ugly scenes that horrified their hosts. The players were divided in their opinions of coach Ron Waldron of Neath and with eight of the squad from the club it is not difficult to work out where the division lay.

Obviously the selection of Ron Waldron was seen in many quarters as the wrong decision. He picked who he thought were the best players in Wales and he was perfectly justified in his selection of so many Neath players as it was undoubtedly the best club in Wales at the time – who wouldn't have done the same? Basically you go for the core of such a team, which is exactly what Ron did. Having said that there was obviously an anti-Ron Waldron, anti-Neath brigade within the squad which included some very senior and well-respected players who I thought should have known better. The problem brewed up during the tour and the fact that Neath were a particularly fit team reflected somewhat badly on others, with the whole thing coming to a head at the final dinner – an experience which reflected badly on me as captain. I have to say that I didn't have a lot of time for some of the players. They let themselves and everyone else down with their lack of commitment, which ultimately brought matters to a head and was the reason I quit. In hindsight I shouldn't have because I was the fittest I'd ever been and probably playing the best rugby of my career, although you wouldn't assume that from the results of the tour. Basically, I'd just had enough.

I saw the team manager Clive Rowlands in his hotel room and told him I was finishing, I broke down I was so upset. People say you should step back and take time to reflect but I knew that things were not going to get any better. I knew people would say get rid of the coach and the problem will be solved but I knew the problem didn't lie with the coach. In fact, I think it's only recently that people have started to take on board what the problems were, that we were not physically fit enough, and it's only now the team actually are fit that you can feel proud looking at a Welsh forward in a jersey. It makes a change from seeing just a beer belly and as a result we are starting to play the game that Wales wants to play. Unfortunately in 1991 people weren't prepared to listen, preferred to blame it on the Ron Waldron era, but it is only quite recently that the drink problem which Welsh rugby had been associated with for far too long has finally disappeared at the highest level.

The tour to Australia highlighted how a captain has to make felt his presence off the field. He must be aware of any division which may occur between his players and act accordingly. Whether Paul Thorburn was actually present at the altercations which followed the Test defeat or not is irrelevant; there should have been enough self-discipline among the players to have prevented the problem arising but in this department Paul Thorburn admits to having been found wanting. Similarly, gesturing and inappropriate slurs should not be seen or heard from any player but when it is the captain who is at fault then questions have to be asked.

I do regret the incident with Stephen Jones, more so perhaps because my family was particularly hurt by it. My father was working in London at the time and the incident had occurred too late for it to be reported in the Sunday papers but when he arrived at the office on Monday the press was full of what I had said and done and I think he was more than a bit embarrassed.

Paul Thorburn had no intention of retiring when he did, his focus firmly on the RWC, only a matter of months away, but after winning thirty-seven caps and leading Wales ten times, he announced his retirement from international rugby following the debacle Down Under. Things had just got too out of hand.

* * *

In 1924 the elected members of the WRU showed much less tolerance than their counterparts would in later years. En route to Paris for the final match of the championship it became clear that the Union's regulations regarding the availability to their clubs of selected players had been contravened the by-law stipulating that in the six days before an international no selected player should appear for his club. Welsh full-back Ossie Male, it turned out, had played for Cardiff against Birkenhead Park on the Saturday before the Paris match, scheduled for the following Thursday, an oversight by Cardiff which saw the player asked to leave the party on arrival in Paddington and return to Wales.

Male won his first cap as a Cross Keys player in 1921 and waited two years before winning a second, by which time he was playing for Pontypool. Then came the move to Cardiff but after adding a further two caps to his total he was forced to spend the next two seasons in the international wilderness. He watched as Cardiff left wing Tom Johnson was transferred to full-back after winning eight caps in his favoured position and then, to add insult to injury, three players in succession win their only cap.

Johnson was Cardiff captain when he was added to the ever-growing list of players to lead Wales during the decade, at Twickenham in 1925, in the first Five Nations selection of the newly appointed panel who had seen their earlier combination seriously exposed by New Zealand two months earlier. Fewer in number they may have been but the Big Five appear to have taken time to harmonise their thinking, judging by the number of changes and new caps that appear in the Welsh line-up between 1924 and 1926, but after opting for almost every other leading full-back in Wales common sense prevailed and Ossie Male was recalled for the 1927 championship. Not that his presence in the side reversed the dreadful results that the public had become used to, far from it, but he went on to win seven more caps over the next two seasons, captaining the side three times but with little distinction other than being the unfortunate man in charge when, after a run of fifteen consecutive defeats, France finally celebrated victory over Wales.

* * *

Penarth RFC now compete in Division Four South-East of the Welsh League. The days that saw the traditional Good Friday fixture with the Barbarians are long gone and it has been a slow decline for one of the clubs which featured on every other's fixture list for 100 years. Some would suggest this was because fixtures with Penarth were usually 'bankers', almost guaranteeing victory, but that would be unfair to a club with such a great tradition and one which can boast John Archibald Bassett as one of its own.

Jack Bassett was one of a handful of players who took the mess that was Welsh international rugby at the end of the 1920s, dragged it into the 1930s and set it on the road to recovery. He was not the quickest full-back ever to play for Wales – his solid build and 13 stone plus certainly prevented him ever being referred to as pacey – but in defence he was unrivalled; not until J.P.R. Williams would his ferocious kind of tackling be seen again. He had all the necessary skills to command the last quarter of the field. In addition to his tackling he was a fine punter of the ball out of hand and fearless when required to fall at the feet of onrushing forwards.

His inclusion in the team to face England at the start of the 1929 championship came after the selectors had held what was seen as an unofficial trial, the visit of Penarth to Newport, before choosing between the two full-backs on display: Bassett and Bill Everson. There followed a run of 15 caps broken only by the player's unavailability for the trip to Paris in 1930, when he was at sea, travelling to New Zealand with the British Isles team, where he performed with great distinction, local press and supporters favourably likening him to their own hero George Nepia.

Bassett's nine matches as Welsh captain began in 1930 and confirm that a revival was under way, with Ireland and Scotland both beaten twice, England and France once, added to which there was also a drawn match with England which prevented a Grand Slam season, but the championship was welcomed by a nation starved of success for a decade. The two defeats saw the best and worst of the captain. In 1931 against South Africa he was magnificent, probably playing his finest ever game, even if tactically he left himself open to criticism by opting to throw the ball about in the wettest of conditions. Then, in 1932 against Ireland, in his final match and with Wales hoping for a victory which would secure the Triple Crown, he played undoubtedly his worst game for his country. Misjudgements, missed tackles and missed kicks at goal all contributed to the nightmare and instead of ending his career on a deserved high Jack Bassett left Cardiff Arms Park for the last time a beaten man, leaving the Irish to celebrate a 12–10 victory.

* * *

Since 1905 the affinity between New Zealand and Wales found through the oval ball has strengthened with each successive meeting. Never mind the fact that results have not gone Wales's way for far too long and never mind the contentious issues which have surrounded some of the high-profile matches; these have just added fuel to the arguments and history of the famous fixture. What 100 years of competition have nurtured is a mutual respect which, despite being put to the test far too often in recent years, has stood the test of time and New Zealanders never take Wales for granted – there are far too many famous names who have made an indelible impression on the All Blacks when visiting New Zealand with the British Lions to ever allow that to happen.

Jack Bassett, Harry Bowcott and Ivor Jones did so in 1930 and in 1950 Ken Jones, Billy Cleaver, R.T. Evans, Bleddyn Williams, Jack Matthews, Malcolm Thomas and Roy John were among a 14-strong Welsh contingent who continually reminded their hosts of the strength of Welsh rugby. The 1959 Lions are held in the highest esteem by all those fortunate to have witnessed their commitment to attack which thrilled the spectators, ensuring record-breaking attendances throughout the land. This time Bryn Meredith, Rhys Williams, Ray Prosser, Malcolm Thomas again, Malcolm Price and a fair-haired full-back who appeared in only nine matches, but nevertheless was included as one of New Zealand's five players of the year, were sufficient reminder that Welsh rugby was something to aspire to. Remember, in 1959 Wales still led New Zealand 3–1 in the series.

Swansea and Devonport Services full-back Terry Davies had started his international career against England in 1953, playing throughout the Five Nations, but a shoulder injury effectively ruled him out of contention for four years and when he was next called upon he was a 'Scarlet'.

I had come out of school at 14 and like most kids in those days, wasn't really going anywhere – a factory job, a year in a colliery, a bit of time on a building site. At 17 I was playing for Swansea but was very much on the light side and when it came to national service I opted for the Marines in the hope that it would give me the chance to build myself up. I went in at five foot ten, weighing eleven and a half stone and came out two stone heavier and an inch taller, but it was in the Marines that I suffered the injury that plagued my career. It occurred climbing a cliff on a night-training exercise. A few of us were linked together, one fell and took the rest with him and I ended up with a badly dislocated shoulder.

Following national service I went on tour to Romania with Swansea and in the first game I dislocated the shoulder again. I was taken to a hospital but I had never seen anything quite like it before; I was familiar with hospitals but nothing like this. It was a run-down building with dead bodies in the corridors and when a doctor came to see me he was wearing a filthy white coat, hadn't shaved for a while and was smoking. He decided to try and put the shoulder back in and spent an hour tugging and pulling. At one point he had his foot under my armpit, but to no avail, and they took me to a much better place where a doctor took one look at the shoulder and within a couple of minutes put it back. He told me to seek medical advice when I got home as the first doctor had broken some bones and it was going to require surgery to insert a plate and pins.

It took me over a year to get over that and when I did start playing again it was for the village team in Bynea. I had really taken umbrage with Swansea. All the time I was in hospital nobody from the club had shown any interest in my progress so I decided to go back to my roots and it was from Bynea RFC that I had three Welsh trials, which was unheard of, a trialist coming from a village team. All of which eventually took me to Llanelli.

Terry Davies was included in the Welsh team to play England in 1957 and only flu interrupted a run of fourteen consecutive appearances, Alun Priday winning the first of two caps against Ireland in 1958. Defeat at Twickenham in 1960 saw Davies dropped for the first time and brought back memories of a conversation with Rex Willis when he was new to international rugby. 'Rex told me that Dai Davies, one of the selectors, would make a point of offering players who were going to be dropped a boiled sweet. It was true. I saw it happen often and spent all my time trying to avoid the man, but my turn finally came.'

Later in the year Davies was included in the team to face the Springboks and when the players took to the field in the most atrocious weather conditions, it was the Llanelli full-back who led Wales onto the field. Much has been written about how the match was decided by the toss of the coin, the Welsh skipper electing to play into the ferocious wind and rain in the first half.

The weather was terrible, the rain pouring down, and the pitch was like a paddy field. The Springboks were a touring team, training twice a day and were obviously much fitter than us, and I felt that in those conditions their pack was going to get the upper hand. Our only chance was to hope to contain them in the first half and then rely on a bit of help from the conditions in the second, so I elected to play against the wind. That was my decision and although it didn't win the game, their forwards dominating much as I had expected, by electing to play against the elements in the first half I'm sure we avoided a much bigger defeat.

The conditions were so bad by the second half that with about 25 minutes remaining the referee asked if we wanted to stop, and at 3–0 up Springbok captain Avril Malan was happy to do so but I said that I would be castrated – not castigated – by the Welsh public if I agreed, but to ask me again if Wales got in front.

The pitch deteriorated into an unplayable mud bath with neither side able to produce anything resembling a constructive game, the outcome decided by the one score, a first-half penalty goal. Wales would have to wait almost 40 years before finally laying the South African hoodoo to rest. Two more low-scoring matches completed Terry Davies's spell as captain before one final appearance brought his tally of caps to twenty-one. He scored a total of 50 points, all with the boot, which included 12 penalties, but it is with a missed penalty that his name will forever be inextricably linked.

Twickenham was the venue, 1958 the year, the final score 3–3.

We turned around at 3–3 – I kicked a penalty and [England's] Peter Thompson scored a try – but in the second half we had to play into the wind and they were expected to go on to win, but it didn't turn out that way. Midway through the half we were awarded a penalty on the halfway line and Clem Thomas called me up. I thought the wind was too strong but gave it a go. I placed the ball, closed my eyes and shunted it and it went like a rocket, cutting straight through the wind, but as the ball approached the posts it veered off, hit the upright, dropped onto the crossbar and was blown back into the field of play. That night three lads from Tenby decided to raid Twickenham. They borrowed a saw, climbed over the wall, got onto the pitch and cut down the offending crossbar.

The next day I travelled back to Wales with my brother and a friend from the village. We stopped in a café and sitting in the corner were three Welsh boys and one of them came over and asked if I would sign something. Outside he went and came back in with this six-foot length of four by two and asked if I could sign it three times, once for each of them.

'What is it?' I asked.

'It's the bloody crossbar,' he said. 'We went and cut it down.'

By Monday the story had made the front page of the *Western Mail*. I was summoned by Eric Evans, the Secretary of the WRU, and it was obvious that I was assumed to be involved. The story rolled for about ten days during which it was raised in Parliament, where opinion was that 'the barbarians who had desecrated HQ should be jailed'. Nobody would believe that I'd had nothing to do with it. In the end I sent the RFU a telegram offering to replace the thing to which I had a reply saying that they would never consider using a crossbar made of Welsh timber.

How many more caps there might have been but for injury we will never know. A.B. Edwards, Viv Evans, Garfield Owen and Gerwyn Evans each had the opportunity to play international rugby during his absence from the team and all performed with distinction but it is Terry Davies who stands out as the leading full-back of the 1950s. His written comment that 'To become a good full-back there is need to practise, practise and then practise again!' should not go unheeded. The techniques of tackling, fielding the ball and kicking out of hand can be improved with regular practice but what are straightforward exercises on the training ground have to be completed with accuracy and at pace in the international arena in front of many thousands of spectators, and no player on the field draws the eye more than the full-back waiting under the high ball with the opposition due to arrive in numbers at or about the same time.

Yes, it certainly takes a special kind of courage to be a full-back, maybe even an element of madness should be included in the mix, and if the recipe still isn't quite right try a bit of psychology, try dressing the part. Roll down the socks. Grow sideburns, big ones, grow the hair to match and hold it in place with a casually tied headband. Have faith, it will work.

* * *

Rugby players are known by a variety of handles. The full name is obvious and there are many nicknames which have become recognised, although recent offerings such as Johnno, Wilko and Robbo show a limited imagination when compared with Pit Bull, Mighty Mouse, The Munch and Merve the Swerve. Then there are the odd occasions when only the first name is necessary. Mention Gareth anywhere in Wales and no further explanation need follow, and then there are the even rarer instances where initials are sufficient, the most recognised among them, JPR.

John Peter Rhys Williams won Junior Wimbledon in 1966, beating David Lloyd 6–4, 6–4 in the final, but it was his love of a very different-shaped ball which, on arrival in London to pursue his medical studies, led him to Old Deer Park, Richmond, home of London Welsh RFC.

In 1968 the IRB introduced the experimental Law which prohibited direct kicks to touch from outside the 22, meaning that players, particularly full-backs, would have to be a bit more innovative and the game would be the better for it. Tackling and fielding the ball were as important as ever but kicking out of hand was suddenly less of a priority, with players expected to look for more entertaining options, which was just as well because JPR loved running with the ball, going in search of the opposition and relishing the physical contact, while his kicking to touch often left much to be desired.

> I had to run with it. At Bridgend Grammar School and Millfield I experienced the restrictions of the old Laws but I couldn't have continued playing under them. It was fine at London Welsh because we never kicked the ball away, always ran with it, but I could never have played full-back at Pontypool, for example, it wasn't my type of game, I would have played in the back row. Before 1968 full-backs were expected to kick for touch and I remember seeing Grahame Hodgson, technically a very good full-back, play for Neath against Bridgend but he would still kick for touch in the last minute of the game, even if Neath were losing, giving the ball away.

It was his ability to fully exploit the dispensation Law that caught the selectors' attention and at Murrayfield in 1969 the 19-year-old J.P.R. Williams won his first cap and in the years that followed only injury prevented him equalling Gareth Edwards's record of 53 consecutive appearances. Only one match was missed in that initial run and it is interesting that on the first occasion he was absent from the team, Wales lost to England, interesting because in his eleven matches against the old enemy JPR was never on the losing side.

On the triumphant British Lions tours of 1971 and 1974 he was a colossus, playing in all eight Tests, a continual reminder of the passion and quality of Welsh rugby, although by 1971 Wales were 5–3 down in their series of matches with New Zealand and in 1974 still had to register a first victory against the Springboks.

Bridgend was JPR's home club and he had promised that when his career in medicine brought him back to Wales it would be at the Brewery Field that he would play his club rugby. He honoured this commitment in 1976 and remained a Bridgend player until retiring from the game in 1981, a period during which the club re-established itself as a major force in Welsh rugby. The Schweppes Challenge Cup was won in back-to-back seasons, 1978–80, added to which Bridgend were club champions in 1980–81, the first time in a decade. This after it had all appeared to have come to an end in 1979 when, following a summer tour to Canada with Bridgend, JPR elected to take some time away from the game, only returning at the end of the season in time to claim his place in the team which defeated Swansea in the Cup final. 'Bridgend captain Meredydd James asked if I would consider returning for the Cup final and I had one game at Cross Keys, felt pretty good and played against Swansea.'

In a magnificent career on the rugby field J.P.R. Williams scaled the heights and finally achieved all the game had to offer in 1978 when the Welsh selectors invited him to lead the team against New Zealand. As he led Wales out at the National Stadium on 11 November there was a collective optimism among the 50,000 present, optimism which would be cruelly dashed. This was the match which saw New Zealand second row Andy Haden throw himself out of a lineout in the closing minutes hoping to con the referee into awarding a penalty, which he did, one which Brian McKechnie goaled to secure an undeserved 13-12 victory. There was an infringement at the front of the lineout for which referee Roger Quittenton confirmed the penalty was awarded, but the antics of Haden in what later materialised was a planned move deserved some action from the man in charge. New Zealand captain Graham Mourie later admitted that as the players prepared for the throw-in Haden confirmed that the plan was about to be hatched and Mourie even went some way toward suggesting that he should probably have stopped it.

We were cheated. I couldn't really see what had gone on at the lineout and wasn't able to comment on it in the immediate after-match interview but when I saw it and when you look at it now, it wasn't even good acting. Speaking to people since, I understand it was something they were practising at their training sessions in Porthcawl. I actually think that Graham Mourie is a decent chap and after the Ashworth incident I had a letter from him. He was the only person who apologised and I should think both incidents sit heavily with him.

The Ashworth incident referred to took place a month on from the Welsh game when it was the turn of Bridgend to meet the tourists who, by December, had gained a reputation as a team which often overstepped the mark with their uncompromising, physical approach. Prop John Ashworth did nothing to sway public opinion when he trampled on the Bridgend full-back's face in the game's opening minutes, leaving him in need of some serious repair work before returning to the fray. But Bridgend suffered the same fate as Wales and all other Welsh opposition the tourists met, only Irish province Munster getting the better of them on their 18-match tour.

J.P.R. Williams led Wales to a fourth consecutive Triple Crown in the 1979 Five Nations, a one-point defeat in Paris preventing a Grand Slam, but his record as Welsh captain is good – the two defeats by the narrowest of margins.

> This was a brand-new side and for some reason I don't think people quite gave it the credit it deserved. We had won the triple Triple Crown with all the well-known names who then retired, but this time there were a lot of the players who had toured Australia in 1978 where they had a bit of a tough ride, but a lot of them grew up on that tour and I think we did very well to win a fourth consecutive Triple Crown in the following year with so many new players. In many ways this made it easier for me as captain because I was now the senior figure and most of the players would actually listen to you, whereas with players you'd been involved with over a period of years it would go in one ear and out the other.

After JPR's sabbatical Welsh coach John Lloyd invited him to return to the Welsh team for the centenary season which included another encounter with the All Blacks. There were no complaints this time when the visitors ran out comfortable 23–3 winners and despite another victory over England, defeat at Murrayfield brought to an end the international career of one of Welsh rugby's greatest players.

> There was an odd reaction to this match because it was the forwards who were beaten on the day but it was among the backs that most changes were made, captain Steve Fenwick included. I thought that was bad selection because he was originally picked as captain for the season, something I agree with. If you are picked as captain, it should be for the season; there should be some stability.

Like all who had gone before, J.P.R. Williams had no input in team selection, barring one occasion in 1979 when Geoff Wheel was forced to miss the England match.

> We had a big dilemma when Geoff pulled out. We needed someone to do a job at the front of the line against Billy Beaumont and I asked the forwards who their preference would be. They all opted for Mike Roberts and when I put this to the selectors, to be fair to them, they listened and Mike played, saw Billy off and even scored a try.

Whoever you speak to who has led a team at whatever level, the one word that is ever present when discussing the attributes needed by a captain is respect.

> My team talks were not of the fire-and-brimstone variety. I tried to get people to think about their own game and we always had a quiet five minutes sat down simply focusing before we went onto the field. The big problem playing at the old Arms Park was it was so atmospheric that when you got out there you were in danger of just running around like a headless chicken. What you had to do was be in charge of the emotion, the occasion, maintain total control. If you looked at yourself before you went onto the field, your eyeballs were huge due to the amount of adrenalin and there are many players who appeared for Wales who can't remember anything about it. Running out of that tunnel in Cardiff you were met by the biggest noise you could imagine and the only ground that came near it was the Parc des Princes in Paris.
>
> After matches I always felt it was important to spend some time together as a team, an hour or so, because once you got to the function you would be split up and the moment was gone. All the Welsh teams that I was involved with got on well together, which is very important because it is much more difficult to get team spirit on the field if players aren't getting on off it.

Like so many of the game's earlier observers J.P.R. Williams frequently uses the word courage in his résumé of full-back play in *An Autobiography* published in 1979. On tackling, he writes:

> The most difficult tackle for a full-back is on a winger with a 15 yard overlap who is running flat out toward you ... Theoretically, if a winger

has room to move then he should always beat a full-back [ref. Rowe Harding]. The full-back's job is to prove that theory wrong. There is nothing better for me in rugby, than pulling off a really good tackle.

On 6 March 1976, Wales met France in Cardiff with a Grand Slam up for grabs. The match was a tight affair between two strong sides and the home team were hanging on to a six-point lead with France throwing everything at the defence as they went in search of a final try which could salvage a draw. Right wing Jean Pierre Gourdon found himself in exactly the circumstances described above. Rowe Harding would have expected him to score, but Williams had different ideas. Was it his greatest tackle? It may well have been, but orthodox it certainly wasn't, more a forearmed-led shoulder charge which 30 years on would probably attract a red card, Gourdon almost ending up in the crowd. Yes, you need courage to be a full-back; courage and honesty, as confirmed by another extract from that 1979 autobiography. On kicking, Williams wrote, 'This is not the most impressive part of my game.'

* * *

In 1981 the Brewery Field, Bridgend, witnessed the end of J.P.R. Williams's glittering rugby career and 13 years later the same venue saw another player set out on the road to rugby fame. From the centre to the wing and finally to full-back Gareth Thomas proved that adaptability was now the name of the game, never looking out of place in any position. Similarly his club rugby has seen him equally mobile, from Bridgend to Cardiff and back again before a season with the ill-fated Celtic Warriors followed by a move to Toulouse which caught everybody out.

Bridgend captain in the last season of professional league rugby in Wales and asked to do a similar job for the Warriors in the inaugural season of regional rugby gave Thomas the necessary foundation when in 2004, together with five other candidates, he was asked to take part in an interview process for the position of Welsh captain. He passed the test and officially took over the squad in preparation for the autumn internationals, a role he had enjoyed once before in a warm-up match against Ireland prior to the 2003 RWC when he led Wales from the right wing. This time would be different, this time 'Alfie', as he is fondly known, was going to lead from full-back, a position he had been introduced to as a replacement for the injured Garan Evans against New Zealand in the 2003 tournament.

Gareth Thomas led Wales to within a whisker of defeating South Africa and New Zealand but the 2005 Six Nations Championship saw the re-emerging Welsh style of play so encouraged by coach Mike Ruddock finally start to pay dividends. Against England, Italy and France it was Gareth Thomas who led the team with an assured style which surprised even the most pessimistic observer. He was a revelation both on and off the field and all of a sudden the players could be seen to be enjoying themselves, enjoying their rugby and doing what Welsh teams do best – entertain.

The best form of recognition is that received from one's peers. Phil Bennett is among those who view the appointment of Gareth Thomas as being critical to the Welsh cause, inspirational even.

He has been absolutely magnificent. He sets an example that the players respond to. He's always got a smile on his face, loves playing for Wales and I think he has been one of the great choices of Welsh captain. Tactically, I don't know how good he is; I don't care, you have others who can take some of that on board. What matters is how good a leader he is and he deserves an enormous amount of credit for the turnaround in Welsh fortunes.

A badly injured thumb saw the captain's championship cut short when he didn't return for the second half in Paris but Wales were on a roll and Thomas continued to impart his infectious enthusiasm at the team's Vale of Glamorgan base and from the sidelines in the remaining matches at Murrayfield and the Millennium Stadium when Scotland and Ireland were beaten to secure all the spoils. It was appropriate that Thomas, together with Michael Owen, received the silverware at the post-match presentation and fitting that this surprise package who had experienced ten years of professional rugby in which Wales had reached several, seemingly ever deepening troughs should be on the rostrum in its finest hour for twenty-seven years.

The summer of 2005 saw Thomas in New Zealand for the eagerly anticipated but ultimately anticlimactic British Lions tour, a tour which promised so much but failed to produce. For Alfie, however, it was to mark yet another milestone in what is slowly unfolding as a significant career in the annals of Welsh rugby history. When tour captain Brian O'Driscoll was controversially injured in the first test and coach Clive Woodward needed another captain, someone who had the utmost respect of the players and someone who would lead by example, it was to Gareth Thomas that he turned. Alfie gave his all in what was, realistically, a lost cause long before the party had left home, but he could hold his head high come the final reckoning.

The dust hadn't settled before the All Blacks arrived in Cardiff to celebrate the centenary of the famous first meeting between the two countries in 1905, but in a match which saw an injury-hit Wales fail to rise to the challenge, Gareth Thomas once again had to accept second best, the New Zealanders winning 41–3. Defeat at the hands of the Springboks was quickly forgotten when Wales registered an exciting 24–22 victory over Australia under Thomas, the first since 1987, meaning his team could look forward to the Six Nations with a certain amount of optimism. It wasn't to be. There was no repeat of the euphoria seen 12 months earlier, Welsh hopes dashed at the first hurdle by a devastating 47–13 defeat at Twickenham. Against Scotland a week later Gareth Thomas added two more tries to his Welsh record as Wales ran out 28–18 winners, but then the proverbial hit the fan, and it was, in many ways, a case of déjà vu for the Welsh captain.

The nation was in shock when, two days after celebrating victory against the Scots, news broke that coach Mike Ruddock had resigned. Allegedly, he had hoped to go at the end of the Six Nations, but the WRU were, allegedly, having none of it, and he was replaced with immediate effect by the Aussie Scott Johnson, who, ironically, was likely to return down under at the end of the campaign. It could only happen in Wales, a rugby nation with a proven track record of self-destruction when it came to the handling of coaches. The media had a field day, and when Gareth Thomas appeared on *Scrum Five*, viewers watched in dismay as accusations of player power being responsible for the demise of Ruddock were vehemently denied by the clearly unhappy Welsh captain.

Watching the recorded programme at home, Gareth Thomas was taken ill and rushed to the local hospital in Bridgend, where scans revealed a damaged vein in his neck, possibly the result of a knock he received playing for Toulouse a few weeks earlier. Complete rest was ordered, and he was told to take the rest of the season off. And Alfie did. He was not seen again in a competitive environment until a huge television audience saw him kicking a football about with the likes of Diego Maradona and Robbie Williams in front of more than 65,000 at Old Trafford in May 2006.

Already the top try scorer in Welsh rugby, with 36 to his credit, Gareth Thomas is now closing in on the record number of caps, a record which, barring serious injury, he must surely break. And then there is the not insignificant matter of Ieuan Evans's 28 matches as

Welsh captain which have previously looked beyond the reach of all candidates, but Alfie is on the case. Could this most unlikely captain of Wales emulate Ieuan Evans and hold all three records simultaneously?

* * *

Unlike those positions which have either been in or out of fashion when it came to the appointment of captains, full-backs have been called upon almost from day one. Charles Lewis was the second Welsh captain and through the Bancroft brothers; Bert Winfield in the first Grand Slam; Joe Rees, Tom Johnson and Ossie Male during the 1920s; Jack Bassett and Terry Davies in the decades before and following the Second World War; J.P.R. Williams and Paul Thorburn in the 1970s and '80s through to Gareth Thomas in the twenty-first century there have been few periods which did not see a full-back lead Wales.

A position considered as unfashionable as prop forward, too distanced from the action, hampered with communication problems and totally ignored in New Zealand closes the discussion on the attributes of leadership on the rugby field with an indirect affirmation that, because of the very shortcomings highlighted above, captaincy may be down to the individual, the charisma and energy of one player which places him above the rest. The jury is out.

CONCLUSION

From James Bevan in 1881 to Duncan Jones in 2006 it has passed through 123 pairs of hands, received for services rendered or as a result of another's misfortune through injury or illness, on merit or out of the sheer desperation of the selectors, or as a result of a one-off gesture – in relation to the ability to speak a foreign language or the equalling of a record haul of caps. Whatever the reason it is the highest honour a Welsh rugby player can aspire to, something intangible for which no mementoes are handed out but which will confirm the player's special place in the history of the game. A single word on the team sheet found between open and closed brackets alongside the player's name. A word more often than not appearing as an abbreviation or simply a single letter but regardless of form, one which confirms the player's additional status – captain.

To help put the importance of such recognition into perspective consider the following: Dewi Bebb, Ray Gravell, Neil Jenkins, Vivian Jenkins, Barry John, Roy John, Allan Martin, Dai Morris, Graham Price, Derek Quinnell, John Taylor, Denzil Williams, J.J. Williams and Bobby Windsor – 14 players who with a bit of poetic licence could be fitted into a competitive line-up, the only omission a scrum-half. What do these distinguished Welsh players all have in common? They never captained their country in a capped match. Many other notables could have been added to the list but two things become apparent when searching for such examples. First, the players listed each received great recognition in the game suggesting they were men possessing the qualities and calibre for the role of captain. Second, the absence of a notable scrum-half tells us that all the outstanding players in this position were at some stage appointed. These two observations sum up what has become the focus of the argument. On the one hand we have a group of players seen as suitable candidates for the captaincy but who were all overlooked; and on the other, we have a key position from which it is impossible to find a player with the necessary qualities who did not captain Wales.

Throughout its history the game of rugby union has laid witness to a host of changes. From the size of the playing field and the number of players, to the introduction of substitutes and the sin bin. So too the Laws relating to every area of play – the scrum, the lineout, the ruck and maul, kicking out of hand, offside, the restart – none has escaped the fine-tuning of the IRB. The ball has changed, jerseys have been the subject of much redesigning, the design of boots appears to have received as much attention as that of the motor car; where shin pads were once in vogue now it is the bodyguard and the gum shield, while headgear has gone full circle – from the early design of the skullcap there followed a phase where forwards wore a simple headband but now the redesigned aerodynamic headguard is the preferred choice.

Where once it was 'boot money', illicit payments which contravened the amateur ethos of the game, now the leading players receive a salary; rugby union is a professional sport. The grounds, the supporters, the media attention, the whole infrastructure – everything about rugby union in the twenty-first century has changed from those heady days when university students with double-barrelled names exercised on the playing fields of rural England in pursuit of an inflated pig's bladder. Amongst all these evolutionary or revolutionary changes it is little surprise that the role of captain has also undergone a transformation, but while we have to accept that his input on the field of play in the modern game is limited as a result of the new-found, all-encompassing status of the coach this in no way alters the basic criteria which are needed to lead a group of men towards the common goal of winning.

It would be wrong to assume that all 123 Welsh captains possessed the required qualities as many were found wanting, and when looking at those players who were overlooked consideration has to be given to the fact that a more suitable candidate may have been available or that the player himself preferred not to take on the responsibility. However, after making these allowances it is still obvious that there have been instances when a suitable candidate wasn't appointed, more often than not because he played in what was perceived as the wrong position.

Let us briefly consider the history of Welsh rugby, specifically where the captain has fitted into the great scheme of things. In the formative years there was much to learn. England and Scotland had played the first international match ten years before Wales ventured onto Richardson's Field in 1881 and Ireland had begun their international history six years earlier in 1875. It was a game of catch up and it took Wales almost 20 years before it was able to regularly compete. The first defining moment came with the introduction of the four three-quarter system which saw Wales gain some ascendancy when the other home unions delayed in adopting it. Arthur Gould nurtured Welsh rugby through this period and come the start of the twentieth century Wales was leading the way for the first time. Gould captained the side from the centre, a position essential to the success of the system, and was succeeded by the experienced full-back Billy Bancroft, but the first Golden Era of Welsh rugby was dominated by the leadership of Gwyn Nicholls, who had been weaned on Frank Hancock's ideal, and that of Billy Trew, who continued in a similar role. Gould, Nicholls and Trew, three centres responsible for overseeing the development of what became a Welsh style of play but was this because they were outstanding leaders or because they played in a position integral to the system favoured?

A change in direction immediately before the First World War saw a dominant Welsh pack sweep all before it. The Revd. Alban Davies was the new captain and on the resumption of international rugby in 1919 the forwards were loath to part with the responsibility and in the 1920s Tom Parker led for seven matches, none of which were lost. There followed a period which saw the fortunes of Welsh rugby plummet and while things began to improve during the 1930s under the leadership of Jack Bassett, Claud Davey and Wilf Wooler among others, it was the 1950s before Wales next enjoyed a sustained period of success.

John Gwilliam and the Welsh captaincy met by accident. Bleddyn Williams's unavailability necessitated a rethink and the selectors invited Gwilliam to lead the team at Twickenham in 1950. Only Watcyn Thomas had previously led Wales from number 8 and with the team able to boast a wealth of talent behind the scrum Gwilliam's appointment certainly brought a new dimension to the role of captain. Here was a man not immediately involved with the perceived strength of the team but who was considered by the Big Five to possess the necessary attributes the responsibility required, and indirectly John Gwilliam was probably the first player appointed because of qualities other than those relating purely to his playing ability or the position he occupied.

Bleddyn Williams had been the preferred choice in 1950, as he was on future occasions when fate in the guise of injury or illness contrived to deny him, but when the opportunities arrived, five of them, he led Wales to victory with great style and authority, victories which included the 1953 defeat of the New Zealand All Blacks.

With the introduction of Clive Rowlands in 1963 the selectors showed a level of patience which few before had tolerated. It appeared that in Rowlands Wales had a captain who was there for the duration. He was given an extended run regardless of initial results and the confidence shown by the Big Five bore fruit in 1965 with a Triple Crown. For a second time a captain was chosen for reasons over and above either position or ability – the focus was changing, moving away from the tried-and-tested bias towards position, the decade ending under the captaincy of Brian Price, a second-row forward of some stature and proven leadership qualities but hardly a man playing in the best position from which to guide a team.

What began in 1967 as a low-key appointment has become the most important playing-related function within the structure of the WRU. David Nash was the first Welsh coach and to date there have been 15 others, including the present incumbent, Gareth Jenkins, who was appointed in 2006. The high-profile position embraces a wide brief and the responsibilities associated with it have increased to a level which has inevitably led to a redefining of the captain's role. It wasn't always so. The successful teams of the 1970s, which fell under the coaching regimes of Clive Rowlands and John Dawes, were very dependent on the abilities of the captains, particularly Dawes himself and latterly Mervyn Davies and Phil Bennett, and we should not forget John Lloyd and J.P.R. Williams who both enjoyed successful tenures during the decade. Such were the results achieved by the various combinations there was every reason to believe that templates had been produced upon which all who followed could be based but life is rarely that simple.

The 1980s and 1990s were difficult periods highlighted by a good performance in the 1987 RWC with Richard Moriarty at the helm which led to a Triple Crown under the captaincy of Bleddyn Bowen in 1988 followed by a championship in 1994, the high point of the Ieuan Evans era. As the day the sport would become professional approached so too did the ideology on where the captain should play come under review. This wasn't necessarily due to any radical rethinking, rather a paucity of star players, but what this enforced change did succeed in doing was to take the emphasis on the position away. From now on the player would be considered first and if he met the laid-down criteria his position on the field became an irrelevance, hence Ieuan Evans on the right wing, in due course David Young at prop, and Gareth Thomas at full-back.

The dawning of professional rugby in 1995 eventually saw this philosophy expanded. The coach now wanted several leaders – individuals to control the lineout, the scrum, the defence and the attacking options – a Southern hemisphere innovation introduced by Graham Henry, scrum-half Robert Howley the first captain to have to work within the new parameters.

Where did this leave the captain, what exactly did his inevitably diminished role now involve? Was he a tactician? No, tactics are sorted out on the training field and if they need changing during the match then the coach presses the button and the message is carried onto the field at the first opportunity. A motivator? This is an area of responsibility often questioned by the men who have led Wales on the basis that pulling on the jersey should be sufficient motivation in itself. But the coach will always have his pre-match speech prepared during which he will introduce any necessary motivation before handing the team over to the captain, who will instil his own particular brand of leadership on the players, the most tangible thing they have to call upon during the 80 minutes' playing time.

Everything a player is comfortable with on the training ground comes under pressure in the high-intensity arena of international rugby. Confidence, attitude, concentration and the ability to rationalise the situation and remain focused. All these are areas of mental preparation which come under threat and it is for the captain to maintain a calming influence. He has to be able to communicate with the players simply and succinctly, be aware of all their little foibles, know when a pat on the back is needed, when a quiet word is appropriate. It has never been any different but where once the focus of the captain was aimed at the skill levels of the players now it leans more towards their minds – the top six inches, keeping the concentration, the discipline, the confidence. What the coach has put in place over many hours of training and analysis the captain has to put into practice and for 80 minutes, in the heat of battle, he has to be almost psychological in his outlook.

Some people are undoubtedly born natural leaders but they are few and far between and for the rest leadership is something which has to be learnt either from personal experience or the experience of others. After two matches it seems unfair to suggest that Duncan Jones has forgotten more about international captaincy than, through no fault of his own, James Bevan ever knew, but it is true simply because Bevan had nobody to refer to, no precedent. Now there are many and it is not only the captains who have learnt from their predecessors but those who appoint them have also become more attuned to the basic attributes of the modern-day rugby captain.

Some of the former captains interviewed for this book felt that far too much was read into the role; that it was a great honour, but one which was elevated to an inappropriate level of importance. They were of the opinion that if a captain was blessed with a team of talented players, he won and if he wasn't, he lost. He called heads or tails, decided whether or not to kick for goal and made the after-dinner speech. It is difficult to argue with men who, having captained Wales, view the responsibility in such a simplistic way but there are many reasons why such self-effacement should be ignored particularly when you expand the discussion to players who never had the opportunity to lead their country but who readily eulogise about the qualities of certain captains and, it must be said, disparage others.

We have to ask ourselves should we even be trying to identify the great Welsh captains? Reference has been made to them all achieving greatness simply through their very involvement with the role but it would be unfair to leave it at that, to treat them as equals. Similarly it would be unfair to identify one above all others as the most outstanding, the top of the pile, numero uno. What is perhaps more acceptable is to try to identify the leaders who influenced all around them, led by example, maintained control when under pressure and as a result led Wales with distinction, but what criteria should we use in an exercise which is so open to opinion and debate? Perhaps it would be advantageous to try and view the argument from the position of the selectors, those who elected the men to lead Wales. What exactly were they looking for?

The position came first. Forget the fact that Richard Mullock chose James Bevan, a back, as the first Welsh captain for reasons which are not apparent and move quickly on to the period when Welsh rugby first had an identity of its own. It made sense to appoint leaders who understood the game Wales wanted to play and they were all found in the backs for patently obvious reasons. When the emphasis moved away from free-flowing, expansive rugby into a forward-orientated game so too did the captaincy change hands, the big men who led the way via the shortest route taking over, but again, appointments made with the position uppermost in the selectors' minds.

For the most part, the 1920s should be ignored, as the selectors, whether of the innumerable variety or the reduced-in-size committee introduced in 1924, struggled to field a team of any note. Neither should the players and captains be absolved of any responsibility at a time when where the latter appeared on the field was of little relevance as no recognised pattern of play seems to have been in place. It is said that if you can remember the 1960s, you weren't there but those who witnessed the 1920s were never given such an opt-out clause: the decade left an indelible scar on the landscape of Welsh rugby. That the 1930s saw an improvement was inevitable, Wales once again moving towards a backs-orientated game and the captains who led with some success were found outside the scrum, position once again playing an important part in the choice of leader.

'Cometh the hour, cometh the man.' In 1950 the selectors were forced to rethink their choice of captain, not once but twice, and probably for the first time in its history Wales was led by a player not immediately involved in the team's dominant faction. This time the selectors, albeit unwittingly, appointed a man who proved himself a great leader over and above his qualities as a player. The position remained the most important factor during the decade but the emphasis on it began to change as selection panels started to look in earnest at another reason to appoint a captain – his qualities as a leader.

Any emphasis on either of the two criteria now became discernible, the 1960s and '70s producing several captains who were selected as much for their undoubted leadership qualities as for where they appeared on the team sheet. But as the influence of the coach increased so did the emphasis shift in favour of the man until the point was reached where his position became a total irrelevance. That certain positions continued to host more captains than others was inevitable but it is early days and if this book's exercise is repeated 50 or 100 years hence the distribution of captains should make interesting reading.

The initial outline for this book indeed suggested that a greatest captain would be found, someone who stood head and shoulders above his peers, but the many interviews conducted with former captains brought to light opinions which made this not only a difficult pursuit but also one which would inevitably be loaded with contention and therefore of no real merit.

To compare Billy Trew with John Dawes, John Gwilliam with Mervyn Davies or any two captains who played the same position but in different eras is impossible other than to say in the case of the above that they all led Grand Slam-winning teams. When thinking of the great Welsh captains it is natural to look first at a player's record, how successful were the teams he led, but this is a direction fraught with danger. That nine Grand Slams have been won is proof of the periods in its history when Welsh rugby has hit the heights but in looking at the most recent success in 2005 there were two captains who each led the team for two and a half matches which obviously indicates that other factors came into play. This is perilous ground we tread. Before getting carried away with the records of the obvious it would be wise to remember Willie Llewellyn, the Revd. Alban Davies, Tom Parker, John Lloyd, Bleddyn Bowen and many others who, as captains, delivered what was expected of them.

One of the captains spoken to made the observation that there have been good captains saddled with poor teams and bad captains getting the benefit of an abundance of talent; a good point, and while the temptation exists to declare a greatest captain or at least an elite group of five or six it is a temptation we are going to ignore. The statistics speak for themselves and if results are allowed to become the determining factor where do the captains who led Wales to victory when making their only appearance in the role come into the equation? You can't get better than a 100 per cent record.

Comparisons are pointless exercises, each captain being presented with a different set of circumstances: the players he leads, the quality of the opposition, the weather, the venue, the referee, the luck of the bounce. And we must also not forget that rugby union is a team game and the measurement of a captain should not be dependent on whether another player succeeds or fails in bisecting the uprights, so often the deciding factor in international rugby matches. It would have been so easy to nominate Gwyn Nicholls, Billy Trew, John Gwilliam, Bleddyn Williams, John Dawes, Mervyn Davies or Phil Bennett as the greatest Welsh captain based purely on results but it would be doing a tremendous disservice to a host of others and, fine captains as those individuals undoubtedly were, they have to take their place alongside many apparent 'lesser' mortals in the roll of honour.

After all the changes, all the discussion and debate somebody still has to lead the team onto the field. Be the first to absorb the charged atmosphere generated by 75,000 people, the one to try and maintain a level of calm among the players when surrounded by such uncontained emotion. To be entrusted with the responsibility, receive such an honour, be chosen to captain Wales, still represents the most sought-after accolade the game can bestow on a player, one which few will be associated with. The due process by which that person is chosen may have changed, from being a decision made by many to one lying in the remit of an individual, but it is a decision which will change the life of the recipient of the honour, elevate him to a level of sporting achievement sought by many but denied to most – it is indeed a priceless gift.

APPENDIX I

THE CAPTAINS' RECORDS:
CAPPED MATCHES
19 FEBRUARY 1881 – 30 JUNE 2006

The captains are listed in chronological order and the matches in which they led Wales are annotated by number, e.g. James Bevan led Wales in match number 1.

The game of rugby union uses a points scoring system which has been amended on many occasions, particularly in the nineteenth century when several variations were adopted before the International Board was able to introduce a format acceptable to all its member unions. From 1890 it became possible to transpose the various methods of scoring into a points equivalent and the results listed reflect this from match number 20. For consistency the winning score is recorded first.

1 BEVAN, JAMES ALFRED
three-quarter back
Cambridge University
1 match

1	19 Feb 1881	England	a	l	7 goals, 1 drop goal, 6 tries to nil

2 LEWIS, CHARLES PRYTHERCH

full-back
Llandovery
3 matches

2	28 Jan 1882	Ireland	a	w	2 goals, 2 tries to nil
3	16 Dec 1882	England	h	l	2 goals, 4 tries to nil
4	8 Jan 1883	Scotland	a	l	3 goals to 1 goal

3 NEWMAN, CHARLES HENRY

half-back
Newport
6 matches

5	5 Jan 1884	England	a	l	1 goal, 2 tries to 1 goal
6	12 Jan 1884	Scotland	h	l	1 drop goal, 1 try to nil
8	3 Jan 1885	England	h	l	1 goal, 4 tries to 1 goal, 1 try
9	10 Jan 1885	Scotland	a	d	no score
10	2 Jan 1886	England	a	l	1 goal from a mark, 2 tries to 1 goal
12	8 Jan 1887	England	h	d	no score

4 SIMPSON, HENRY JOSEPH

forward
Cardiff
1 match

7	12 April 1884	Ireland	h	w	1 drop goal, 2 tries to nil

5 HANCOCK, FRANCIS ESCOTT

three-quarter back
Cardiff
1 match

11	9 Jan 1886	Scotland	h	l	2 goals, 1 try to nil

6 GOULD, ROBERT

forward
Newport
1 match

13	26 Feb 1887	Scotland	a	l	4 goals, 8 tries to nil

7 CLAPP, THOMAS JOHN SERCOMBE

forward
Newport
3 matches

14	12 Mar 1887	Ireland	h	w	1 drop goal, 1 try to 3 tries
15	4 Feb 1888	Scotland	h	w	1 try to nil
16	3 Mar 1888	Ireland	a	l	1 goal, 1 drop goal, 1 try to nil

8 HILL, ALGERNON FRANK
forward
Cardiff
4 matches

17	22 Dec 1888	Maoris	h	w	1 goal, 2 tries to nil
18	2 Feb 1889	Scotland	a	l	2 tries to nil
20	1 Feb 1890	Scotland	h	l	5-1
34	10 Mar 1894	Ireland	a	l	3-0

9 GOULD, JOSEPH ARTHUR
centre
Newport
18 matches

19	2 Mar 1889	Ireland	h	l	2 tries to nil
21	15 Feb 1890	England	a	w	1-0
22	1 Mar 1890	Ireland	a	d	3-3
26	2 Jan 1892	England	a	l	17-0
27	6 Feb 1892	Scotland	h	l	7-2
28	5 Mar 1892	Ireland	a	l	9-0
29	7 Jan 1893	England	h	w	12-11
30	4 Feb 1893	Scotland	a	w	9-0
31	11 Mar 1893	Ireland	h	w	2-0
32	6 Jan 1894	England	a	l	24-3
33	3 Feb 1894	Scotland	h	w	7-0
35	5 Jan 1895	England	h	l	14-6
36	26 Jan 1895	Scotland	a	l	5-4
37	16 Mar 1895	Ireland	h	w	5-3
38	4 Jan 1896	England	a	l	25-0
39	25 Jan 1896	Scotland	h	w	6-0
40	14 Mar 1896	Ireland	a	l	8-4
41	9 Jan 1897	England	h	w	11-0

10 BOWEN, WILLIAM ARNOLD
forward
Swansea
1 match

23	3 Jan 1891	England	h	l	7-3

11 THOMAS, WILLIAM HENRY
forward
Llanelli
2 matches

24	7 Feb 1891	Scotland	a	l	15-0
25	7 Mar 1891	Ireland	h	w	6-4

12 BANCROFT, WILLIAM
full-back
Swansea
11 matches

42	19 Mar 1898	Ireland	a	w	11–3
43	2 Apr 1898	England	a	l	14–7
44	7 Jan 1899	England	h	w	26–3
45	4 Mar 1899	Scotland	a	l	21–10
46	18 Mar 1899	Ireland	h	l	3–0
47	6 Jan 1900	England	a	w	13–3
48	27 Jan 1900	Scotland	h	w	12–3
49	17 Mar 1900	Ireland	a	w	3–0
50	5 Jan 1901	England	h	w	13–0
51	9 Feb 1901	Scotland	a	l	18–8
52	16 Mar 1901	Ireland	h	w	10–9

13 NICHOLLS, ERITH GWYN
centre
Newport/Cardiff
10 matches

53	11 Jan 1902	England	a	w	9–8
54	1 Feb 1902	Scotland	h	w	14–5
55	8 Mar 1902	Ireland	a	w	15–0
58	14 Mar 1903	Ireland	h	w	18–0
59	9 Jan 1904	England	a	d	14–14
65	16 Dec 1905	New Zealand	h	w	3–0
66	13 Jan 1906	England	a	w	16–3
67	3 Feb 1906	Scotland	h	w	9–3
68	10 Mar 1906	Ireland	a	l	11–6
69	1 Dec 1906	South Africa	h	l	11–0

14 PEARSON, THOMAS WILLIAM
wing
Newport
1 match

56	10 Jan 1903	England	h	w	21–5

15 LLOYD, GEORGE LLEWELLYN
outside-half
Newport
1 match

57	7 Feb 1903	Scotland	a	l	6–0

16 LLEWELLYN, WILLIE
wing
Newport
5 matches

60	6 Feb 1904	Scotland	h	w	21–3

258

61	12 Mar 1904	Ireland	a	l	14–12
62	14 Jan 1905	England	h	w	25–0
63	4 Feb 1905	Scotland	a	w	6–3
64	11 Mar 1905	Ireland	h	w	10–3

17 OWEN, RICHARD MORGAN
scrum-half
Swansea
3 matches

70	12 Jan 1907	England	h	w	22–0
90	20 Jan 1912	England	a	l	8–0
91	3 Feb 1912	Scotland	h	w	21–6

18 TREW, WILLIAM JAMES
wing/outside-half/centre
Swansea
14 matches

71	2 Feb 1907	Scotland	a	l	6–3
77	12 Dec 1908	Australia	h	w	9–6
78	16 Jan 1909	England	h	w	8–0
79	6 Feb 1909	Scotland	a	w	5–3
80	23 Feb 1909	France	a	w	47–5
81	13 Mar 1909	Ireland	h	w	18–5
82	1 Jan 1910	France	h	w	49–14
83	15 Jan 1910	England	a	l	11–6
84	5 Feb 1910	Scotland	h	w	14–0
86	21 Jan 1911	England	h	w	15–11
87	4 Feb 1911	Scotland	a	w	32–10
89	11 Mar 1911	Ireland	h	w	16–0
96	1 Feb 1913	Scotland	a	w	8–0
97	27 Feb 1913	France	a	w	11–8

19 GABE, REES THOMAS
centre
Cardiff
1 match

| 72 | 9 Mar 1907 | Ireland | h | w | 29–0 |

20 HARDING, ARTHUR FLOWERS
forward
London Welsh
1 match

| 73 | 18 Jan 1908 | England | a | w | 28–18 |

21 TRAVERS, GEORGE
hooker
Pill Harriers
1 match

| 74 | 1 Feb 1908 | Scotland | h | w | 6–5 |

22 MORGAN, EDWARD
wing
London Welsh
1 match

75	2 Mar 1908	France	h	w	36–4

23 WINFIELD, HERBERT BEN
full-back
Cardiff
1 match

76	14 Mar 1908	Ireland	a	w	11–5

24 GIBBS, REGINALD ARTHUR
wing
Cardiff
1 match

85	12 Mar 1910	Ireland	a	w	19–3

25 WILLIAMS, JOHN LEWIS
wing
Cardiff
1 match

88	28 Feb 1911	France	a	w	15–0

26 BANCROFT, JOHN (JACK)
full-back
Swansea
1 match

92	9 Mar 1912	Ireland	a	l	12–5

27 VILE, THOMAS HENRY
scrum-half
Newport
4 matches

93	25 Mar 1912	France	h	w	14–8
94	14 Dec 1912	South Africa	h	l	3–0
95	18 Jan 1913	England	h	l	12–0
109	5 Feb 1921	Scotland	h	l	14–8

28 JONES, JOHN PHILLIPS
centre
Pontypool
1 match

98	8 Mar 1913	Ireland	h	w	16–13

29 DAVIES, REVD. JENKIN ALBAN
forward
Llanelli
4 matches

99	17 Jan 1914	England	a	l	10–9
100	7 Feb 1914	Scotland	h	w	24–5
101	2 Mar 1914	France	h	w	31–0
102	14 Mar 1914	Ireland	a	w	11–3

30 STEPHENS, GLYN
forward
Neath
1 match

103	21 Apr 1919	New Zealand Army	h	l	6–3

31 UZZELL, HENRY
forward
Newport
4 matches

104	17 Jan 1920	England	h	w	19–5
105	7 Feb 1920	Scotland	a	l	9–5
106	17 Feb 1920	France	a	w	6–5
107	13 Mar 1920	Ireland	h	w	28–4

32 WETTER, JOHN JAMES
outside-half/centre
Newport
3 matches

108	15 Jan 1921	England	a	l	18–3
122	8 Mar 1924	Ireland	h	l	13–10
124	29 Nov 1924	New Zealand	h	l	19–0

33 PARKER, EDWIN THOMAS
forward
Swansea
7 matches

110	26 Feb 1921	France	h	w	12–4
111	12 Mar 1921	Ireland	a	w	6–0
112	21 Jan 1922	England	h	w	28–6
113	4 Feb 1922	Scotland	a	d	9–9
114	11 Mar 1922	Ireland	h	w	11–5
115	23 Mar 1922	France	a	w	11–3
118	24 Feb 1923	France	h	w	16–8

34 LEWIS, JOHN MORRIS CLEMENT
outside-half
Cardiff
2 matches

116 20 Jan 1923	England	a	l	7–3
117 3 Feb 1923	Scotland	h	l	11–8

35 JENKINS, ALBERT EDWARD
centre
Llanelli
2 matches

119 10 Mar 1923	Ireland	a	l	5–4
140 10 Mar 1928	Ireland	h	l	13–10

36 REES, JOSEPH
full-back
Swansea
1 match

120 19 Jan 1924	England	h	l	17–9

37 WHITFIELD, JOHN JAMES
forward
Newport
1 match

121 2 Feb 1924	Scotland	a	l	35–10

38 HARDING, ROWE
wing
Swansea
4 matches

123 27 Mar 1924	France	a	w	10–6
129 16 Jan 1926	England	h	d	3–3
131 13 Mar 1926	Ireland	h	w	11–8
138 21 Jan 1928	England	h	l	10–8

39 JOHNSON, TOM ALBERT
full-back
Cardiff
1 match

125 17 Jan 1925	England	a	l	12–6

40 MORRIS, STEPHEN
hooker
Cross Keys
1 match

126 7 Feb 1925	Scotland	h	l	24–14

41 CORNISH, ROBERT ARTHUR
centre
Cardiff
2 matches

127 28 Feb 1925	France	h	w	11–5
130 6 Feb 1926	Scotland	a	l	8–5

42 JONES, WALTER IDRIS
hooker
Llanelli
1 match

128 14 Mar 1925	Ireland	a	l	19–3

43 DELAHAY, WILLIAM JAMES 'BOBBY'
centre
Cardiff
1 match

132 5 Apr 1926	France	a	w	7–5

44 TURNBULL, BERNARD RUEL 'LOU'
centre
Cardiff
1 match

133 15 Jan 1927	England	a	l	11–9

45 MALE, BENJAMIN OSWALD
full-back
Cardiff
3 matches

134 5 Feb 1927	Scotland	h	l	5–0
139 4 Feb 1928	Scotland	a	w	13–0
141 9 Apr 1928	France	a	l	8–3

46 POWELL, WILLIAM CHARLES
scrum-half
London Welsh
2 matches

135 26 Feb 1927	France	h	w	25–7
136 12 Mar 1927	Ireland	a	l	19–9

47 JONES, IVOR EGWAD
forward
Llanelli
3 matches

137 26 Nov 1927	New South Wales	h	l	18–8
142 19 Jan 1929	England	a	l	8–3
147 1 Feb 1930	Scotland	a	l	12–9

48 MORGAN, WILLIAM GUY
centre
Swansea
4 matches

143	2 Feb 1929	Scotland	h	w	14–7
144	25 Feb 1929	France	h	w	8–3
145	9 Mar 1929	Ireland	a	d	5–5
149	21 Apr 1930	France	a	w	11–0

49 BOWCOTT, HENRY MORGAN
centre
Cardiff
1 match

146	18 Jan 1930	England	h	l	11–3

50 BASSETT, JOHN ARCHIBALD
full-back
Penarth
9 matches

148	8 Mar 1930	Ireland	h	w	12–7
150	17 Jan 1931	England	a	d	11–11
151	7 Feb 1931	Scotland	h	w	13–8
152	28 Feb 1931	France	h	w	35–3
153	14 Mar 1931	Ireland	a	w	15–3
154	5 Dec 1931	South Africa	h	l	8–3
155	16 Jan 1932	England	h	w	12–5
156	6 Feb 1932	Scotland	a	w	6–0
157	12 Mar 1932	Ireland	h	l	12–10

51 THOMAS, WATCYN GWYN
number 8
Swansea
3 matches

158	21 Jan 1933	England	a	w	7–3
159	4 Feb 1933	Scotland	h	l	11–3
160	11 Mar 1933	Ireland	a	l	10–5

52 EVANS, JOHN RAYMOND
hooker
Newport
1 match

161	20 Jan 1934	England	h	l	9–0

53 DAVEY, CLAUD
centre
Swansea
8 matches

162	3 Feb 1934	Scotland	a	w	13–6

163 10 Mar 1934	Ireland	h	w	13–0
164 19 Jan 1935	England	a	d	3–3
165 2 Feb 1935	Scotland	h	w	10–6
166 9 Mar 1935	Ireland	a	l	9–3
167 21 Dec 1935	New Zealand	h	w	13–12
169 1 Feb 1936	Scotland	a	w	13–3
171 16 Jan 1937	England	a	l	4–3

54 REES, JOHN IDWAL
centre/wing
Swansea/Edinburgh Wanderers
3 matches

168 18 Jan 1936	England	h	d	0–0
170 14 Mar 1936	Ireland	h	w	3–0
172 6 Feb 1937	Scotland	h	l	13–6

55 WOOLER, WILFRED
centre
Cardiff
4 matches

173 3 Apr 1937	Ireland	a	l	5–3
177 21 Jan 1939	England	a	l	3–0
178 4 Feb 1939	Scotland	h	w	11–3
179 11 Mar 1939	Ireland	a	w	7–0

56 JONES, WILLIAM CLIFFORD
outside-half
Cardiff
3 matches

174 15 Jan 1938	England	h	w	14–8
175 5 Feb 1938	Scotland	a	l	8–6
176 12 Mar 1938	Ireland	h	w	11–5

57 TANNER, HAYDN
scrum-half
Cardiff
12 matches

180 18 Jan 1947	England	h	l	9–6
181 1 Feb 1947	Scotland	a	w	22–8
182 22 Mar 1947	France	a	w	3–0
183 29 Mar 1947	Ireland	h	w	6–0
185 17 Jan 1948	England	a	d	3–3
186 7 Feb 1948	Scotland	h	w	14–0
187 21 Feb 1948	France	h	l	11–3
188 13 Mar 1948	Ireland	a	l	6–3
189 15 Jan 1949	England	h	w	9–3
190 5 Feb 1949	Scotland	a	l	6–5
191 12 Mar 1949	Ireland	h	l	5–0
192 26 Mar 1949	France	a	l	5–3

58 TAMPLIN, WILLIAM EWART
lock
Cardiff
1 match

184	20 Dec 1947	Australia	h	w	6–0

59 GWILLIAM, JOHN ALBERT
number 8
Edinburgh Wanderers/Gloucester
13 matches

193	21 Jan 1950	England	a	w	11–5
194	4 Feb 1950	Scotland	h	w	12–0
195	11 Mar 1950	Ireland	a	w	6–3
196	25 Mar 1950	France	h	w	21–0
197	20 Jan 1951	England	h	w	23–5
198	3 Feb 1951	Scotland	a	l	19–0
199	10 Mar 1951	Ireland	h	d	3–3
201	22 Dec 1951	South Africa	h	l	6–3
202	19 Jan 1952	England	a	w	8–6
203	2 Feb 1952	Scotland	h	w	11–0
204	8 Mar 1952	Ireland	a	w	14–3
205	22 Mar 1952	France	h	w	9–5
206	17 Jan 1953	England	h	l	8–3

60 MATTHEWS, JACK
centre
Cardiff
1 match

200	7 Apr 1951	France	a	l	8–3

61 WILLIAMS, BLEDDYN
centre
Cardiff
5 matches

207	7 Feb 1953	Scotland	a	w	12–0
208	14 Mar 1953	Ireland	h	w	5–3
209	28 Mar 1953	France	a	w	6–3
210	19 Dec 1953	New Zealand	h	w	13–8
215	22 Jan 1955	England	h	w	3–0

62 STEPHENS, JOHN REES
number 8/lock
Neath
6 matches

211	16 Jan 1954	England	a	l	9–6
212	13 Mar 1954	Ireland	a	w	12–9
217	12 Mar 1955	Ireland	h	w	21–3
218	26 Mar 1955	France	a	w	16–11

225 9 Mar 1957	Ireland	h	w	6–5
226 23 Mar 1957	France	a	w	19–13

63 WILLIS, WILLIAM REX
scrum-half
Cardiff
2 matches

213 27 Mar 1954	France	h	w	19–13
216 5 Feb 1955	Scotland	a	l	14–8

64 JONES, KENNETH JEFFREY
wing
Newport
1 match

214 10 Apr 1954	Scotland	h	w	15–3

65 MORGAN, CLIFFORD ISAAC
outside-half
Cardiff
4 matches

219 21 Jan 1956	England	a	w	8–3
220 4 Feb 1956	Scotland	h	w	9–3
221 10 Mar 1956	Ireland	a	l	11–3
222 24 Mar 1956	France	h	w	5–3

66 THOMAS, MALCOLM CAMPBELL
centre
Newport
2 matches

223 19 Jan 1957	England	h	l	3–0
224 2 Feb 1957	Scotland	a	l	9–6

67 THOMAS, RICHARD CLEMENT CHARLES
wing forward
Swansea
9 matches

227 4 Jan 1958	Australia	h	w	9–3
228 18 Jan 1958	England	a	d	3–3
229 1 Feb 1958	Scotland	h	w	8–3
230 15 Mar 1958	Ireland	a	w	9–6
231 29 Mar 1958	France	h	l	16–6
232 17 Jan 1959	England	h	w	5–0
233 7 Feb 1959	Scotland	a	l	6–5
234 14 Mar 1959	Ireland	h	w	8–6
235 4 Apr 1959	France	a	l	11–3

68 WILLIAMS, RHYS HAYDN
lock
Llanelli
1 match

236	16 Jan 1960	England	a	l	14–6

69 MEREDITH, BRINLEY VICTOR
hooker
Newport
4 matches

237	6 Feb 1960	Scotland	h	w	8–0
239	23 Mar 1960	France	h	l	16–8
247	24 Mar 1962	France	h	w	3–0
248	17 Nov 1962	Ireland	a	d	3–3

70 BRACE, DAVID ONLLWYN
scrum-half
Llanelli
2 matches

238	12 Mar 1960	Ireland	a	w	10–9
243	11 Mar 1961	Ireland	h	w	9–0

71 DAVIES, TERENCE JOHN
full-back
Llanelli
3 matches

240	3 Dec 1960	South Africa	h	l	3–0
241	21 Jan 1961	England	h	w	6–3
242	11 Feb 1961	Scotland	a	l	3–0

72 WILLIAMS, LLOYD HUGH
scrum-half
Cardiff
3 matches

244	25 Mar 1961	France	a	l	8–6
245	20 Jan 1962	England	a	d	0–0
246	3 Feb 1962	Scotland	h	l	8–3

73 ROWLANDS, DANIEL CLIVE THOMAS
scrum-half
Pontypool
14 matches

249	19 Jan 1963	England	h	l	13–6
250	2 Feb 1963	Scotland	a	w	6–0
251	9 Mar 1963	Ireland	h	l	14–6
252	23 Mar 1963	France	a	l	5–3
253	21 Dec 1963	New Zealand	h	l	6–0
254	18 Jan 1964	England	a	d	6–6

255	1 Feb 1964	Scotland	h	w	11–3
256	7 Mar 1964	Ireland	a	w	15–6
257	21 Mar 1964	France	h	d	11–11
258	23 May 1964	South Africa	a	l	24–3
259	16 Jan 1965	England	h	w	14–3
260	6 Feb 1965	Scotland	a	w	14–12
261	13 Mar 1965	Ireland	h	w	14–8
262	27 Mar 1965	France	a	l	22–13

74 PASK, ALUN EDWARD ISLWYN
number 8
Abertillery
6 matches

263	15 Jan 1966	England	a	w	11–6
264	5 Feb 1966	Scotland	h	w	8–3
265	12 Mar 1966	Ireland	a	l	9–6
266	26 Mar 1966	France	h	w	9–8
267	3 Dec 1966	Australia	h	l	14–11
268	4 Feb 1967	Scotland	a	l	11–5

75 WATKINS, DAVID
outside-half
Newport
3 matches

269	11 Mar 1967	Ireland	h	l	3–0
270	1 Apr 1967	France	a	l	20–14
271	15 Apr 1967	England	h	w	34–21

76 GALE, NORMAN REGINALD
hooker
Llanelli
2 matches

| 272 | 11 Nov 1967 | New Zealand | h | l | 13–6 |
| 273 | 20 Jan 1968 | England | a | d | 11–11 |

77 EDWARDS, GARETH OWEN
scrum-half
Cardiff
13 matches

274	3 Feb 1968	Scotland	h	w	5–0
276	23 Mar 1968	France	h	l	14–9
280	12 Apr 1969	England	h	w	30–9
284	24 Jan 1970	South Africa	h	d	6–6
285	7 Feb 1970	Scotland	h	w	18–9
286	28 Feb 1970	England	a	w	17–13
287	14 Mar 1970	Ireland	a	l	14–0
300	24 Mar 1973	France	a	l	12–3
301	10 Nov 1973	Australia	h	w	24–0

302 19 Jan 1974	Scotland	h	w	6–0
303 2 Feb 1974	Ireland	a	d	9–9
304 16 Feb 1974	France	h	d	16–16
305 16 Mar 1974	England	a	l	16–12

78 DAWES, SYDNEY JOHN
centre
London Welsh
6 matches

275 9 Mar 1968	Ireland	a	l	9–6
288 4 Apr 1970	France	h	w	11–6
289 16 Jan 1971	England	h	w	22–6
290 6 Feb 1971	Scotland	a	w	19–18
291 13 Mar 1971	Ireland	h	w	23–9
292 27 Mar 1971	France	a	w	9–5

79 PRICE, BRIAN
lock
Newport
6 matches

277 1 Feb 1969	Scotland	a	w	17–3
278 8 Mar 1969	Ireland	h	w	24–11
279 22 Mar 1969	France	a	d	8–8
281 31 May 1969	New Zealand	a	l	19–0
282 14 Jun 1969	New Zealand	a	l	33–12
283 21 Jun 1969	Australia	a	w	19–16

80 LLOYD, DAVID JOHN
prop
Bridgend
3 matches

293 15 Jan 1972	England	a	w	12–3
294 5 Feb 1972	Scotland	h	w	35–12
295 25 Mar 1972	France	h	w	20–6

81 THOMAS, WILLIAM DELME
lock
Llanelli
1 match

| 296 2 Dec 1972 | New Zealand | h | l | 19–16 |

82 LEWIS, ARTHUR JOHN LLEWELLYN
centre
Ebbw Vale
3 matches

297 20 Jan 1973	England	h	w	25–9
298 3 Feb 1973	Scotland	a	l	10–9
299 10 Mar 1973	Ireland	h	w	16–12

83 DAVIES, THOMAS MERVYN
number 8
Swansea
9 matches

306 18 Jan 1975	France	a	w	25–10
307 15 Feb 1975	England	h	w	20–4
308 1 Mar 1975	Scotland	a	l	12–10
309 15 Mar 1975	Ireland	h	w	32–4
310 20 Dec 1975	Australia	h	w	28–3
311 17 Jan 1976	England	a	w	21–9
312 7 Feb 1976	Scotland	h	w	28–6
313 21 Feb 1976	Ireland	a	w	34–9
314 6 Mar 1976	France	h	w	19–13

84 BENNETT, PHILIP
outside-half
Llanelli
8 matches

315 15 Jan 1977	Ireland	h	w	25–9
316 5 Feb 1977	France	a	l	16–9
317 5 Mar 1977	England	h	w	14–9
318 19 Mar 1977	Scotland	a	w	18–9
319 4 Feb 1978	England	a	w	9–6
320 18 Feb 1978	Scotland	h	w	22–14
321 4 Mar 1978	Ireland	a	w	20–16
322 18 Mar 1978	France	h	w	16–7

85 COBNER, TERENCE JOHN
wing forward
Pontypool
1 match

323 11 Jun 1978	Australia	a	l	18–8

86 DAVIES, THOMAS GERALD REAMES
wing
Cardiff
1 match

324 17 Jun 1978	Australia	a	l	19–17

87 WILLIAMS, JOHN PETER RHYS
full-back
Bridgend
5 matches

325 11 Nov 1978	New Zealand	h	l	13–12
326 20 Jan 1979	Scotland	a	w	19–13
327 3 Feb 1979	Ireland	h	w	24–21
328 17 Feb 1979	France	a	l	14–13
329 17 Mar 1979	England	h	w	27–3

88 SQUIRE, JEFFREY
number 8/wing forward
Pontypool
6 matches

330 19 Jan 1980	France	h	w	18–9
331 16 Feb 1980	England	a	l	9–8
332 1 Mar 1980	Scotland	h	w	17–6
333 15 Mar 1980	Ireland	a	l	21–7
337 21 Feb 1981	Ireland	h	w	9–8
338 7 Mar 1981	France	a	l	19–15

89 FENWICK, STEVEN PAUL
centre
Bridgend
3 matches

334 1 Nov 1980	New Zealand	h	l	23–3
335 17 Jan 1981	England	h	w	21–19
336 7 Feb 1981	Scotland	a	l	15–6

90 DAVIES, WILLIAM GARETH
outside-half
Cardiff
5 matches

339 5 Dec 1981	Australia	h	w	18–13
340 23 Jan 1982	Ireland	a	l	20–12
341 6 Feb 1982	France	h	w	22–12
342 6 Mar 1982	England	a	l	17–7
343 20 Mar 1982	Scotland	h	l	34–18

91 BUTLER, EDWARD THOMAS
number 8
Pontypool
6 matches

344 5 Feb 1983	England	h	d	13–13
345 19 Feb 1983	Scotland	a	w	19–15
346 5 Mar 1983	Ireland	h	w	23–9
347 19 Mar 1983	France	a	l	16–9
348 12 Nov 1983	Romania	a	l	24–6
349 21 Jan 1984	Scotland	h	l	15–9

92 WATKINS, MICHAEL JOHN
hooker
Newport
4 matches

350 4 Feb 1984	Ireland	a	w	18–9
351 18 Feb 1984	France	h	l	21–16
352 17 Mar 1984	England	a	w	24–15
353 24 Nov 1984	Australia	h	l	28–9

93 HOLMES, TERENCE DAVID
scrum-half
Cardiff
5 matches

354 2 Mar 1985	Scotland	a	w	25–21	
355 16 Mar 1985	Ireland	h	l	21–9	
356 30 Mar 1985	France	a	l	14–3	
357 20 Apr 1985	England	h	w	24–15	
358 9 Nov 1985	Fiji	h	w	40–3	

94 PICKERING, DAVID FRANCIS
wing forward
Llanelli
8 matches

359 18 Jan 1986	England	a	l	21–18	
360 1 Feb 1986	Scotland	h	w	22–15	
361 15 Feb 1986	Ireland	a	w	19–12	
362 1 Mar 1986	France	h	l	23–15	
363 31 May 1986	Fiji	a	w	22–15	
366 7 Feb 1987	France	a	l	16–9	
367 7 Mar 1987	England	h	w	19–12	
368 21 Mar 1987	Scotland	a	l	21–15	

95 MORIARTY, RICHARD DANIEL
lock
Swansea
7 matches

364 12 Jun 1986	Tonga	a	w	15–7	
365 14 Jun 1986	W. Samoa	a	w	32–14	
370 25 May 1987	Ireland	a	w	13–6	RWC
371 29 May 1987	Tonga	a	w	29–16	RWC
373 8 Jun 1987	England	a	w	16–3	RWC
374 14 Jun 1987	New Zealand	a	l	49–6	RWC
375 18 Jun 1987	Australia	a	w	22–21	RWC

96 JAMES, WILLIAM JOHN
hooker
Aberavon
1 match

369 4 Apr 1987	Ireland	h	l	15–11	

97 DAVIES, JONATHAN
outside-half
Neath/Llanelli
4 matches

372 3 Jun 1987	Canada	a	w	40–3	RWC
382 11 Jun 1988	New Zealand	a	l	54–9	
383 12 Nov 1988	W. Samoa	h	w	28–6	
384 10 Dec 1988	Romania	h	l	15–9	

98 BOWEN, BLEDDYN
centre
South Wales Police
5 matches

376	7 Nov 1987	USA	h	w	46–0
377	6 Feb 1988	England	a	w	11–3
378	20 Feb 1988	Scotland	h	w	25–20
379	5 Mar 1988	Ireland	a	w	12–9
380	19 Mar 1988	France	h	l	10–9

99 NORSTER, ROBERT LEONARD
lock
Cardiff
1 match

381	28 May 1988	New Zealand	a	l	52–3

100 THORBURN, PAUL HUW
full-back
Neath
10 matches

385	21 Jan 1989	Scotland	a	l	23–7
386	4 Feb 1989	Ireland	h	l	19–13
387	18 Feb 1989	France	a	l	31–12
388	18 Mar 1989	England	h	w	12–9
396	6 Oct 1990	Barbarians	h	l	31–24
397	19 Jan 1991	England	h	l	25–6
398	2 Feb 1991	Scotland	a	l	32–12
399	16 Feb 1991	Ireland	h	d	21–21
400	2 Mar 1991	France	a	l	36–3
401	21 Jul 1991	Australia	a	l	63–6

101 JONES, ROBERT NICHOLAS
scrum-half
Swansea
5 matches

389	4 Nov 1989	New Zealand	h	l	34–9
390	20 Jan 1990	France	h	l	29–19
391	17 Feb 1990	England	a	l	34–6
392	3 Mar 1990	Scotland	h	l	13–9
393	24 Mar 1990	Ireland	a	l	14–8

102 PHILLIPS, KEVIN HUW
hooker
Neath
2 matches

394	2 Jun 1990	Namibia	a	w	18–9
395	9 Jun 1990	Namibia	a	w	34–30

103 EVANS, IEUAN CENNYDD
wing
Llanelli
28 matches

402	4 Sep 1991	France	h	l	22–9
403	6 Oct 1991	W. Samoa	h	l	16–13	RWC
404	9 Oct 1991	Argentina	h	w	16–7	RWC
405	12 Oct 1991	Australia	h	l	38–3	RWC
406	18 Jan 1992	Ireland	a	w	16–15
407	1 Feb 1992	France	h	l	12–9
408	7 Mar 1992	England	a	l	24–0
409	21 Mar 1992	Scotland	h	w	15–12
410	21 Nov 1992	Australia	h	l	23–6
411	6 Feb 1993	England	h	w	10–9
412	20 Feb 1993	Scotland	a	l	20–0
413	6 Mar 1993	Ireland	h	l	19–14
414	20 Mar 1993	France	a	l	26–10
418	16 Oct 1993	Japan	h	w	55–5
419	10 Nov 1993	Canada	h	l	26–24
420	15 Jan 1994	Scotland	h	w	29–6
421	5 Feb 1994	Ireland	a	w	17–15
423	19 Mar 1994	England	a	l	15–8
424	17 May 1994	Portugal	a	w	102–11
425	21 May 1994	Spain	a	w	54–0
426	11 Jun 1994	Canada	a	w	33–15
427	18 Jun 1994	Fiji	a	w	23–8
428	22 Jun 1994	Tonga	a	w	18–9
429	25 Jun 1994	W. Samoa	a	l	34–9
430	17 Sep 1994	Romania	a	w	16–9
434	18 Feb 1995	England	h	l	23–9
435	4 Mar 1995	Scotland	a	l	26–13
436	18 Mar 1995	Ireland	h	l	16–12

104 LLEWELLYN, GARETH OWEN
lock
Neath
7 matches

415	22 May 1993	Zimbabwe	a	w	35–14
416	29 May 1993	Zimbabwe	a	w	42–13
417	5 Jun 1993	Namibia	a	w	38–23
422	19 Feb 1994	France	h	w	24–15
431	12 Oct 1994	Italy	h	w	29–19
432	26 Nov 1994	South Africa	h	l	20–12
433	21 Jan 1995	France	a	l	21–9

105 HALL, MICHAEL ROBERT
centre
Cardiff
3 matches

437 27 May 1995	Japan	a	w	57–10	RWC
438 31 May 1995	New Zealand	a	l	34–9	RWC
439 4 Jun 1995	Ireland	a	l	24–23	RWC

106 HUMPHREYS, JONATHAN MATTHEWS
hooker
Cardiff/Bath
19 matches

440 2 Sep 1995	South Africa	a	l	40–11
441 11 Nov 1995	Fiji	h	w	19–15
442 16 Jan 1996	Italy	h	w	31–26
443 3 Feb 1996	England	a	l	21–15
444 17 Feb 1996	Scotland	h	l	16–14
445 2 Mar 1996	Ireland	a	l	30–17
446 16 Mar 1996	France	h	w	16–15
447 8 Jun 1996	Australia	a	l	56–25
448 22 Jun 1996	Australia	a	l	42–3
449 24 Aug 1996	Barbarians	h	w	31–10
451 5 Oct 1996	Italy	a	w	31–22
452 1 Dec 1996	Australia	h	l	28–19
453 15 Dec 1996	South Africa	h	l	37–20
455 18 Jan 1997	Scotland	a	w	34–19
456 1 Feb 1997	Ireland	h	l	26–25
457 15 Feb 1997	France	a	l	27–22
458 15 Mar 1997	England	h	l	34–13
519 22 Feb 2003	England	h	l	26–9
521 22 Mar 2003	Ireland	h	l	25–24

107 DAVIES, NIGEL GARETH
centre
Llanelli
1 match

450 25 Sep 1996	France	h	l	40–33

108 GIBBS, IAN SCOTT
centre
Swansea
1 match

454 11 Jan 1997	USA	h	w	34–14

109 JONES, RHODRI GWYN
wing forward
Cardiff
5 matches

459	5 Jul 1997	USA	a	w	30–20
460	12 Jul 1997	USA	a	w	28–23
462	30 Aug 1997	Romania	h	w	70–21
463	16 Nov 1997	Tonga	h	w	46–12
464	29 Nov 1997	New Zealand	h	l	42–7

110 JOHN, PAUL
scrum-half
Pontypridd
1 match

461	19 Jul 1997	Canada	a	w	28–25

111 HOWLEY, ROBERT
scrum-half
Cardiff
22 matches

465	7 Feb 1998	Italy	h	w	23–20	
466	21 Feb 1998	England	a	l	60–26	
467	7 Mar 1998	Scotland	h	w	19–13	
468	21 Mar 1998	Ireland	a	w	30–21	
469	5 Apr 1998	France	h	l	51–0	
470	6 Jun 1998	Zimbabwe	a	w	49–11	
472	14 Nov 1998	South Africa	h	l	28–20	
473	21 Nov 1998	Argentina	h	w	43–30	
474	6 Feb 1999	Scotland	a	l	33–20	
475	20 Feb 1999	Ireland	h	l	29–23	
476	6 Mar 1999	France	a	w	34–33	
477	20 Mar 1999	Italy	a	w	60–21	
478	11 Apr 1999	England	h	w	32–31	
479	5 Jun 1999	Argentina	a	w	36–26	
480	12 Jun 1999	Argentina	a	w	23–16	
481	26 Jun 1999	South Africa	h	w	29–19	
482	21 Aug 1999	Canada	h	w	33–19	
483	28 Aug 1999	France	h	w	34–23	
484	1 Oct 1999	Argentina	h	w	23–18	RWC
485	9 Oct 1999	Japan	h	w	64–15	RWC
486	14 Oct 1999	Samoa	h	l	38–31	RWC
487	23 Oct 1999	Australia	h	l	24–9	RWC

112 JONES, PHILIP KINGSLEY BRIAN
wing forward
Ebbw Vale
1 match

471	27 Jun 1998	South Africa	a	l	96–13

113 YOUNG, DAVID
prop
Cardiff
12 matches

488 5 Feb 2000	France	h	l	36–3
489 19 Feb 2000	Italy	h	w	47–16
490 4 Mar 2000	England	a	l	46–12
491 18 Mar 2000	Scotland	h	w	26–18
492 1 Apr 2000	Ireland	a	w	23–19
496 3 Feb 2001	England	h	l	44–15
497 17 Feb 2001	Scotland	a	d	28–28
498 17 Mar 2001	France	a	w	43–35
499 8 Apr 2001	Italy	a	w	33–23
502 22 Sep 2001	Romania	h	w	81–9
503 13 Oct 2001	Ireland	h	l	36–6
504 10 Nov 2001	Argentina	h	l	30–16

114 TAYLOR, MARK
centre
Swansea/Sale
4 matches

493 11 Nov 2000	Samoa	h	w	50–6
494 18 Nov 2000	USA	h	w	42–11
551 4 June 2005	USA	a	w	77–3
552 11 June 2005	Canada	a	w	60–3

115 QUINNELL, L. SCOTT
number 8
Llanelli
7 matches

495 26 Nov 2000	South Africa	h	l	23–13
505 17 Nov 2001	Tonga	h	w	51–7
506 25 Nov 2001	Australia	h	l	21–13
507 3 Feb 2002	Ireland	a	l	54–10
508 16 Feb 2002	France	h	l	37–33
509 2 Mar 2002	Italy	h	w	44–20
510 23 Mar 2002	England	a	l	50–10

116 MOORE, ANDREW PAUL
lock
Swansea
2 matches

500 10 Jun 2001	Japan	a	w	64–10
501 17 Jun 2001	Japan	a	w	53–30

117 CHARVIS, COLIN LLOYD
number 8/wing forward
Swansea/unattached/Tarbes/Newcastle
22 matches

511 6 Apr 2002	Scotland	h	l	27–22	
512 8 Jun 2002	South Africa	a	l	34–19	
513 15 Jun 2002	South Africa	a	l	19–8	
514 1 Nov 2002	Romania	h	w	40–3	
515 9 Nov 2002	Fiji	h	w	58–14	
516 16 Nov 2002	Canada	h	w	32–21	
517 23 Nov 2002	New Zealand	h	l	43–17	
518 15 Feb 2003	Italy	a	l	30–22	
528 30 Aug 2003	Scotland	h	w	23–9	
529 12 Oct 2003	Canada	a	w	41–10	RWC
530 19 Oct 2003	Tonga	a	w	27–20	RWC
531 25 Oct 2003	Italy	a	w	27–15	RWC
532 2 Nov 2003	New Zealand	a	l	53–37	RWC
533 9 Nov 2003	England	a	l	28–17	RWC
534 14 Feb 2004	Scotland	h	w	23–10	
536 7 Mar 2004	France	h	l	29–22	
537 20 Mar 2004	England	a	l	31–21	
538 27 Mar 2004	Italy	h	w	44–10	
539 12 Jun 2004	Argentina	a	l	50–44	
540 19 Jun 2004	Argentina	a	w	35–20	
541 26 Jun 2004	South Africa	a	l	53–18	
545 26 Nov 2004	Japan	h	w	98–0	

118 WILLIAMS, MARTYN ELWYN
wing forward
Cardiff/Cardiff Blues
5 matches

520 8 Mar 2003	Scotland	a	l	30–22
522 29 Mar 2003	France	a	l	33–5
523 14 Jun 2003	Australia	a	l	30–10
524 21 Jun 2003	New Zealand	a	l	55–3
535 22 Feb 2004	Ireland	a	l	36–15

119 THOMAS, GARETH
wing/full-back
Celtic Warriors/Toulouse
12 matches

525 16 Aug 2003	Ireland	a	l	35–12
542 6 Nov 2004	South Africa	h	l	38–36
543 12 Nov 2004	Romania	h	w	66–7
544 20 Nov 2004	New Zealand	h	l	26–25
546 5 Feb 2005	England	h	w	11–9
547 12 Feb 2005	Italy	a	w	38–8
548 26 Feb 2005	France	a	w	24–18

553	5 Nov 2005	New Zealand	h	l	41–3
555	19 Nov 2005	South Africa	h	l	33–16
556	26 Nov 2005	Australia	h	w	24–22
557	4 Feb 2006	England	a	l	47–13
558	12 Feb 2006	Scotland	h	w	28–18

120 JONES, STEPHEN MICHAEL
outside-half
Llanelli Scarlets
1 match

| 526 | 23 Aug 2003 | England | h | l | 43–9 |

121 DAVIES, MEFIN
hooker
Celtic Warriors
1 match

| 527 | 27 Aug 2003 | Romania | h | w | 54–8 |

122 OWEN, MICHAEL
number 8
Newport-Gwent Dragons
6 matches

549	13 Mar 2005	Scotland	a	w	46–22
550	19 Mar 2005	Ireland	h	w	32–20
554	11 Nov 2005	Fiji	h	w	11–10
559	26 Feb 2006	Ireland	a	l	31–5
560	11 Mar 2006	Italy	h	d	18–18
561	18 Mar 2006	France	h	l	21–16

123 JONES, DUNCAN
prop
Ospreys
2 matches

| 562 | 11 June 2006 | Argentina | a | l | 27–25 |
| 563 | 17 June 2006 | Argentina | a | l | 45–27 |

APPENDIX II

CLUB REPRESENTATION
OF WELSH CAPTAINS:
CAPPED MATCHES
19 FEBRUARY 1881 – 30 JUNE 2006

The statistics are based on the total number of matches in which players representing the respective clubs and regions captained Wales.

CARDIFF	146
SWANSEA	107
LLANELLI	76
NEWPORT	71
PONTYPOOL	28
NEATH	27
EDINBURGH WANDERERS	13
BRIDGEND	11
TOULOUSE	11
LONDON WELSH	10
PENARTH	9
ABERTILLERY	6
NEWPORT-GWENT DRAGONS	6
SOUTH WALES POLICE	5
EBBW VALE	4
NEWCASTLE	4
TARBES	4

LLANDOVERY	3
BATH	2
CELTIC WARRIORS	2
OSPREYS	2
SALE	2
ABERAVON	1
CAMBRIDGE UNIVERSITY	1
CARDIFF BLUES	1
CROSS KEYS	1
GLOUCESTER	1
LLANELLI SCARLETS	1
PILL HARRIERS	1
PONTYPRIDD	1
UNATTACHED	6

BIBLIOGRAPHY

Bennett, Phil and Williams, Martyn, *Everywhere for Wales*, Stanley Paul, 1981

Billot, John, *History of Welsh International Rugby*, Roman Way Books, 1999

Chester, Rod, McMillan, Neville and Palenski, Ron, *The Encyclopaedia of New Zealand Rugby*, Hodder Moa Beckett, 1998

Chester, Rod, McMillan, Neville and Palenski, Ron, *Men in Black*, Hodder Moa Beckett, 2000

Davies, D.E., *Cardiff Rugby Club: History and Statistics 1876–1975*, Starling Press, 1975

Davis, Jack, *One Hundred Years of Newport Rugby*, Starling Press, 1974

Donovan, Edward, Crane, Arthur, Smith, Allan and Harris, John, *Pontypool's Pride: The Official History of Pontypool RFC 1868–1988*, Old Bakehouse Publications, 1988

Evans, Howard, *Welsh International Matches 1881–2000*, Mainstream Publishing, 1999

Frost, David, *The Bowring Story of the Varsity Match*, MacDonald Queen Anne Press, 1988

Gadney, C.H., *The History of the Laws of Rugby Union Football 1949–1972*, RFU, 1973

Griffiths, John, *The Phoenix Book of International Rugby Records*, Phoenix House, 1987

Harding, Rowe, *Rugby: Reminiscences and Opinions*, Pilot Press, 1929

Hughes, Gareth (compiler), *One Hundred Years of Scarlet*, Llanelli RFC, 1983

Hughes, Gareth, *The Scarlets: A History of Llanelli Rugby Club*, Llanelli RFC, 1986

Jenkins John M., Pierce, Duncan and Auty, Timothy, *Who's Who of Welsh International Rugby Players*, Bridge Books, 1991

Lewis, Steve and Griffiths, John, *The Essential History of Rugby Union: Wales*, WHS, 2003

Marshall, Revd. F. (ed.), *Football: The Rugby Union Game*, Cassell and Co. Ltd, 1892

Morgan, Cliff with Nicholson, Geoffrey, *Beyond the Fields of Play*, Hodder and Stoughton, 1996

Rice, Grantland, *The Tumult and the Shouting: My Life in Sport*, Cassell, 1956

Royds, Admiral Sir Percy, *The History of the Laws of Rugby Union*, RFU, 1949

Sewell, E.H.D., *Rugby Football Today*, John Murray, 1931

Smith, David and Williams, Gareth, *Fields of Praise*, University of Wales Press, 1980

Thomas, Clem, *The History of the British Lions*, Mainstream Publishing, 1996

Thomas, Watcyn, *Rugby-Playing Man*, Pelham, 1977

Townsend Collins, W.J., *Rugby Recollections*, R.H. Johns, 1948

Wakefield, W.W. and Marshall, H.P., *Rugger*, Longmans, Green and Co., 1930

Wakelam, Captain H.B.T. (ed.), *The Game Goes On*, Arthur Barker Ltd, 1936

Williams, J.P.R., *JPR: An Autobiography*, Collins, 1979

Yearbooks
(Various editions publishers and editors)
International Rugby Yearbook
Playfair Rugby Football Annual
Rothmans Rugby Yearbook
Rugby Almanack of New Zealand
Rugby Annual For Wales
South African Rugby Annual

INDEX